UNFIT & IMPROPER PERSONS

UNFIT & IMPROPER PERSONS

An Idiot's Guide to Owning a Football Club

Kevin Day, Kieran Maguire & Guy Kilty

BLOOMSBURY SPORT
LONDON • OXFORD • NEW YORK • NEW DELHI • SYDNEY

BLOOMSBURY SPORT
Bloomsbury Publishing Plc
50 Bedford Square, London, WC1B 3DP, UK
29 Earlsfort Terrace, Dublin 2, Ireland

BLOOMSBURY, BLOOMSBURY SPORT and the Diana logo are trademarks
of Bloomsbury Publishing Plc

First published in Great Britain in 2023

A catalogue record for this book is available from the British Library

Library of Congress Cataloguing-in-Publication data has been applied for

ISBN: 978-1-3994-0754-0; eBook: 978-1-3994-0753-3;
ePDF: 978-1-3994-0752-6

2 4 6 8 10 9 7 5 3 1

Typeset in Adobe Garamond Pro by Deanta Global Publishing Services,
Chennai, India
Printed and bound in Great Britain by CPI Group (UK) Ltd, Croydon, CR0 4YY

To find out more about our authors and books, visit www.bloomsbury.com
and sign up for our newsletters

*This book is dedicated by Guy to Sarah, Owen
and Emmeline.*

*By Kevin to Ali, Ed, Molly, Smudge and the Pawsons Arms
who all bring me great joy.*

*By Kieran to Andy Hill, from one dweeb to another,
Rest In Peace.*

Contents

Contents

Introduction

*Well if you know so much about it, why don't you buy
a club yourselves?*

Ah, if only we at *The Price of Football* podcast had a pound for every time that's been said to us we'd have... Hang on, as you are aware, I'm not good with numbers, I'll ask Kieran... Right, turns out we'd have £27, which is not a funny amount, but as Kieran says, it's better to be accurate than funny. That's why he's an accountant and I'm a comedian.

We would absolutely love to buy a football club. And Kieran and Producer Guy would absolutely love to run a football club. They genuinely enjoy arranging and managing things. They have tidy, organised minds. Give Producer Guy some admin to do and he is a happy man. Kieran finds numbers and accounts so sexy I suspect he has satin spreadsheets. I, on the other hand, haven't got the attention span needed for business and am very easily distracted – my wife, Ali, often leads me away from dangerous situations by dangling a set of shiny keys in front of me. Plus, I am seriously bad with money. I'm not allowed a credit card and Ali, along with Bobby Numbers, my accountant, agreed long ago that I should not be given the details of the account my VAT gets paid into.

So my role as the co-owner of a football club would be very much PR. I'd be the one glad-handing the media, right up to the moment I accidentally reveal that our manager is having an affair with the physio. I'd also be the one who mixes with the fans until, after an away game in Oldham, I end up on the lash with five of our Ultras and am inevitably photographed draping a half and half scarf round a lap-dancer's neck in a dodgy club.

Between us, though, I think Kieran, Producer Guy and I would be brilliant club owners.* For a start, we would see ourselves merely as temporary guardians of the club, respectful of its past, mindful of its future and always aware that if a football club truly belongs to anyone, it's the fans. We would be financially responsible; we would be open and honest with both facts and figures. We would communicate with our fans, explaining to them why difficult decisions may have to be made on and off the field, and acting quickly to resolve any issues they may have with the club. And we would certainly not try to exploit the fans through ticket prices, cryptocurrencies or a range of garden gnomes in both home and away kits.†

We would ensure the club was sustainable both economically and environmentally, and we would actively seek to recruit staff from outside the traditional white male workforce still so prevalent in modern football. Perhaps most importantly, we would make the ground a community hub, so that everyone in the area, regardless of whether they supported us or not, would feel welcome at our fitness sessions for the elderly, social clubs for the lonely, foodbanks for the hungry etc. And we would do those things, because over the past few years on *The Price of Football* we have not only learned all the ways not to run a football club, we have also heard from hundreds of fans about the things that make them even more proud of the football clubs they love.

It was at the end of 2019 that Guy Kilty, a BBC radio business presenter and producer, approached me to suggest I host a podcast that shone a light on the finances of the beautiful game at every level, along with a 'groovy' accountant he knew called Kieran Maguire, an expert in the subject who taught it at Liverpool University. I listened politely, then asked two very important questions. First, how did you get my number? Second, are you mad? Who's going to listen to that? Producer Guy, who had obviously done some research, suggested we meet for a drink and halfway through my second bottle of wine I apparently agreed to take part.

Two weeks later we recorded our first episode and two weeks after that Kieran plucked up the courage to tell me he was a Brighton

*Of a football club, that is, not a dodgy establishment in Oldham.
†Well, that would be the theory anyway.

and Hove Albion fan, which to me as a Crystal Palace fan was a shocking and depressing revelation, especially as, up until then, he had seemed quite a decent bloke. Let's just say that was the quietest show we've ever done. However, as we had already had a surprising amount of interest in the show, both from fans and from inside the game, I decided to be a grown-up and continue.

And thank goodness I did, because not only has the podcast become hugely successful and slightly influential, but the three of us have also become very close friends. We are roughly the same age and from roughly similar backgrounds. We are all happily married with children, and we are united by a deep love of football and a shared passion for its history and its culture. You'll have to go a long way before you find three middle-aged men more obsessed with football kits. We are also united by our fears for, and worries about, the future of football.

I absolutely love doing the pod, but it scares the bejesus out of me sometimes as Kieran reveals yet another tale of a greedy and ignorant owner driving a club to near-extinction or being so blinded by a cheque offered by a cryptocurrency company they forget to check whether it actually exists.

But much as I believe we would be brilliant at it, there are several reasons why we don't buy a club ourselves. For a start, we probably wouldn't pass the fit and proper person test or, as it is more officially known, the owners' and directors' test. Producer Guy would be disqualified, because he wouldn't give his real name for reasons known only to his accountant. I imagine I'd be disqualified because I don't have any money, and Kieran would be disqualified because he is very sensible and knows all about the finances of football. If there is one thing we have learned on the podcast, it's that the Premier League and English Football League seem rather hesitant about letting capable and financially solvent people take over a club.

As it happens, in my case, I imagine wrong, because the irony is that my lack of money would be less of a hindrance than Kieran's financial common sense. In fact, as I am currently not in prison, I have already passed the owners' and directors' test with flying colours. And trust me, that is a subject we will be coming back to.

Another reason why we can't buy a club ourselves is that we are all passionately in love with our own teams: Guy is a Manchester United fan, which is fine, because he's from there. Well, I think he is. He's got an accent, but he's as cagey about where he's from as he is about his real name: I'm beginning to think he may be on a witness protection scheme. As you've heard, I support Crystal Palace and for reasons known only to himself, but possibly related to his love of posh matchday sandwiches, Kieran supports Brighton and Hove Albion.

Obviously, I daydream about owning Palace, if only because I want to buy Kevin de Bruyne and Harry Kane, but just as obviously I don't daydream about the bit where me buying those players bankrupts the club. The only thing Kieran daydreams about is spreadsheets and Panini stickers, but we both agree that buying another real club means we would have to go and watch them play on a Saturday afternoon, so that ain't going to happen.

Also, both our partners have made it very clear that they think we've spaffed enough money on football in our lives already, so taking out a £200 million loan to buy an actual club would be seriously frowned on, plus even the dodgiest of pay-day loan companies isn't going to cough up just so we can buy a football team. I could probably rustle up enough cash for one of those clubs like Bury which changed hands for £1 (yes, a whole quid), but Kieran wouldn't let me, for reasons that will become apparent later in this book.

Now at this stage, some of you may be thinking 'Hang on, what about Producer Guy? According to your podcast he lives in a solid gold house and is richer than Prince Andrew's lawyer. Surely he can help?' Fair point, except for one thing. Producer Guy does exist, but we may have exaggerated how much money he makes out of the pod and even if he had made that much, one thing we don't exaggerate is his, ahem, care with cash. Producer Guy is certainly not going to offload any of his hard-earned on something flippant like a football club or, indeed, a solid gold house. Too impractical, apparently, and very difficult to keep clean.

But we do love the idea of owning a club, so, after much thought and several more hours in the pub, we decided that instead of buying one we'd start a fictional one from scratch. That way we could prove to all those doubters that we can talk the talk, walk the walk, and sign the cheques for eye-watering amounts of money.

Speaking of which, I'm actually quite looking forward to being an out and out capitalist. I reckon it's going to be fun. I haven't told the others that part. They still think I plan to be the caring, sharing sort of club owner they will be, but I don't get the chance to spend millions on an unnecessary full-back in real life or to be taken for a weekend in Paris by a grateful agent off the back of it, so sod it, I'm going rogue.

I know from experience as a Palace fan and from talking to decent club owners on the pod that we may be embarking on an interesting and perilous journey. Actually, as it's me writing the book, I know for a fact we are. Fortunes could be made and lost, along with reputations (and hair); family time could become a thing of the past as owning a football club can be an all-consuming affair. There will be local FAs to deal with, as well as unscrupulous agents, silver-tongued lawyers and angry fans chasing us with pitchforks and burning torches. Or the modern equivalent: calling us pricks on Twitter. To be fair, there will also be scrupulous agents and, if we can find one, we may even introduce them to you. It may also turn out that the local FAs are modern-thinking, warm-hearted and generous, just as it may also turn out that Crystal Palace win the Champions League one day.

Who knows, maybe our fans will all be sensible, intelligent people fully aware of the dangers of short-term spending sprees. I doubt it, though, especially as I'm a football fan and I'm definitely not like that, but along the way we will meet people like Gary Lineker, Clare Balding and Gabby Logan, as well as people who operate at every level of the game, on and off the pitch. We will learn how to organise play-offs, how to smile politely on Sky TV, how much beer costs in Vaduz, how to secretly poach a manager and exactly how big a corner flag needs to be. Hopefully you will also learn something useful that you can casually drop into a conversation in the pub before a game, like the cost of collecting rainwater to irrigate a football pitch or exactly how West Ham got away with that stadium deal.

I'm all excited now, so let's get this show on the road. Whether you play on a pitch in Croydon that's more dog-poo than grass or on a pitch in Madrid kept green by the tears of tiny children, we are coming for you. Whether your broadcast deal is worth fifty quid with BBC Radio East Surrey or £50 million with BT Sport (now TNT Sports), we are coming for you. Whether your trophy cabinet is full of silverware or beer and crisps, we are coming for you. Football, we are coming for you!

1

FOUNDING A NEW FOOTBALL CLUB

From here you have to look up to see the grassroots

Kieran, God bless him, is a teetotaller, and Producer Guy can make a pint of Guinness last all evening, so I woke up this morning in the unusual position of having two people to remind me of the brilliant idea we came up with last night. I sometimes worry that during a session in the pub, my mates and I come up with an idea to end all world poverty and the blueprint for a self-assembly jetpack, but have absolutely no recollection the following morning. A couple of months ago I came downstairs after a night out to find a packet of cheese wrapped in a Scottish £5 note on top of the microwave and I still have no idea how they got there.

Luckily, all I found this morning were emails from both of them saying how much they had enjoyed chucking ideas around and they couldn't wait to get started on building our football team. Even more luckily, it turns out that I told Ali all about it when I got home last night ('twice') so she was able to fill me in. And, you know what, I still think it's a good idea, so let's get this show on the road. Just as soon as I've been to the café for double bacon and eggs and a giant cup of strong tea.

We decided to start a team at the lowest level possible in the FA pyramid, get it promoted all the way to the EFL, the Premier League and into Europe, then have an almighty argument about whether to join the inevitable European Super League Mark Two. And, because we are generous and thoughtful people, along the way we would share our experience on the podcast – and possibly make a few bob from our listeners by selling half and half scarves online.

Now Kieran is firmly of the opinion that generous and thoughtful people like us are not always best suited to owning a football club, but we would be different. As our team rose to global domination, we would show everyone how a football club should be run. We would involve fans in every decision. Our recruitment policy would be faultless, our financial structure sustainable yet successful, our community outreach second to none, our commitment to the environment exemplary and we would lead the fight against the unjust distribution of money in a game awash with the stuff; and if we could trouser a bit of cash through being exemplary owners, so much the better.

Then, of course, we realised the snag with that idea. Time. Even allowing for our innate optimism (except when watching Palace and Brighton) it would probably take, what, at least 15 years to get from a park pitch to Le Parc des Princes. My attention span is short enough as it is ... Ooh, there's a squirrel ... I'd never last 15 years. Plus the chances are that by then we'd be living together in sheltered accommodation remembering the glory days of 3pm kick-offs and singing Sex Pistols songs round the old piano.

Instead, determined to prove the doubters wrong, we decided to start a fictional team, write a book about it and do all those things we had planned, but in the space of chapters not decades. That way we could still show everyone how to run a club and, hopefully, we'd get some lovely book money while we were still young enough to shift it into an offshore account. (Calm down, Kieran. I know it's not ethical, but it's a book about the murky world of football finance. Some of the money has to 'rest' in a private account somewhere along the line or it wouldn't be authentic.)

In fact, running a fictional football club actually makes this book even more accessible. After all, we know that many club owners and chief executives listen to the podcast, but the vast majority of you will never reach those lofty heights, whereas all of you are capable of inventing your own team and this book will be the perfect way to learn how make it a success. Especially if you ignore my suggestions which, according to Kieran, amount to a pretty useful guide on how not to run a football club, which in its own way, I suppose, is just as important. Incidentally, the first suggestion that Kieran would prefer you to ignore is keeping a separate set of books for HMRC.

So, let us introduce you to a brand-new football club: West Park Rovers. It took some time to settle on that compromise of a name, let me tell you. Kieran suggested we call it Crystal Albion, but that sounds like someone who might support Dolly Parton at a country music festival in Tennessee,* so I put my foot down. Producer Guy wanted the name to represent his club as well, so he came up with Hovechester Eagles, but that's the sort of name a middle-class script writer would come up with if *Midsomer Murders* ever did a football episode, so my foot went down again. The club name discussion went on for some time, but then Guy and Kieran did what they always do: wait until I've had a third glass of wine, after which I'm always much more amenable to other people's ideas. So West Park Rovers it is.

Now, you may be wondering how we stand on that name legally, containing as it does elements of other football team names. Well, football clubs can, and do, trademark their names, logos and badges (Tottenham Hotspur and Liverpool, for example), but we were advised that as long as we make it ABSOLUTELY clear that ours is a fictional side with ABSOLUTELY no link whatsoever to West Ham, Queen's Park Rangers or Blackburn Rovers then we are fine (although I haven't told the others yet that the person who said we would be fine was a bloke I met in the pub and not an actual lawyer).

Incidentally, although Liverpool FC were able to successfully trademark that name, their effort to legally claim the sole right to use the name 'Liverpool' was met with short shrift in court – a decision that saved Jamie Carragher a fortune, because if he'd had to pay every time he told people where he was from he'd have been skint by now.

Kieran and Guy reckon the name West Park Rovers represents a sort of generic national spread: 'West' for the, erm, west, 'Park' is sort of London-y and, according to Guy, 'Rovers' is the sort of

---

*I hate C&W due to my mum's habit of spending most Sundays crying her way through songs that mainly appeared to be about messy divorces and dogs dying.

down-to-earth, no-nonsense name that immediately makes you think of the north. To readers from the east of England I can only apologise. If it's any consolation I'm a big fan of your fens and your turkeys.

Before we go any further, there's one very important thing you need to know. Our football team may be fictional, but everything that happens to it will be based on hard facts from the real world, which, I'm guessing is not the same as the Real Madrid world. We may be showing you how to run (or not) a football team, but in doing so, we will be showing you the real price of football.

Now you may think that it would be sensible to start our fictional team halfway up the football pyramid, so we can really get into the nuts and bolts of football finances, but much to my amazement it turns out that even at the lowest level possible there are decisions to be made about surprisingly high levels of spending.

We did toy with the idea of starting West Park Rovers as a fictional pub team, but, and not without reason, Producer Guy reckoned I would spend too much time doing research in an actual pub. Luckily, Kieran knows a few people near his gaff down Crawley way, so he called in some favours with the local FA and got us a place in the Sussex, Surrey and Gatwick League; a league that is obviously fictional, but represents the reality of life so far down the pyramid you may well burn your toes on the sand.

I played Sunday football back in the day. Because I looked about 12 years old right up to the day I reached 30, a lot of opposition left-wingers assumed they'd be in for an easy game until word got round that I was actually quite a dirty little cherub. I once got sent off twice in the same game, because I sneaked back on and it took the ref a while to notice. I remember those days with fondness, but I don't remember a large number of hoops that had to be jumped through before our team could play – legal and financial hoops that is, not training hoops, as we weren't the fittest team in the league.

Roy, who organised and administered Venn Street FC, is still a dear friend, so I asked him why I had no recollection of anything other than playing. He said it was because, like all the other players, I had no interest in helping with anything that required even minimal effort, up to and including washing the kit, carrying the crossbar, paying subs and turning up for disciplinary hearings after being sent off twice in one match. Well, words to that effect anyway. In my defence, and that of the other players, Roy did seem to enjoy doing all that grown-up stuff and he is still the only man I know who irons his Palace scarf before a game.

It seems nothing has changed. I simply assumed we would invent a club and crack on with our first game, but Kieran and Guy insist that if our fictional team is to reflect real life then we have to fulfil all the requirements necessary to do so. And I mean *all* the requirements. If Roy was setting up a team now he'd be in clerical heaven, because the Amateur Football Alliance (AFA) thoughtfully provides a 15-page PDF with all the details you need and many more that I reckon you don't. It even starts by explaining that you can use the guide 'whether you are setting up a team in a new club or if you are an established club setting up a new team' – a level of detail that Roy would have framed and hung in the toilet.

After that helpful start we are still some way from kicking a ball in anger. First we are told to contact our local FA to agree a name and to have several options in case there are already clubs with a similar title. Interestingly, unlike the Jockey Club, say, who are very diligent in banning rude names for racehorses like Hoof Hearted, there seem to be no rules about inappropriate names. So in the event that there is already a West Park Rovers, I have suggested Twat United as our second choice.

With your name ratified you have to call a general meeting of all intended members to elect a chairman, secretary, treasurer and others to form a management committee. And in a blow to those of us who would happily shirk such duties, the chairman, secretary and treasurer need to be three different people. I'd better put myself down as secretary. I'm not responsible enough to chair or numerate enough to treasure, but I'm alright at typing. Oh, and if you plan to have players younger than 18 or you are starting a youth team, it is also compulsory to appoint a club welfare officer.

They also suggest who some of the 'others' should be on that management committee. For example, a 'discipline secretary' – a title that interested Kieran just a little bit too much for my liking; a 'groundsman' – and notice it says 'man'; and, my favourite, an 'emergency aid kit co-ordinator', which on closer inspection turns out to be someone who knows where the first-aid kit is.

Now you have to agree a set of club rules and the AFA are kind enough to provide some model examples to help, such as, 'The members of the club from time to time shall be those persons listed in the member of registers (the membership register) which shall be maintained by the club secretary' and 'The quorum for the transaction of business for the club committee shall be three'. I don't remember Venn Street FC having a club committee, but if they did I'd be amazed if anyone other than Roy ever turned up. Then, and only then, can you apply to join a league, which you are recommended to do in January in order to give you time to start in August.

I assume those rules are there to deter those people who suddenly decide to start a football team halfway through a night in the pub and are now regretting it in the cold light of day. If so, then they are very effective, because in real life I would have got bored and given up long ago.

If you are still determined to see it through, you now have to identify ways of fundraising through the first season and you have to establish a home ground. That bit at least is easy. Kieran's Uncle Terry, a businessman well known locally (especially to the Police) has very kindly given us as a 'few bob' as the down payment for the rent on our new ground, which we are grandly calling Whitestone Park, even though a more accurate name would be the pitch furthest from the changing rooms right under the Gatwick flightpath.

About halfway through, the AFA document takes time for a moment of quiet reflection: 'It can be a daunting task to set up a new football club, but help is at hand to support you through the process. It is through affiliation that the family of football is brought together and correct standards are maintained.' Er, OK, but you have sort of helped to make it daunting with all these meetings and rules you insist upon.

It then continues with a long list of the benefits of affiliation, including 'being legally affiliated to the Amateur Football Alliance – AFA', 'access to advice from FA staff', 'access to purchase public liability and personal injury insurance', 'opportunities to participate in FA football development schemes' and the rather vaguer 'discipline, fair play and respect'. I mean, all very laudable, but the tone seems somewhat similar to Uncle Terry's when he explained the very many reasons why he was giving us the money for ground rent and why it should maybe sit in a separate account until things blew over. He used the word 'respect' as well. In other words, it came across as slightly threatening: 'Look, you don't have to be affiliated, but I can't be responsible for what happens if you're not. Oh, is that your new crossbar I just accidentally broke?'

Interestingly, the guide doesn't mention what the cost of FA affiliation actually is, which is strange because the FA is not usually coy about mentioning money or, indeed, asking for it. They charge you £325 just to register your name with them and charge more on top of that to register for leagues and cup competitions. In fact, the FA have ways of taking money off you that even Uncle Terry hasn't thought of. All it says is that 'an annual fee payable by each member shall be determined from time to time by the club committee and set at a level that will not pose a significant obstacle to community participation. Fees shall not be re-payable.' In other words, pay what you think you can afford, a principle I intend to suggest to the guvnor of the Pawsons Arms.

One financial rule is made very clear: 'The club can sell and supply food, drink and related sports clothing and equipment' and for that purpose can 'employ members and remunerate them (although not for playing).' In other words, you can pay someone for making tea, but not for playing football, which may make recruitment in one area slightly trickier than the other. Incidentally, when you decide how much you are going to remunerate your tea-maker, the FA suggest that the tea-maker is not in the room at the time. Especially, I imagine, if the tea-maker has been sent by Uncle Terry.

To be fair to the FA (and, trust me, you won't hear that from many other people in the game) it turns out the members of the local Football Association are sharper than I thought. I was expecting a collection of crusty old geezers all in the job solely for freebies and the company of other blazer-wearing buffoons. In reality, only a few of them are like that and, even at this local level, the FA are doing their best to drag themselves into the 20th century – so much so that it feels churlish to tell them that we are already nearly a quarter of the way through the 21st century.

And when I say local, I mean local. There are 43 Football Associations covering what is a pretty small country, although it doesn't feel that small when you're trying to travel from London to Newcastle for a game that Sky has somehow decided should be at 4pm on a Sunday afternoon. The 43 are mainly county FAs, although it seems a bit unfair that Berkshire and Buckinghamshire have to share one between them, while Yorkshire gets four of its own: East Riding, North Riding and West Riding plus a separate one for Sheffield, presumably because Sheffield is acknowledged as the home of the first ever football club.

But there are other Football Associations as well: Guernsey, Jersey, and the Isle of Man each have their own (sorry Isle of Wight, I don't make the rules). There is an English Schools FA, plus separate FAs for the Army, the Royal Navy and the RAF, which is rather pleasingly entitled the RAFFA, and it's only because I suspect they've heard them all before that I don't bung in a BENITEZ joke here. There is also the Amateur Football Alliance, which, I guess, is there to hoover up the few people left who aren't in a county or the armed forces, and, as it turns out, us.

The Football Association itself was formed on 26 October 1863 and legend has it there are still a couple of committee members knocking about who were at that very first meeting. The original aim of the FA was 'forming an association with the object of establishing a definite code of rules for the regulation of the game.' In other words, they wanted to make sure that every game was played under the same set of rules rather than the local rules, which may have varied from town to town or school to school. Indeed, the first two meetings were dominated by whether 'hacking' or deliberately kicking an opponent on the shin should be allowed, as Blackheath FC vigorously demanded. It was decided that it should not, although no one ever seems to have passed that message on to Leeds United.

In fact, the first two years of the FA were characterised by clubs arguing about how the game should be played, with many insisting that catching the ball and running with it should be part of the newly organised game. Luckily, those clubs were eventually shouted down and buggered off to form their own game, which I believe is still called rugby.

Annual membership of the FA was set at one guinea, which is roughly £129.56 today, but there was no real clamour to join and even the FA's own official history admits that no one really took any notice of it until an advert appeared in *The Sportsman* newspaper on 20 July 1871, announcing the establishment of 'The Football Association Challenge Cup'. Even then only 15 of the 50 member clubs applied to take part, with many of the others worrying that it would 'lead to unhealthy rivalry and even bitterness.' As someone who has been on the wrong end of two FA Cup finals, I can certainly testify to the 'even bitterness' part, my only consolation being that Palace have been to twice as many finals as Brighton, although come to think of it, I'm not sure it is a consolation to have had your heart broken more often than your bitterest rivals. And it was bloody Manchester United who won the cup all three times!

Nevertheless, despite that initial lack of enthusiasm, the inauguration of the FA Cup and games against other nations saw the FA gradually become football's ultimate authority, which it remains, despite the introduction of a professional football league in 1888 and the Premier League in 1992. For men and women, from the England national team to West Park Rovers, the governance of the beautiful game is still in the hands of the Football Association. Everything we do has to be sanctioned by the local FA, which, of course, takes a bit of funding, as we soon found out.

Essentially, as we will also find out, the FA partly exists to take all the blame for things that are wrong in the game and to get none of the credit for things that are right. We promise that the owners, staff and players of West Park Rovers will treat FA officials with every respect, although some owners do take a more robust approach. Andy Holt, the admirable owner of Accrington Stanley, told us that the FA tried to fine him when he referred to Ipswich Town player Sam Morsy as a 'shithouse'. Andy apologised for using that term, but said that until the FA could prove Sam Morsy *wasn't* a shithouse, he wouldn't pay the fine. 'In fact,' he said, 'I don't pay most of the fines. They've stopped asking now.'

If I'm being honest that AFA guide to setting up West Park Rovers was actually very helpful and being affiliated to the FA makes us all feel very grown-up. The bad news is that having come so far we are now sort of committed to carrying on: 'A resolution to dissolve the club shall only be proposed at a general meeting and shall be carried by a majority of at least three-quarters of the members present.' I'll work out what three quarters of three is when the time comes, but at the moment I am still flushed with enthusiasm, excitement and the remnants of a hangover. So, congratulations everybody, we are now the proud owners of a brand-new football club. Well, the owners of a name and the tenants of a pitch. All we need now is players, a manager and coaches, balls, nets and a kit.

KITTY KITTY BANG BANG

Now, most people starting a new football team would probably prioritise getting some actual footballers, but, as you know, all three of us are in love with football kits, so choosing one of those was always going to be the first thing we did. Kieran, obviously, wants a fully sustainable, recyclable and environmentally friendly kit made of bamboo that can double up as bedding for orphaned rabbits, like Forest Green Rovers have. But unlike Forest Green Rovers, we aren't bankrolled by an eco-millionaire so, for the moment, polyester it is.

I do share Kieran's conviction that the football industry should be more aware of the environment. It was shocking to be told on the pod by Thom Rawson of campaign group Football for Future that if climate change is not tackled soon then 24 league clubs will be under water within decades. Kieran was horrified. Even more so when I said, 'Great, let's build our ground on a hill and that's 24 clubs we won't have to compete with.'

You'd imagine an accountant would share my view that scarcity will create demand for those clubs that are still on dry land, but apparently not. However, we can console ourselves that, for now at least, we are doing our bit. For example, like Forest Green Rovers, we are using rainwater to irrigate our pitch, the only difference being that they collect and store theirs in state-of-the-art butts and we collect ours on the pitch when it rains.

We will be discovering much more about the economics of football kits (and football's impact on the environment) as we rise up the pyramid and, personally, I can't wait for that glorious day when we are in the Premier League and we can make a fortune by changing our first, second and third kits every season and selling tens of thousands of them in the club shop. And I've promised Kieran that if we can do that and save the planet at the same time then, of course, we will, but, like most Premier League clubs, not if it costs us extra,* although I am prepared to compromise and offset the carbon costs of flying the kits in from a sweatshop in

---

*When we get to the Premier League, you're going to be amazed to learn how little the top clubs are actually prepared to spend on fripperies like sustainable energy and saving the planet.

Bangladesh. Sorry, did I say 'sweatshop'? I meant to say 'affordably priced low overheads manufacturing unit'.

So, in terms of material, we have settled for the cheapest option, but what colour will our kit be? Again, economics play a part. Our budget doesn't yet run to asking Adidas or Nike to make us up a bespoke nectarine and lemon zest striped number. Our budget doesn't even run to off-the-shelf at Sports Direct. In fact, our budget limits our choices to one: a mate of ours called Tony, who runs what can best be described as a semi-legitimate pop-up football kit outlet, AKA an unlicensed market stall.

Doing business with Tony is difficult, because he's constantly got one eye out for anyone in uniform or carrying an official-looking clipboard, but he did concentrate enough to offer us an all-red strip that was actually rather natty. However, we turned it down, because on closer inspection you could quite clearly see grass stains and they already had players' names on the back. We could just have recruited players with the same names, but that would have taken some time and the chances are they could be the very same players the kit had clearly been nicked from in the first place.

Luckily, as we were talking, two middle-aged police officers popped into the market for a mid-morning sausage roll and before he legged it Tony was willing to do us a deal on a set of green and black striped shirts he had somehow 'acquired' from an open prison. And if older readers think that all sounds a bit like an episode of *Only Fools and Horses*, you'll have to take my word that it's actually based on a Sunday football team I knew only too well, because I played for it.

I wasn't bad actually. I wasn't actually good either, but that never stopped me thinking the strange old man watching the game on Mitcham Common was a scout from a league club, rather than the more likely explanation that he was somebody from an open prison looking for their stolen kit. In fact, Kieran still plays football, only he plays 'walking football' with some other elderly reprobates. I have pointed out to him that it's not a new phenomenon. I was playing 'walking football' when I was 25. In fact, as one unkind opposition winger once said, I was so slow it looked like I was running backwards.

I once talked Gary Lineker in detail through the only goal I ever scored, then very graciously offered to let him talk me through a couple of his goals in Sunday football. He said, 'We'll be a long time, I scored 161 in one season'. He also revealed the team travelled to games in his dad's fruit and veg van. The image of infant Lineker sitting on a bag of potatoes is a very pleasing one.

OK, we have a kit. A kit. Unfortunately, the FA say we need two kits, which is a bugger. I was rather hoping that if there was a colour clash with our green and black stripes, we could just turn the shirts inside out and have a black and green away kit, but the FA saw through that.

So as Kieran is colour blind, and it seems only fair that the co-owner of a club can tell which of the two teams on the pitch he actually owns, we have decided on an all-white one, which will be helpful for him even if it's ruinous for our laundry bill. Sadly, as we will discover, the higher up the league we go, the less football, and especially broadcasters, care about the roughly 8% of fans who are unable to distinguish between colours.

However, the expensive modern football kit has now become a way of making money too. These days no team, at any level, takes to the pitch without a sponsor's name splashed across their pristine green and black or all-white shirts. We cannot be an exception. It's not only a handy source of income, but we don't want other teams laughing at us, because we have plain shirts. What is this, the 1960s? Even primary school teams have front-of-shirt sponsorship now. And I'm not saying that Kieran comes from a hard part of South London, but his old primary school are currently sponsored by Golden Virginia...

Of course, it will be some time yet before we reach the level where a Far Eastern gambling site like ManBetX are offering us top dollar for our shirt fronts (and our integrity), but in the meantime there will hopefully be plenty of local businesses only too willing to offer at least medium dollar to sponsor us. In fact, by the time we hit the Premier League, sponsorship by betting companies will be on the verge of being banned, just as tobacco and alcohol sponsorship was, so there is no point approaching our local Paddy Power, even though, in the current climate, gambling companies are one of the few who can cough up the readies. Bet365, for example, who sponsor Stoke City, generate 13 times as much money from wagers in a season than the entire Premier League earns, although it still hasn't enabled them to spend their way back into it.

The website discountfootballkits.com has some handy tips on 'how to spice up your sponsorship pitch' and 'identifying a unique selling point, something that conveys a strong message, holds mass appeal and will attract publicity.' It also has some less handy tips, such as approaching a local driving school and offering to wear a kit consisting of a red shirt, amber shorts and yellow socks. Or, as Kieran would call it, all grey.

Of course, there was one obvious potential source of sponsorship: we are, after all, 'The Price of Football, the show that looks at the money behind the beautiful game,' so why don't we sponsor our own football team?

Well, it's partly because that would be a lot of words to fit across the front of a shirt, even allowing for our new striker, who is so big he has his own postcode, but it's mainly because Producer Guy, the self-styled chief executive officer of The Price of Football, is reluctant to commit to a sponsorship deal 'at this moment in time' but 'going forward' he 'may review his options vis-à-vis some sort of financial tie-in to our mutual benefit.' He certainly speaks like a chief executive, but I think he's missing a trick, because a) it's not real money and b) his name is on the cover of this bloody book!

So we took that website's advice and had a session to identify one of those unique selling points that holds mass appeal. We concluded that everyone likes pizza, mainly because we'd just had one delivered, and that is why our shirt sponsor is a brand-new local food outlet called Omino's Pizza, who want their name on the front of our shirts and are willing to pay a fair price, which at our level is around £500. However, in the world of professional football, a 'fair price' can mean many things, such as Everton receiving an estimated £30 million from a former business associate of the club owner for an option on naming rights for a new stadium, which at the time did not have planning permission. Five hundred quid is not a bad deal for us, providing, of course, that Omino's have any money left after the possible court case that may be coming their way from a similarly named dough-based food product delivery company.

HUMAN ASSETS

Right, I reckon West Park Rovers are just about ready to take our place on the legendary pyramid of English football and start our first season as a fully FA-accredited team with proper kits, a pitch to play on and joint owner/managers in me and Kieran, plus an owner/chief executive in the shape of Producer Guy. Is there anything we've forgotten? Oh yes, actual players.

Turns out that giant striker I mentioned is a friend of Uncle Terry's who may be here to keep an eye on that money he 'lent' us. Luckily he's also quite a handy player and his loyalty to Terry means he should be reliable, because I was amazed to learn from Kieran that at this level players can register for as many clubs as they want, provided they are in different leagues. This could present us with a problem, because we need players with 100% commitment and loyalty, and Kieran also tells me that we 100% cannot buy that commitment with cash. I assumed he meant because we didn't have any, but it's actually against the rules as I have already explained. Told you I had a short attention span.

I did suggest that perhaps we could just bung them a little bit of money to keep them loyal and buy their silence, but Kieran went a bit quiet and a funny colour at the same time. As Kieran is rarely quiet and has the lovely complexion of a teetotaller, I guessed that I'd said the wrong thing.

So, in the absence of cash inducements we recruited a squad by virtue of assuring them of our ambition and promising some of the better players that they would never have to take their place on the kit-cleaning rota. Actually, it's a consolation that at this level we don't have to pay the players' wages. In fact, they pay us. I've often thought that Premier League clubs should try the same scam. When we eventually get there and offer fifty million quid for Real Madrid's star striker, I intend to say to his agent, 'Look, he's getting a lovely house in the countryside, he'll be playing the game he loves in front of millions of people worldwide who all adore him, he's going to win trophies and make shed loads in image rights, and you still want us to actually pay him wages?! The deal is he pays us ten quid a week subs, take it or leave it.'

So we're ready and raring to go, and the good news is, we have enough spare money to fulfil the FA requirement that we keep our sprinkling of new, yet dedicated fans safely away from the pitch. As it happens, at this level keeping fans safely away from the pitch mainly involves four lengths of rope, but let's start as we mean to go on and make it good rope. And when we upgrade and need to sell it we can actually make money for old rope! Sorry, but every now and then I reserve the right to chuck in a terrible joke. Writer's perks.

BRASS TACKS

For all you accountants and pod fans, or those of you out there who are using this as a genuine guide to setting up a football club, here is Kieran's breakdown of our starting costs, together with my response (in brackets) when he made me concentrate enough to listen to what he was telling me.

League registration: £80 (That's a one-off right? What, every season? Swindlers.)

FA registration: £325 including mandatory public liability and personal accident insurance (Why is the insurance mandatory? Can't we just tell the players to be careful? Although I will concede that having seen some of them in the first training session they are indeed public liabilities.)

Cup registration: £32 (No worries, we'll make that back at Wembley.)

Player registration: 24 x £4 = £96 (We don't need that many players. Let's just get 12 really fit ones.)

Home and away kit: £1600 (Such a shame Tony got banged up as we'd have saved six hundred quid right there. Still, he may come out with a new set of shirts, so fingers crossed.)

Balls: 12 x £15 = £180 (That's a lot of balls... Sorry, had to be done.)

Pitch hire for home games: 15 x £70 = £1050 (Does that include rope?)

Rope: £100 (Oh.)

Training ground fees: once a week x 28 weeks = £40 x 28 = £1120 (Once a week! How fit do they need to be?)

Travel: £300 (Most of that will be cab fares for me. The players can jog. That'll save on training costs as well.)

Referees: 15 x £26 match fee and 35p a mile fuel costs = £35 x 15 = £525 (Can't they walk? Most refs look like they could use the exercise.)

Miscellaneous: £200 to cover pumps for balls, £12 fine per yellow card and £40 per red card, plus fines for everything, from not having numbers on the back of the shirt to not sending in your grading of the referee (Judging by the look of our centre-backs I reckon we may be shelling out a lot of forty quids.)

Total: £4448

So we've already forked out upwards of five grand and even though it's made-up money Guy has still kept the receipts. Of course, we'll get some of that back in player subs, but that won't be a steady source of income, because Kieran and I are both suckers for a sob story involving a player not being able to afford it this week, because he bought a kitten for a lonely old lady. They wouldn't try that with Guy, mainly because of the sign on his wall that says: 'No chance. Pay up or piss off.'

Now, let's get this party started and get ourselves up the leagues to where the real fictional money can be made and where, as Guy points out, we will have to travel further, which costs money, install floodlights, which costs money, pay the floodlight electricity bill, which costs a lot of money, put seats and a roof in, which costs... Alright I get the point. It's expensive.

For the moment let's just enjoy this brief moment of calm before the journey begins: West Park Rovers are established in the newly named EasyJet Sussex, Surrey and Gatwick Airport Sunday League, playing at Whitestone Park in a resplendent kit of green and black stripes. We have a badge consisting of a bird with the body of a seagull and the head of an eagle, and we have a motto – Nam Civitas Non Pecuniam – which translates as For the Community Not the Money and which is very admirable, but my inner capitalist has taken the precaution of checking that a motto is not actually legally binding.

We don't have a nickname yet, but it's early days. I'm suggesting the Titans, although knowing football fans it will probably end up being the Rovers or the Eagulls.* We do have a squad, though, and we have a captain in the form of throwback Scottish hardman centre-back Malky Porter. Self-appointed captain I should add, but trust me, he's not someone you argue with.

Most importantly, we have an ethos. We will foster a culture of respect, especially to match officials. We will create positive teams and environments. We will expect our players to win, lose or draw with dignity and decency, and we will do those things because we think they are right, not just because the FA handbook suggests it. We will be open and honest with our fans about matters on and off the pitch. We will reach out to local people and make sure Whitestone Park is a place of safety, security and, hopefully, fun. We will do our utmost to make sure that all fans feel welcome there regardless of ethnicity, religion or sexual identity.

We will recognise that times are hard financially and try to reflect that in the price of tickets, refreshments and merchandise. Our recruitment policy will be such that our staff fully reflect our community. In other words, we will be like no other team in the league. And we will have bowls of dog food in the bar for our four-legged fans.

So here we go. Ref, and I say this with the utmost respect, earn your twenty-six quid and blow that whistle!

---

*Actually, Eagulls is quite clever. So it will never catch on.

2

OWNERS

Prototypes, paragons and pricks

So, here we are on the first rung of the ladder of success, but what sort of owners are we going to be? Apart from responsible ones, of course, who will use any money we make purely for the benefit of the team and to improve facilities for our beloved fans, because they are the beating heart of our community.

If this was a text I would have included a winky face emoji at the end of that, although it turns out Kieran genuinely does believe this stuff. As do I in real life, but I'm already quite enjoying channelling my hidden capitalist. I also reckon that every multi-millionaire football club owner probably believes that stuff as well – right up until the moment they actually buy the club and start to become less and less of a multi-millionaire with each week that passes.

But before we discuss the many paragons of virtue* who constitute the club-owning class and which of them may be potential role models, let's have a brief history lesson. Many books have been written about child psychology, mainly for the benefit of middle-class parents who hope to spend as little actual time with their kids as possible, but are still keen to tell their mates down the gastropub how it should be done.

In truth, there is only one thing you really need to know about the infant human being: as soon as they can stand on their own

---

*Sarcastic face emoji…

two feet, they will use their own two feet to start kicking things. By the age of 18 months, any child with an ounce of self-respect will be kicking a toy, tin can or ball towards some sort of hole. It's why football was always going to win the evolutionary war to become our national sport and, for many of us, our national obsession.

By the way, if you are a new parent whose child likes to toddle down the corridor with an egg under its arm before slamming the egg down on the doorstep, then you have my condolences. Rugby is a fine sport, so I'm told, but I won't watch it on principle – the principle being that you should be able to see the bloody ball occasionally.*

That toddler instinct to kick is followed a few years later by the instinct to divide your mates into teams and take part in those 73-goal thrillers we remember so fondly from school playtimes. It's also around this stage when some children start to realise that while they love the whole kicking a ball thing, they may not be very good at it. That's when you'll spot the bossy kids who want to be managers, the sinister kids who want to be referees, the occasional really weird kid who wants to be a football accountant and the kid standing on the side thinking, 'Well, I clearly can't play this game, but I wonder if I can make money out of it?'

That's the kid we're interested in and that kid has always been with us. You will have seen the images of those mediaeval games that took place on Shrove Tuesday when hundreds of lads beat the crap out of each other in an attempt to transport a pig's bladder from one church to another. I use the word 'lads' for historical accuracy. Women and girls, as far as we know, weren't allowed to take part. Sadly, as we will see when we set up our women's team, it took an awfully long time for male attitudes to females in football to change. An *awfully* long time.

Anyway, you can bet your bottom groat that one likely lad will have spotted the chance to make money out of that Shrove Tuesday kickabout chaos. He will have started by making a few coppers holding cloaks for lords and ladies, then he will have progressed to

---

*It's not even a ball though, is it? Balls are round.

selling team parchments with the names of all the players, adverts for the local tavern and a sure-fire cure for rickets, and by the time you can say Peasants' Revolt he'll have bought one of the village teams and sold the tapestry rights to an overseas weaver. Because where there's football, there's money, and where there's money, there's someone trying to make more of it.

Early in the 19th century, in an attempt to civilise the mayhem, rules started to emerge from the public schools of England. Gradually these rules were codified and, as we've already discussed, in 1863 the Football Association was formed to oversee all aspects of the game in England. And it was a game for amateurs. There may have been handball and hacking, but there was no prize money and players weren't paid. It was all very gentlemanly until someone realised you could bung a fence round the pitch and charge people to get in. And then you could use some of that money to 'accidentally' pay a couple of hefty lads from the local factory who were not only good players, but only too keen to give a kicking to some effete Oxbridge graduates.

When the Factory Acts of 1874 and 1878 restricted the working hours of Industrial England, leaving millions of (mainly) men with nothing to do on a Saturday afternoon, canny business owners in the north, which was where so much of Industrial England was, realised that they not only had a bored workforce on their hands, but they also had a bored workforce who had just been paid on their hands.

The Football League – the *professional* Football League – was founded in 1888 with 12 clubs from the West Midlands and Lancashire who paid the players, charged the punters and immediately realised they could make money from every aspect of this new Saturday ritual. For example, the oldest existing movie footage of a match is from 1902, Burnley v Manchester United. As the flickering action begins your eye is immediately drawn to an advert for Bulldog Flake Tobacco, which runs across the entire length of the roof on the rudimentary stand. It's with those entrepreneurs that the game as we know it really begins.

Kieran has made a list of the main types of club owner. Actually, he made a spreadsheet and I turned it into a list, and first on it is the man who dreamed up the Football League all those years ago.

THE PIONEER

Aston Villa have a fair claim to be the most influential club in English football, because it was their director, William McGregor, who forever shattered the uneasy footballing truce between south and north, amateur and professional, kickabout and competition, top hat and cloth cap.

McGregor was a proud Scot who moved to Birmingham in 1870 to open a draper's (for those under the age of 90, that's a shop selling cloth). Despite looking like the sort of Victorian who would happily send a child up a chimney, he was a teetotal Christian, and passionate about football and its potential to turn boozy young tearaways into fine upstanding young men. In 1877 he was invited to become a committee member of Aston Villa and went on to serve the club as a director, chairman, president and occasional match umpire for over 20 years.

He sounds exactly like the sort of busy bugger that every Sunday football team has; the one who wants to organise everything and will then happily run the line waving a carrier bag as a flag (yes, Roy, I'm looking at you). They are very handy to have around, but tend to be equally annoying, especially when, like McGregor, they also try to stop the players from having a decent drink before kick-off.

McGregor was certainly a visionary. It's nigh-on impossible to say anything with certainty about the early days of organised football, but it was almost absolutely 100% definitely him who adopted the Scottish lion rampant as Villa's badge and it's believed that he sold an early form of football merchandise in his shop. I like to think these were a claret and blue top hat for the gentleman fan and a claret and blue corset for the lady fan. Or the cross-dressing gentleman fan.

In 1885, along with Major William Sudell, chairman of Preston North End, McGregor confirmed the long-held suspicions of snooty southern amateurs by admitting to a shocked FA committee that they were paying their players actual cash money. It was the death knell for amateur football. The FA caved in and allowed professional footballers 'but only under certain restrictions', the main one being you could only pay players who were born, or who had lived for two years, within 6 miles of the ground. Presumably this was to stop something else the FA disliked: the import of big hairy Scottish players into English teams.

Like so many FA regulations, this one was very easy to get around. All you had to do was import the big hairy Scottish players then give them a really well-paid job in a local mill, while allowing them to take every day off to train and play football.

Of course, to pay players you need money and McGregor became increasingly frustrated that the only games in which he was guaranteed matchday income were competitive cup ties. So, in 1888, after five friendly games in a row were cancelled at short notice, McGregor invited a number of other club owners to discuss the idea of starting a league, with the teams playing home and away fixtures, and ticket revenue being shared equally between the clubs.

Professional football as we know it had arrived, although the idea of sharing ticket revenue was quickly shelved – come on, it was the height of Victorian capitalism and what was the point of having more money than everyone else if you couldn't use it to buy success? Which is an ethos many club owners have stuck to ever since. By the way, I'm sure the newly professional Villa team must have been delighted to be paid to play football, but there was one drawback – William McGregor now obliged them to attend temperance meetings every Monday night.

Naturally, the early days of football were full of pioneers, like the owners of Chelsea, who started the club in 1905 simply because they had built a football ground intending to lease it to one of the growing number of teams in the capital, but couldn't find anyone willing to pay the extortionate rent. And Sir Henry Norris, owner of Woolwich Arsenal FC, who, fearing they faced too much competition in South London, moved the club to North London in 1913, then bribed their way into the first division, where they've been ever since.

Football soon became part of the weekly experience for working men and women all over the country. Well, all over those parts of the country where you couldn't see for smog. Even now, when you look at a map of the 92 English clubs they are mainly based in urban industrial conurbations. The more rural a town is, the more likely it will be that rugby is their sport, possibly because those areas were owned and influenced by the aristocracy who, for the most part, preferred the more gentlemanly game. You know, the one where 'gentlemen' stick their thumbs into an opponent's eye, but then call the referee 'Sir'.

In truth, once football had established itself as the national game it stayed pretty much the same on and off the pitch until the 1960s, that decade of glamour and free love we hear so much about; although my dad reckoned the glamour and free love didn't arrive in Tooting until about 1979, by which time he had a dodgy back, so it was too late.

We'll be hearing a lot about Jimmy Hill later, but in between being the man who abolished the minimum wage and TV's most annoying pundit, from 1961 to 1967 he was manager, then managing director, of Coventry City FC. Hill was a true pioneer, determined to put the comfort of fans at the heart of everything the club did. He introduced the country's first electronic scoreboard and the first club radio station. He booked local bands to perform pre-match and at half-time. He produced the first colour matchday programme and, even more impressively, he commissioned the Sky Blue Special, a chartered train that took fans to away games, complete with an on-board canteen and disco!

Granted, he wrote the 'Sky Blue Song', one of the worst football ditties ever, but in 1981, now chairman, he turned Highfield Road into the league's first all-seater stadium, because, he said, 'You can't be a hooligan sitting down.' By the way, you may have noticed that he was quite keen on the whole 'Sky Blue' branding. That's because it was him who changed Coventry City's kit from blue and white stripes to that iconic colour they still wear today.

I interviewed him on a live radio show towards the end of his life and he was still passionate and fascinated about football, but when I was praising him for his many innovations, he was keen to point out that they were about business as much as the comfort of the fans. The pre-match entertainment encouraged people to arrive early, which meant they had more time to buy refreshments. The innovative matchday programme always sold out and all the takings from the disco-train canteen also went to the club.

Modern football has thrown up its own pioneers. In 2012, a professional gambler called Matthew Benham bought Brentford and brought to Brentford a brand-new culture of analytics, relying on the examination of key performance indicators for player recruitment, rather than the recommendations of a scout or a YouTube clip sent by an agent. And modern football has produced pioneers of a more basic sort; men who have looked around for a suitable club to buy then shoved a funnel into its mouth and poured in the vast amounts of money needed to buy success.

Jack Walker was a Blackburn-born childhood fan of Blackburn Rovers. In 1991, having made around £600 million from the steel industry, he bought his beloved hometown club. They were 19th in the second tier of English football, which made it all the more surprising when he appointed as new manager the legendary Kenny Dalglish, winner of six league titles as a player for Liverpool and three more as manager.

In 1995, having spent big money on players like Alan Shearer and Chris Sutton, Blackburn Rovers won the Premier League title or, as many fans and journalists said at the time, they bought the Premier League title – mainly, I reckon, fans and journalists who supported the traditional big clubs. It's amazing how badly they take it when someone else wins, like Leicester, in 2016, who got lucky by amassing more points than the others in just 38 short games.

Walker resented the accusation, pointing out that runners-up Manchester United had spent more on players than he had that season and that Liverpool had bought one defender, Phil Babb, who cost more than his entire back four. Walker also spent a lot of money turning Ewood Park into a ground fit for a title-winning team and, as someone who got soaking wet there one night in 1989 and was then covered in glass when a brick came through the train window on the way back, I can testify that returning there a few years later was a much more pleasant experience. He must have spent a *lot* of money.

Despite the snootiness of some fans there was still an element of romance in Blackburn's title win. For later exponents of Walker's pioneering approach, I suspect the word 'romance' rarely came up. Roman Abramovich took over at Chelsea in 2003 and in 2005, for the first time in 50 years, they won the Premier League. Before he was forced out of the club following the Russian invasion of Ukraine, Chelsea won the Premier League four more times and the Champions League twice, as well as many other trophies that he probably left in the taxi on his way back from the final. I don't think maths has a number high enough to describe the money he spent doing so, but I'd suggest it was a shitloadillion.

We can be clearer on the numbers elsewhere. When the Sovereign Wealth Fund of Abu Dhabi, headed by Sheikh Mansour, took over at Manchester City in 2008 their squad was worth £76 million. Four years later they won the Premier League title with a squad worth £438 million and a wage bill that had quadrupled. Similarly, in one of the most unlikely club takeovers ever, Hollywood legend Ryan Reynolds and his sidekick Rob McElhenney are now the proud owners of Wrexham FC, and have embarked on their own spending spree, filming themselves every step of the way. They have started by lifting the club from the fifth tier of English football and will be wanting to replicate the success of Luton Town in the ultimate aim of being part of the Premier League.

The Brentford model seems a bit modern for us here at West Park Rovers and clearly we don't have the funds to emulate those other contemporary pioneers, so let's look at a type of club owner more familiar to our generation.

THE LOCAL BOY MADE GOOD

Anyone who grew up watching football on telly in the 1970s will recognise this image. During a lull in the game the camera would inevitably pan to the directors' box for a lingering shot of a man in a camel-hair coat and trilby barely visible through a plume of cigar smoke. This was the owner. The commentator would chuckle, tell us who we were gazing at and possibly mention his glamorous wife, who would almost certainly be the only woman in the directors' box and quite possibly the only woman in the entire stand. The owner would inevitably spot the camera, then lift his hat and smile benevolently, whereupon the commentator would tell us what a good sport he was, before invariably adding, 'He's a local boy made good, of course – the fans love him.'

As a kid I was a bit bemused by this. I was a local boy and I had definitely never seen the Crystal Palace owner, Raymond Bloye, hanging around anywhere that I knew, even allowing for the fact that a middle-aged man in a trilby lingering outside a youth club wouldn't have been a good look. I did, however, know how he made his money, because the matchday programme never lost an opportunity to tell us he was the accountant for London's biggest wholesale meat supplier, and every now and then would have an 'amusing' photo of him writing a cheque next to an upside down and extremely dead cow.

In November 1974, because of floodlight concerns, Palace played an away FA Cup game at non-league Tooting and Mitcham* on a Wednesday afternoon. A couple of us duly bunked off school to attend and on the long walk there we were caught in a torrential downpour, when a very posh car pulled up alongside us and the driver asked if we were going to the game. Personally, I would have thought the Palace scarves round our wrists would have been a clue, but we nodded politely and said we were, whereupon he offered us a lift.

We weren't supposed to get into a stranger's car, but sod that, it was bloody pouring, so in we got and the kindly gentleman introduced himself as Raymond Bloye. He did look vaguely familiar and seemed to have an extensive knowledge of the accounting side of the meat business, so we went along with that while he drove us right up to the main entrance of Tooting and Mitcham's tiny ground. A man in a blazer rushed to open the car door and said, 'Good afternoon, Mr Bloye, are these your children?' to which he replied, 'Christ, no', gave us a quid each and disappeared inside. Kinder, gentler times...

Kind and gentle were not words you would use about the archetypal local boy made good, Bob Lord of Burnley,[†] the first club owner with a truly national profile. Like Sid James, Angel Delight and flared trousers, it's almost impossible to imagine Bob Lord existing outside the 60s and 70s. And, like Raymond Bloye, he was also big in meat, establishing a successful chain of Lancashire butchers before buying Burnley FC, where he oversaw a period of great on-field success and great off-field controversy. He was the classic example of a man who saw himself as plain-speaking and honest, but who was, in general, ignorant and rude. He revelled in being a thorn in the side of the football authorities, asking rhetorically, 'Who was the butcher's boy to be telling the big shots how to run their mismanaged business?'

---

*I'm ashamed to say that T and M's ground, Sandy Lane, was actually much closer to my flat than Selhurst Park, but in my defence I only found that out when I was six and already a Palace fan.
[†]That's Bob Lord, of Burnley. Not Bob, Lord of Burnley.

I wondered how much it cost Bob Lord to run his well-managed football club. Luckily, I wondered aloud near Kieran, who needs no excuse to forensically examine a balance sheet and he dived straight in. Sadly, it turns out that shortly before his death, Bob Lord ordered his daughter to burn all his business papers, but we can show you what an albeit much bigger team was spending at the time:

Liverpool FC	1973/74	2021/22
TV revenue	Nil	£260,841,000
Total revenue	£847,149	£594,271,000
Transfer fees spent	£62,000	£68,651,000
Wages	£365,874	£366,092,000

Source: The Liverpool Football Club and Athletic Grounds Annual Report

Kieran worked out (with great pleasure) that in 2018/19, the last season before the Premier League's revenues were impacted by Covid, it took Liverpool 13 hours and 54 minutes to earn as much as they did in the whole of the 1973/74 season, and in that time wages rose by 100,060%.

Of course, the biggest difference between then and now is TV income, which proves that the butcher's boy didn't always know better than the big shots. Lord was a fierce opponent of televised football, explaining in 1963 that it would 'damage and undermine attendances' and he banned *Match of the Day* cameras until 1969. He also predicted that allowing cameras in would inevitably lead to 'a world of television football fans looking on as Manchester United won the title every year' and then, in 1974, he went further, making antisemetic implications about who ran football. Incredibly, the FA and the Football League saw no need to sanction him, and when an offended Manny Cussins, the Jewish owner of Leeds United, said he would walk out of the Elland Road boardroom if Lord visited, Lord complained to the press about *his* mistreatment. As a postscript to that, in 2022, Burnley FC conducted a six-month investigation after the Board of Deputies of British Jews suggested that the Bob Lord Stand at Turf Moor be renamed. After consulting with Jewish representatives, communities and supporters they decided to retain the name, but did officially adopt the International Holocaust Remembrance Alliance's definition of antisemitism.

Many football club owners back then smoked cigars, but Sam Longson smoked cigars with a capital C and had the jowly demeanour of a man who probably looked 75 when he was born, although, let's be honest, all babies look 75 when they're born. By the age of 21 he owned a fleet of lorries and claimed to be the first man ever to deliver milk by road to Manchester from the Peak District. He went on to build one of the biggest haulage companies in the country, which he sold to take control of his boyhood club, Derby County, in 1967.

Sam Longson was the man who brought the untried managerial duo of Brian Clough and Peter Taylor to Derby from Hartlepool United, ushering in half a decade of amazing success. Unfortunately, he is better known as the man who then forced Clough out of the club, ushering in a very bitter and public dispute. Longson had grown increasingly tired of Clough's outspokenness and when the manager signed David Nish from Leicester without consulting the board, Longson had had enough and demanded that they cancelled all extra-curricular activity and did no transfer business without permission. Clough and Taylor resigned, expecting Longson to back down, but he didn't. He banned them from the ground.

The players threatened to strike and Clough used a mate's season ticket to attend the next home game to tumultuous applause, but there were ugly mob scenes outside the ground and Longson's home. This was 1973, a time of terrible industrial unrest, and Longson was seen as representing the boss class, unable to deal with a maverick working-class talent, an image that he seemed happy to feed with his cigars and his Rolls-Royce. It didn't help that, according to Taylor, Longson offered Taylor alone a huge amount of money to stay on, then cancelled the insurance on his and Clough's cars, and informed the police they should stop and arrest them for driving without insurance!

Many clubs are still owned by local boys made good and, who knows, as we hurtle towards the middle of the 21st century we may see some more clubs owned by a local girl made good. At the moment, Carol Shanahan, owner of Port Vale, is one of only three women who have a stake of more than 10% in a Premier League or EFL club. The others are Joy Seppala, owner of hedge fund Sisu, who retained 15% of their stake in Coventry City after a recent takeover, and Amanda Staveley, who owns 10% of Newcastle United.

Shanahan is an award-winning businesswoman, noted for her dedication to corporate social responsibility, and since buying the club in 2019 that dedication has been seen in action. Not only did Port Vale (admittedly like just about every club in the country) become a community hub during the pandemic, but it has continued doing sterling work, particularly for local children. And why did she buy the club when it was in severe financial difficulties? Simple: 'We really viewed it as almost a loved one being held hostage and someone had to pay the ransom.'

She is a reminder that the local-person-made-good model tends to be a much more benevolent style of ownership. Rather than investing in a club as an act of self-aggrandisement, the likes of Andy Holt at Accrington and Simon Hallett at Plymouth Argyle have invested their own money into clubs in the communities they were raised in, because, yes, they want success, but also because they recognise the importance of those clubs to those communities, both economically and psychologically.

Salford City are owned by not one, but six, local boys made good. *Very* good. David Beckham, Nicky Butt, Ryan Giggs, Paul Scholes and the Neville brothers – the so-called Class of '92 – are ex-Manchester United stars who wanted to 'put something back' into an area that meant so much to them. They have achieved the extraordinary feat of establishing a tiny club in the Football League *and* making Gary Neville seem like a decent lad. However, when they set up Project 92 Ltd to buy the club, they probably didn't envisage it would lose £92,000 a week by 2020/21, which is an astonishing sum for a club at that level with an average crowd of 2274.*

It seems those losses are being sustained not by the local lads, but by a Singaporean businessman, who purchased a 50% stake in the club in 2014. Peter Lim also owns Spanish club Valencia and at the last home match of the 2021/22 season the entire crowd walked

---

*For those who see destiny in numbers, I guess the Class of '92 setting up Project 92, which went on to lose 92 grand a week in a 92-club league, is almost too good to be true.

out of their famous Mestalla stadium during the game. All of them, every single one, abandoned the game to hold a 'Lim out' protest in a local square.

Regardless of who is doing the funding, Andy Holt is one of many other owners who loudly complain that the wealth of Salford's local boys made brilliant makes it impossible for Accrington's boy made good to compete. He may have a point. In September 2022, Salford City announced they had received an extra £2.5 million in investment from existing shareholders in the previous six months, which was an interest-free loan on top of a further £2.5 million generated by issuing new shares in the 12 months before that. Meanwhile, Accrington Stanley's entire wage bill for 2022 was £1.8 million.

When it comes to West Park Rovers, Kieran and I may be local, but you would have to extend the definition a bit to argue that we have made good. And let's face it, we're no longer boys either, although we are both constantly being asked to grow up by our partners. Let's see, then, if we fit into the next category.

THE TIGHTWAD

There's a very strange sort of club owner in modern football and I suspect it's the sort Producer Guy secretly admires: the sort who is wealthy enough to buy a football club in the first place, but then seems to begrudge every single penny he has to spend to keep that club going. 'It's called careful cost management, Kevin,' says Producer Guy.

When a consortium led by Steve Parish bought Crystal Palace in 2010 (saving the club from almost certain liquidation) they were honest enough to admit that most of their money had gone on the actual purchase and there was none left to buy Lionel Messi. Overjoyed at still having a club to support, we Palace fans were perfectly happy to have our expectations managed, but managing the expectations of Newcastle fans is a completely different matter. Despite not winning a trophy since 1969, Newcastle fans have recently lived in a permanent state of optimism about the future tinged with fury at under-achievement in the present.

In 2019, according to the *Sunday Times* Rich List (in which I believe you can find Producer Guy at around number 11), Mike

Ashley, owner of Sports Direct, was worth £1.976 billion. Yes, billion. So, when he bought Newcastle United in 2007 for around £134 million, Toon fans finally started to plan for those inevitable trips to Barcelona and Munich.

At first, all went well. Ashley paid off most of the club's outstanding debts and turned up in the directors' box wearing a Newcastle shirt. It's amazing how fans are impressed by a billionaire wearing a £44.99 shirt that he certainly didn't pay for because a) he owned the club and b) he owned the shops that sold the shirts. However, Newcastle fans are a savvy bunch and after a while they noticed that their away trips were still to places like Norwich rather than the Nou Camp. As the *Newcastle Chronicle* put it: 'Fans of the Magpies have been left frustrated and often infuriated by the businessman's decisions.' Indeed.

To be fair to Mike Ashley (not words you hear often) he put millions into the club to keep them viable, he just didn't put in enough millions to keep them ambitious, although every now and then he would have a rush of blood to the head, like spending a fortune prising manager Steve Bruce away from Sheffield Wednesday.

During the 14 years between buying and selling the club, Mike Ashley's Newcastle United made an operating profit of over £30 million. However, during that period the club was relegated twice and won no silverware, unless you count the EFL Championship in 2010 and 2017; as that second one prevented Brighton from winning it, they definitely are worth counting.

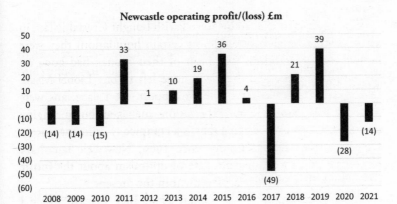

Newcastle operating profit/(loss) £m

Source: Kieran Maguire

One area that was very noticeable during Ashley's reign at St James' Park was the spending on infrastructure, or, more accurately, the lack of spending on infrastructure. Newcastle spent £8 million on new facilities, machinery, IT equipment etc. in the period from 2010 to 2021, the lowest amount in the Premier League. This was despite some other clubs not spending much (or in the case of Brentford, any) time in that division during the period and other clubs, like West Ham, renting rather than owning their stadium for part of that time.

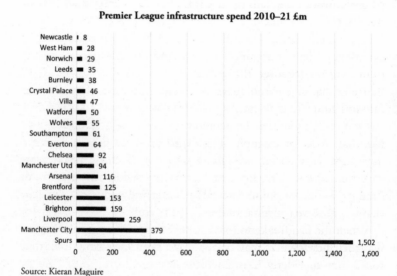

Premier League infrastructure spend 2010–21 £m

Source: Kieran Maguire

Ashley's diminishing rearguard of supporters pointed out how sensible his approach was, but 'sensible' isn't sexy, as I explained to Kieran and Guy when I took that cruise down the Loire last week to source new wines for the executive lounges and possibly bump into Kylian Mbappé's agent on the way.

THE SOVEREIGN STATE

If Newcastle fans got excited when a wealthy individual bought their club, imagine the thrill when word got round that a wealthy country was about to buy it. Super-wealthy, in fact, and with a sudden desire to spend big on sport-washing its image. This is one ownership model you won't find at our level. Even the smallest country isn't looking to improve its global branding by acquiring a glorified Sunday League team, even one that's handy for the airport, although for a while South London non-league team Peckham Town were sponsored by the Jamaican Embassy, which we all thought was really cool.

The Kingdom of Saudi Arabia, however, claimed it wasn't them that actually wanted to buy Newcastle United, it was their Public Investment Fund (PIF), which had over $600 billion in assets and whose directors were all, by an amazing coincidence, members of the Saudi royal family.

The purchase was a protracted one, with the Premier League claiming, despite appearances to the contrary, that they didn't try to prevent the takeover, they just didn't get round to approving it. Basically, that's the corporate version of putting your fingers in your ears and going 'la-la-la' until a problem goes away.

Of course, there may be people who aren't uneasy about things like that. Me, for example. Personally, now I'm a club owner I don't care what Kieran says about integrity. If the North Korean government is looking for a way into English football, I, for one, think it would be polite to at least hear them out. And possibly charge a massive consultation fee in the process.

When the Saudi takeover was complete, Geordie fans, delighted that their new owners may be about to invest the sort of cash that could lure an elderly Cristiano Ronaldo to the north-east in an all-out bid to qualify for the Europa Conference League, justifiably pointed out the glaringly obvious hypocrisy of all those who criticised the new owners for their country's values: to all intents and purposes, Manchester City are owned by the ruling family of Abu Dhabi.

Yes, technically, they too are owned by a private investment company, but it's a company set up specifically to privately invest on behalf of the ruling family of Abu Dhabi; and as their attitude to new-fangled things like homosexuality and women walking alongside men are highly questionable, then you can't blame those Newcastle fans who smelled double standards.

It has to be said, though, that Sheikh Mansour and his family have not just bought incredible success to Manchester City, they have also galvanised the run-down, economically deprived eastern part of the city itself with a programme of construction and job creation, and they seem very aware of their corporate community responsibility. If the Saudis can do something similar in Newcastle then people outside the city may perhaps question their motives a little less. Perhaps.

It's been interesting (and mildly amusing) to watch the reaction of fans of the traditional big six clubs to the idea of Newcastle muscling their way into the gang at their expense. Although some are more philosophical. Arsenal nut Ian Stone is a very fine comedian and the host of BT Sports chat show *The Football's On* and he's actually quite looking forward to the idea. 'Of course, because if Newcastle do buy their way in it could only be at the expense of Spurs and how entertaining would that be?!' I asked Ian if he would accept a similar takeover at Arsenal? 'Well, nation states do have very deep pockets but I'd rather not be owned by a despot. But these days the most you can hope for is that the owner of your club is less of a dick than all the other dicks'. Hmm, that could be Kieran's motto.

Things get a little more nuanced when your club is acquired by an individual whose personal attitudes to human rights have never been ascertained, but who certainly doesn't look like he'd be bothered if his henchmen threw someone into a shark pool in their underground volcano lair. Roman Abramovich, for example, whose CV almost certainly contains the words 'legitimate businessman'.

THE OLIGARCH

Your attitude to Roman Abramovich will probably depend on what team you support, because it is a sad fact of footballing life that the more successful your team becomes, the fewer awkward questions your fans will ask. For example, those Everton fans who spent years accusing Chelsea of artificial success bankrolled by a Bond villain were probably less critical when the naming rights for their training ground were bought by a company controlled by another oligarch, Alisher Usmanov, for way above the expected price.

In December 2019 Everton sacked manager Marco Silva and replaced him two weeks later with the master of the raised eyebrow, Carlo Ancelotti. Some observers queried how Everton, who had racked up pre-tax losses of £112 million the previous season, could afford to pay Silva's redundancy and meet Ancelotti's wage demands. They also wondered how Everton could stay within the Premier League's Profitability and Sustainability Limits, which replaced Financial Fair Play, but may promote neither profitability nor sustainability.

In what was no doubt just another amazing coincidence, in January 2020, Usmanov's USM Holdings then agreed a naming-rights option, *not* a commitment, for Everton's new stadium at Bramley Moore Dock, at an estimated fee of £30 million. This was despite the fact that planning permission had yet to be granted (it was eventually given, but more than a year later). Usmanov was a close associate of Everton's owner, Farhad Moshiri, and between them they had wonderful plans for Everton's future and the funding of a range of brilliant local projects.

However, Usmanov, from Uzbekistan, once spent six years in a Russian prison for 'fraud and theft of socialist property'. He then made his money 'acquiring' metal mines in the aftermath of the collapse of the Soviet Union. He is also a 'close associate' of Vladimir Putin. Does any of that matter? As I said, depends on who you support. And, of course, events in Ukraine have conspired to make that a rhetorical question.

It's very difficult to tie down exactly when and how Roman Abramovich went from selling dolls on the street for a couple of roubles at a time to buying aluminium mines for millions of dollars at a time, but by his own admission a lot of those millions went on bribes and protection money. As a BBC investigation noted, Abramovich told a journalist he was initially reluctant to enter the world of aluminium because, 'Every three days someone was murdered in that business.' And as the BBC investigation also noted, after Abramovich did arrive, the aluminium industry became a lot safer.

That, naturally, is a coincidence, as our lawyers are only too keen for us to point out, and Roman Abramovich has certainly donated a lot to charity. He probably sleeps at night. He probably slept at night even when someone other than Chelsea was winning the Champions League, because, of course, there would be other nights in other seasons. All he had to do was spend even more money to buy even more success, secure in the knowledge that while he was spending it, he was making it all back in interest at the same time.

Roman Abramovich bought Chelsea in 2003 via a company called Fordstam Limited and 'loaned' the club approximately £1.5 billion via companies based in the Channel Islands and British

Virgin Islands called Camberley International Investments and Lindeza Worldwide. In the eyes of some fans that money was well spent in terms of delivering two Champions League titles and many domestic trophies, as well as the occasional chance to see Danny Drinkwater and Adrian Mutu play at Stamford Bridge.

Roman's riches bought Chelsea a lot of success, but as we know there was a sting in the tail. On 24 February 2022, Vladimir Putin ordered his troops across the border to launch an unprovoked and undeclared war on Ukraine. On the same day Chelsea, one of the richest football clubs in the world, were third in the Premier League and still very much in contention for the Champions League. A few weeks later they were still third in the Premier League, but they were out of the Champions League and were most emphatically *not* one of the richest football clubs in the world.

On 10 March, as a response to the invasion, the UK government sanctioned a number of Russian businessmen who had financial interests in this country. Roman Abramovich was one of them and ownership of Chelsea Football Club passed temporarily into the hands of ... well, no one knew whose hands really. And no one in the government or Civil Service was showing much desire for this giant hot potato to be thrust into their mitts.

Nevertheless, Chelsea were now trading only by virtue of a special government licence. As Mr Abramovich was now unable to profit from his asset, then no more matchday tickets would be sold to home or away fans. Those who already had season tickets could attend Stamford Bridge for home games, but they would not be allowed to buy any form of merchandise, although the licence was hastily amended to allow food and drink to be purchased (especially in the executive lounges, naturally).

It didn't take long for the government to decide it was sensible to allow the matchday experience to return to some sort of normal with away fans allowed to attend games again, while they got on with the serious business of finding a new billionaire owner for the club once Abramovich had publicly agreed that any profit from the sale would go to charity and not to him. And no asking for that £1.5 billion loan back, eh Roman? There's a good chap.

Turns out that finding a new billionaire quickly *was* a serious business. One of the richest clubs in the world now only had enough liquid cash for the next monthly wage bill and possibly the one after that. To use Kieran's technical accounting term, they were fucked. Under Abramovich, Chelsea went from having the fifth highest wage bill in the Premier League in 2003, behind Manchester United, Arsenal, Leeds United and Newcastle United, to having the highest in history. In 2020/21 Chelsea's wage bill was £28 million a month – not an issue when the club is being bankrolled by a multi-billionaire such as Abramovich, but when Chelsea had their assets frozen and no revenues coming in, paying that sort of dosh became a challenge. And Chelsea weren't the only club affected. Everton, already in financial difficulty, were now stripped of that potential investment from Alisher Usmanov.

The UK government relaxed the terms of the licence under which Chelsea could trade, allowing the club to borrow £30 million to address the cash flow problems. This gave enough breathing space to allow a successful sale to new owners, on the condition that none of the proceeds went to Abramovich or 'any other sanctioned individual' and went instead to a foundation that would channel it to humanitarian aid causes in Ukraine.

Chelsea were duly acquired by a consortium led by US businessman Todd Boehly for a fee reported to be in the region of £2.5 billion, a sum that, according to which sources you believe, is either a billion more or a billion less than Boehly himself is worth. As to where that £2.5 billion went, it does seem clear that none of it ended up in an oligarch's pocket, but, at time of writing, the UK government is exceptionally cagey about how much has gone to support victims of the war in Ukraine, because the sum is precisely zero.

Naturally, many fans of other clubs enjoyed the plight that Chelsea fans were now in, but to me it was a frightening indication of how quickly a club's fortunes can turn (and disappear).

Still, if you're reading this, Mr Abramovich, and you're still having your little local difficulty with the British authorities, one third of us here at West Park Rovers doesn't judge. What happened in post-Soviet Russia stays in post-Soviet Russia as far as we're concerned. Give me a call. We can find a way round. Unless we've already done a deal with the North Koreans by then.

At least Abramovich bought Chelsea with his own money. It turns out that's not always the case. In 2021, Burnley (until then always top of Kieran's list of best-run teams in the Premier League) were bought by an American consortium called ALK Capital using the club they didn't own yet as collateral; and, incredibly, a few years earlier Malcolm Glazer had used the same process to acquire Manchester United, one of the biggest and most successful clubs in the world.

THE LEVERAGED BUYER

United were actually bought using leveraged loans, which is money borrowed to buy a company based on the fact that you *will* be able to pay it back, because the company you are borrowing the money to buy is enormously profitable and has lots of lovely assets you can sell if it all goes tits up. (Kieran tells me that's not quite the language accountants use, but it's close enough.)

Oddly enough, the sale of Manchester United was partly due to a horse. The then owners of Manchester United were in a syndicate with legendary club manager Alex Ferguson, but they fell out over who owned the most legs on Rock of Gibraltar, winner of the 2000 Guineas in both England and Ireland in 2002, and therefore worth a fortune in stud fees. It all got so heated that they decided to sell the club.

Malcolm Glazer was the classic all-American boy made good. Born in New York State in 1928, the son of Lithuanian immigrants, he began by selling watches door to door, a job he was very good at and, presumably, never late for. He raised enough money to buy a watch repair concession for the US Air Force (apparently G-forces can play havoc with the big hand), before investing in real estate, healthcare provision and TV channels.

In 1995 he spent a then record sum of $192 million buying the NFL franchise Tampa Bay Buccaneers and in 2003 began to acquire shares in Manchester United, buying his first 2.9% for £9 million. By 2005 he had enough money to buy the club outright. How did he have enough money? By borrowing huge sums against the huge sums Manchester United would earn in the future. Except it wouldn't be Manchester United earning the huge sums of money, it would be Malcolm Glazer and his family.

The purchase caused a seismic rift among the club's enormous fanbase and, for some, damaged the integrity of Sir Alex Ferguson, who fully backed the purchase. Overnight, a debt-free Manchester United was now saddled with six hundred million quid's worth of debt, which initially increased, partially due to the Glazers using payment-in-kind (PIK) loans, in which interest is added to the amount borrowed as one of the means of financing the club. By March 2023 United owed banks over £100 million more than the original amount borrowed.

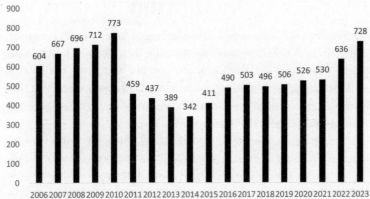

Manchester United Borrowings £m

Source: Kieran Maguire

If this doesn't sound like a great business strategy, there were certainly some winners from the Glazers' acquisition of Manchester United – the banks. Indeed, since 2005 Manchester United has incurred interest costs of £855 million, enough to sign 10 more Harry Maguires and still have enough change left over for a Donny van de Beek.

Malcolm Glazer died in 2014, leaving the club to his five sons and a daughter, who between them take out an annual dividend of around £18 million. Thanks, Dad! Early in 2021, Avram Glazer sold five million of his shares for around $100 million. Was that money re-invested in the club? Of course it bloody wasn't!

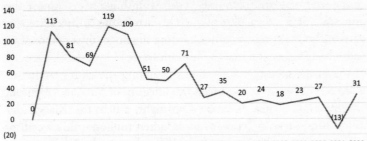

Manchester United interest expense £m

Source: Kieran Maguire

There has been some on-field success under the Glazers, but there would have been anyway, even if I was in charge. In the meantime, Old Trafford has been left to stagnate and has been taken off UEFA's list of approved venues to host European finals, which are a potential source of income not just for the club, but for the hospitality industry in the city. Paint is peeling and there are holes in the roof letting in rain, and United fans are left to reflect that the debt belongs to the club, but the earnings belong to the Glazers.

There are some people whose motives for buying a football club in the first place don't seem to be about bringing success, but about making as much money as possible before someone notices the chaos they have caused; people who care nothing for a club's fans or its place in the community. On *The Price of Football*, these people are known as 'wrong'uns'. Actually, they are known as many things, but 'wrong 'un' is the closest we can get without our lawyers having kittens.

THE WRONG'UN

Sadly, there are so many candidates for inclusion in this section, many of whom seem to have an almost cartoon-like roguish charm until you properly examine what they did *to* their clubs, while claiming they were doing it *for* their clubs. Ken Richardson, for example, former owner of Doncaster Rovers, was jailed for four years in 1999 after hiring someone to burn down his own stadium, so he could claim the insurance and sell the land to property developers. He claimed he only did it because the local council refused him planning permission to actually build a new ground, but it was a plot of such an intellectually low level that even without Velma, Scooby-Doo could have foiled it. Richardson was arrested after the man he hired to start the fire left his mobile phone at the scene!

Ken is obviously a good name for, shall we say, the more 'robust' type of club owner. In 2007 Ken Bates put Leeds United into administration with debts of more than £35 million, then headed a consortium that bought it back from the administrators for just £1.5 million, but now, of course, as a new company that was debt-free.

However, his status as a wrong'un is based mainly on his erection of an actual electric fence to keep the fans off the pitch at Stamford Bridge when he owned Chelsea. Luckily, the fence had to be taken down when he was refused permission to switch it on. He consoled himself by declaring that all football fans were 'parasites' who gave nothing to the game. Unless you counted all that money they spent on tickets, merchandise, travel, beer and pies.

Leeds United haven't had much luck when it comes to owners. In 2014 they were acquired by Italian businessman Massimo Cellino, even though he had prior criminal convictions for embezzling millions from the Italian Minister of Agriculture and false accounting when he was the owner of Cagliari. Less importantly, he also hated the number 17, so much so that all seats numbered 17 had to be changed to 16b, and was terrified of the colour purple. Clearly the EFL owners' and directors' test did not have a clause preventing oddly superstitious people from buying a football club, and it sure as hell didn't have one that prevented a convicted fraudster buying Leeds. Maybe his 15-month prison sentence being suspended was a tick in the plus column. His many cost-cutting plans included stopping free lunches at the training ground and making the players pay to have their kits washed. Whether that covered the expense of changing all the seat numbers to 16b we shall never know.

Cellino's time at Leeds is best described as 'colourful'. In the space of three years at the club he sacked managers Darko Milanič, Brian McDermott, Dave Hockaday, Neil Redfearn, Uwe Rösler, Steve Evans and Garry Monk.

Cellino also tried to ban Sky Sports cameras from Elland Road and once planned to drastically alter away ticket allocations. He also introduced the infamous 'pie tax' – South Stand ticket prices went up by £5, but now came with a food voucher, although he denied it was to punish fans there who booed him (and no, Guy, a pie tax is not a good idea). He sold his investment in the club in 2017 and when he left he told those fans, 'If you can survive working with me, you can survive anything.'

And before him at Elland Road there was Peter Ridsdale, who in six years, from 1997 to 2003, took Leeds United from the Champions League to mid-table in League One. Doing that the other way round would have been a hell of an achievement, but even the way he did it took some doing and, according to which financial sources you believe, in the same period Leeds went from being worth £12 million on the Stock Exchange to being anywhere between £70 and £103 million in debt. That was partly because the club borrowed £60 million against future gate receipts and partly because Ridsdale sanctioned such ludicrously high transfer bids that he became affectionately known to agents as 'Father Christmas'.

Fear not, though, for the vagaries of English football are such that despite being disqualified as a company director for seven years between 2013 and 2020 after he diverted payments meant for his business to a personal account, he was happily back in the game as chairman of, and then adviser to – but not director of, so that's alright then – Preston North End.

Sadly, there isn't room here to discuss a whole host of eccentric club owners around the world, but special mention must go to Maurizio Zampini, owner of Palermo, who once threatened to cut off and eat his players' testicles (possibly why hot dog sales slumped in the Stadio Renzo Barbera). Another Italian owner, though, did his damage closer to home. Musician and music producer Domenico Serafino took less than three years to bring down Welsh club Bangor City, which was founded way back in 1876 and which, not that long ago, had faced Napoli and Atlético Madrid in European competition.

The most cursory of checks by local journalists uncovered the fact that when Serafino bought Bangor in 2019, the man he brought along as his 'business adviser', one Ignazio Spinnato, was an ex-jailbird, imprisoned for his part in a drug trafficking and money laundering operation run by the Mafia. You'd think Serafino's links with a man like that would have rung alarm bells somewhere in the Welsh FA, but apparently not. And when Bangor City, in Cymru North, the second tier of Welsh football, suddenly started recruiting players on professional contracts from as far away as Argentina and South Africa, those bells still stayed resolutely unheard.

Then along came the pandemic, a time of uncertainty and fear for football clubs all over the world. Welsh football was, of course, suspended and Serafino, as he was perfectly entitled to do, put the players on furlough and received furlough money of £375,000. The only problem was that he didn't pass all of it on to the team.

Stories emerged of players struggling to feed their families and those foreign recruits having to turn to fans and foodbanks for help. In 2021, Bangor were suspended from the league and in 2022 Serafino withdrew from the league completely with debts of £55,000. The club's results were expunged and 146 years of history was over, just like that.

It's not a ringing endorsement, but whatever else the Glazer family are, at least they are not the Oyston family. Estate agent Owen Oyston bought Blackpool FC in 1988 for the princely sum of £1 and, as Kieran says, every time a club changes hands for a token amount like that you may as well use the money to call the administrators now and save time later. He kept the club ticking over until he was convicted and imprisoned for rape and indecent assault. Horrible crimes, but not so horrible that the Football League didn't happily allow him to continue as a club director, even from behind bars.

While Oyston was 'away', first his wife Vicki and then his son Karl took charge of the club, and despite running it on a shoestring* they were promoted to the Premier League in 2010. They stayed there just one season; perhaps not surprisingly given they spent only £1 million on new players and had the lowest Premier League wage bill this century. Then, also perhaps not surprisingly, it turned out that despite their claims to the contrary, money for players and higher wages had been available all along. An investigation of the accounts revealed that an un-named director, possibly called Oyston, had been paid £11 million across the season.

Definitely not surprisingly, the fans were furious and began a campaign called 'Not A Penny More', boycotting Blackpool games and merchandise. The Oystons were unperturbed, because they had several seasons of Premier League parachute payments to fall back on, or stash away, whichever technical term you prefer. It was a terrible time of tension, claim and counterclaim as the name of one of England's most famous football clubs was dragged through the donkey-shit on the Golden Mile while silver-tongued lawyers coined it in from both sides.

---

*Kieran has yet to define how much a 'shoestring' actually is.

Then another shareholder, club president Valeri Belokon, sued Karl Oyston over irregular payments and the court found that a cool £26 million had made its way from the club to the Oyston family. They were forced to relinquish ownership; the club went into receivership and the Oystons were forced to pay Mr Belokon a lot of money, which they are still doing. The club is still not faring brilliantly financially, but until recent relegation they were in the Championship and no one in that league is doing brilliantly financially. In fact, I can't wait until West Park Rovers get there, because it seems like a brilliant place to bury bad news.

Which brings us to a man who was very bad news for Bury. Meet Steve Dale, patron saint of wrong'uns. He was *The Price of Football*'s big story in our first weeks and he remains our biggest villain, as well as being one of the most hated men in football. He drove Bury FC into the ground, then into extinction. What his motivation was I have no idea, although God knows we tried to find out.

We invited him to be a guest on the pod, just to try and discover whether he genuinely thought he was doing the right thing, but he ignored our requests – possibly for the best, in case he *was* genuinely suffering from a personality disorder. After all, *Chitty Chitty Bang Bang* wouldn't have been half as disturbing if the Child Catcher suddenly turned to the camera and said, 'I think I may be sublimating my own separation anxiety here, you know?' Whatever his reasons, when he took over, the small town of Bury had a football club with a proud heritage. And a year later, it didn't.

Steve Dale bought the club for £1 (uh-oh) in December 2018. Before that, 43 of the 51 companies he'd been associated with had been liquidated, but the EFL's constitution at the time allowed him to buy shares and therefore control the club before submitting proof of funds in terms of being able to cover the operating losses. And initially, it seemed, he was. Dale paid part of an outstanding tax bill in February 2019 to avoid a winding-up order, but then decided there was no pressing need to pay other outstanding debts or indeed the players' wages and pension contributions.

Dale's predecessor as owner, Stewart Day, did come up with some unorthodox money-raising schemes though, such as offering fans a mortgage on their own parking space, but Dale continued his deliberate policy of non-payment, claiming in April 2019 that the club's financial problems were 'far in excess' of what he understood when he took over (you bought the club for a pound – that must have been a clue!).

Then Dale said he was open to offers to sell the club and suggested a Company Voluntary Arrangement where football creditors were paid in full and others, including HMRC, would receive 25%. This was agreed and a winding-up order was dismissed, but league rules meant an automatic 12-point deduction. When creditors were not paid, Dale was told the club would be expelled from the league if proof were not given that the club was in a financial position to fulfil its fixtures for the upcoming season. Bury fans, local politicians, the press and football fans everywhere implored the league and Dale to work together to find a solution, but both parties insisted the other was being stubborn. On 27 August, Bury FC were expelled from the EFL.

Surprise, surprise, an 'independent' EFL investigation later announced that 'a lack of owner funding' caused Bury's demise, even though the EFL had turned down an offer of £1 million from Bill Kenwright, the co-owner of Everton, to keep the club alive. It would have compromised the EFL's 'conflict of ownership interest rules', you see. And it turned out that the 'lack of owner funding' was entirely the fault of Steve Dale. At least two viable companies had made credible bids for the club while they were still in the league; bids that were turned down by Dale because he wanted to make a bigger profit on his £1 purchase. Both Steve Dale and Stewart Day were declared bankrupt in 2022, leaving many small local creditors out of pocket.

The saga dragged on before, during and after the Covid lockdowns as two phoenix entities fought for the soul of the club in a bid to retain its identity. As the *Manchester Evening News* said, 'With no players, no league to play in and no employees to speak of, it is little more than a hollow shell of the club fans knew and loved.' After a protracted and bitter civil war between the two sets of fan groups, football returned to Gigg Lane for the 2023/24 season.

Before we move on, maybe we should have a closer look at how the owners' and directors' test works and why it obviously doesn't in so many cases. As the Law In Sport website helpfully explains, 'The owners' and directors' test (also known as the "fit and proper person test") is a test that is applied to directors and prospective directors of English football clubs to ensure those appointed are appropriate people to act as directors at football clubs. It is designed to protect the image and integrity of the relevant league and the clubs that play in it.' Speaking as a football fan, I'm not sure that image and integrity are the first things I want protecting.

The Premier League has its own separate but similar tests, although they share the same legalese language that I'm sure is designed to prevent us oiks from examining them too closely. However, you can't be the owner and director if you have a 'significant interest' in any other club. The size of that interest is not defined, but is generally considered to be 10%. I have a 'significant interest' in Brighton and Hove Albion being relegated, but I don't think that counts. You can't be the owner or director if you have 'a current conviction in respect of any offence involving any act which could be considered to be dishonest in respect of which an unsuspended of at least 12 months has been imposed.' I'm only a pub lawyer, but are there any criminal offences involving acts that could considered to be honest? The key word here, though, is 'current'. If you went to prison for fraud 10 years ago, you'll be welcomed in with open arms.

You can't continue to be the owner or director if you are struck off by a professional body, but, again, if you were struck off previously you should be fine now. You can't be the owner or director if you were previously the owner or director of one club that went into administration twice or two clubs that went into administration once. Oh, but you can be removed as a director if, within two weeks of the season starting, you fail to provide a copy of the owners' charter signed by your good self.

This doesn't seem to me to be a watertight set of rules for ensuring only fit and proper people become owners or directors of your club. In fact, they seem more about removing people already there if they do something wrong, which, by extension, means they have already done a lot of damage. And it's slightly depressing to note that in the 346 pages of Premier League rules and regulations, almost as much space is given to allocating an area for the away side's analysis team than preventing wrong'uns taking over a club.

Fair enough, you could argue that the amount of money needed to buy a Premier League club is a sort of self-weeding-out process, but are the rules substantially tighter in the EFL where a club could change hands for £2 million or, as we have seen, for just a quid? Not really. To be fair, the EFL regulations are more comprehensive, but they amount to the same thing.

And they are only more comprehensive because they describe things in more detail. For example, if you want a definition of a dishonest act they helpfully provide one: 'Any act which could reasonably be considered to be dishonest.' They also elaborate on the types of unspent criminal offence that are likely to debar you, including 'dishonestly receiving a programme broadcast from within the UK to avoid payment under the Copyright, Designs and Patents Act of 1988.' I think that means watching a game on a dodgy stream, which seems a bit harsh, considering... although this might explain why Kieran's Uncle Terry is so keen not to be a director of West Park Rovers as he has a wholesale interest in such dodgy streams.

If you have recently been convicted and sent to prison for allowing spectators to watch a football match at unlicensed premises don't even consider buying an EFL club, although despite extensive research I haven't managed to ascertain how many people are currently serving time at His Majesty's Pleasure for that heinous offence. Ticket touting and hate crime are also on the list though, which I thoroughly endorse.

Luckily, however, most people don't buy a football club with malign intent. Quite often they buy a club and *accidentally* fuck it up. And, amazingly, there are people who acquire a club to save it being broken by somebody else, or because it's their childhood team, or they are Hollywood film stars who stuck a pin in a map and came up with Wrexham, or they just fancied the idea of owning a football club and are happy to cough up some money on the way to keep it solvent and responsible. These are Kieran's favourite type of owner and they are...

THE BENEVOLENT DICTATOR

The ultimate benevolent dictator was, of course, Roman Abramovich, but there is another example just down the road from Stamford Bridge. Shahid Khan, known as Shad, is the owner of the most splendid moustache in football and Fulham Football Club. He arrived in the US from Pakistan at age 16 to study engineering and must have studied hard, because he found his way into the car-part supply business and now owns a company that generated around $8.9 billion a year in 2020.

He is also the owner of Jacksonville Jaguars NFL team and has tried to do in West London what he has done for years in East Florida: use the club as a centre to invest not only in the team, but in local community causes. Shad seems happy to keep investing in Fulham, the ultimate yo-yo club, while equally as happily keeping his nose out of on-pitch matters. His mantra is: 'The hard road is almost always the right road' and as the English game has very few easy roads, he is clearly in the right place.

For the first 11 decades or so of English professional football the game was constantly evolving, but changes were mainly small and cosmetic. Referees got whistles instead of flags, nets were added to goals and numbers to shirts. Shorts got shorter and tighter, balls got rounder and tighter, but the essence of the game remained the same. Players weren't paid much and there were no fortunes to be made by owners, who, for the most part, would have been local businessmen and fans of the club.

It may be too simple to blame the creation of the Premier League for altering all that, but I'm happy to suggest that when it kicked off at 3pm on Saturday 15 August 1992 everything changed forever, often for the better (especially for players and agents), but in terms of financial responsibility and economic management off the pitch, very much for the worse.

One of Kieran's mantras right from the start of the pod was that owners are only temporary custodians of a football club and the real guardians of its heritage are the fans. To be fair, there are some club owners, like Steve Parish, owner of my own club Crystal Palace, who share that sentiment. But whereas in the past those local businessmen tended to be the custodians of the club for decades (and were often replaced by their sons when they died), today's owners tend to come and go much quicker than that, and are determined to make as much money in that time as possible.

Indeed, many clubs, mainly in the Premier League and Championship, are owned by overseas investors or hedge funds who, despite what they may have learned from Wikipedia in the back of the car on their way to the press conference, had probably never heard of the club they have just spent tens of millions buying in the hope of making hundreds of millions. Football clubs that for a century or more were probably millstones around the neck of a local businessman are now sexy global brands, followed by millions all over the world because of hugely rewarding broadcasting deals and all eager to buy merchandise from the club they have been supporting since yesterday.

Far Eastern conglomerates buy clubs to help them tap into local markets, Middle Eastern countries buy clubs as an exercise in soft power, Eastern European billionaires buy clubs for, well, many reasons, some of which I'm sure are altruistic and benevolent, and some of which our lawyers would prefer I didn't speculate about. Does it matter who owns your club if their huge investment buys it a place in the Premier League or turns it into a Champions League contender? Maybe not, but then maybe I'm lucky as a Palace fan not to have had my hypocrisy levels tested, because so far not even the smallest state in the United Arab Emirates (Ajman, since you ask) has shown the remotest interest in buying the club.

But if you think it will never matter, then you are wrong. The number of Premier League clubs majority owned by Americans is creeping slowly but surely towards the 14 needed to outvote the rest of the clubs. That means the only thing between them and a no-relegation, franchise-based top league would be government legislation, which, if considered to be state interference, would see England kicked out of FIFA, or an Independent Regulator, the potential creation of which has resulted in a smouldering relationship between a former Sports Minister and a teetotal lecturer.

The ownership types we have just been discussing by no means represent the full range, but in 20 years' time do you think there will be any, for example, fan-owned teams in whatever the top league is called then? I reckon it's much more likely that every team there will be either owned by nation states or people with Elon Musk levels of wealth. Who knows, maybe 2043 will be the year that West Park Rovers People's Democratic Football Club, wholly owned by the

North Korean government, finally wins the European Super League. In the meantime, Kieran, Guy and I intend to be the kindly, open, honest and charitable type of club owners we promised to be, intent on bringing joy to our fans and help to our community, so let's get back to some actual football. It's time to start climbing the pyramid and swanning around some actual directors' boxes looking for free wine and pies. Come on you Rovers!

3

RULES

This is getting serious

Even when we're going through the inevitable cool and rebellious phases we all go through, we still find ourselves living by rules, written and unwritten. You may have an eye tattooed on your eye, but you still go up the ladders and down the snakes, you don't put ice in red wine and you never wear white socks with black trainers. You hear that, Producer Guy? Never! Regulations, laws, guidelines – they can all seem a bit tiresome sometimes, but they are usually there for a reason. My dad lived his life by two main rules – don't put buttons up your nose and try not to eat anything bigger than your head – and he lived to the age of 87, so they clearly worked, but there are rules and there is jumping through hoops, and I'm not convinced the FA are fully aware of the difference.

Well, now, doesn't time fly? After a stunning run of victories we find ourselves already in the heady heights of the National League South. And to think, some doubters thought it would take us until at least Chapter 5 for that to happen. By the way, I can't thank our fans enough for turning out in such numbers. During our brief stay in the Southern Combination League we were getting crowds of nearly 200 per game, which doesn't sound a lot, but comfortably topped the average attendance for the league of 90.7. Just think, if Kieran and I had seen a few more games rather than bunking off to watch Palace and Brighton, we could have got that average all the way up to 91.

And if any of those fictional West Park Rovers fans are reading this, then thank you, but, cards on the table, growing your fictional football team has been much more time-consuming and energy-sapping than any of us imagined, especially as we want to make it as realistic as possible. There are just so many things to consider, so many plates to keep spinning, so many ways for money to disappear before I've even had a chance to spend it. Sorry, I mean before we've even had a chance to invest it.

There's the FA and their regulations, of course, plus the local council and their regulations, which means that even simple things like where we put the bins out on a Monday morning are the subject of form-filling and site visits. Then there's the police, who want to know how many away fans are coming and where their coaches will be parking, even in the early days when the answer is usually, 'Three and they'll be in a cab.'

Player welfare is now a concern. Back in the day when Kieran and I were turning out for pub teams at the weekend, player welfare pretty much consisted of checking whether anyone had a hangover. Now, we have a responsibility to ensure that our players are physically and mentally well, and we have a similar responsibility to make sure that they are aware of, and comply with, FA regulations around racism, homophobia, sexual harassment, bullying etc, which brings us to safeguarding.

Who knew that even at this level we'd need policies to ensure that everyone involved in the club can enjoy the experience in what the FA define as 'a safe, positive and enjoyable environment'. Absolutely right, but it means that everything we do, from recruitment to training to catering to seating, everything, has to be viewed through a safeguarding lens and we need a safeguarding officer to ensure that happens.

As you'll discover, even though we are now a few rungs up the pyramid (I know, I'm not sure how you climb an actual pyramid either), the FA are still short on detail when it comes to disabled access, but we have a moral duty to ensure that those fans can travel, park, access the ground safely and watch in comfort, and much as we don't resent it, it doesn't come cheap.

In short, there are hundreds of things that we didn't consider when we came up with that grand plan in the pub and it became obvious quite early on that being ambitious to grow a club as quickly as possible meant that we weren't quite going to have the carefree fun we remembered so fondly from our own Sunday football playing days. Back then, a crowd of 90 would have been a cause for amazement and celebration, and was probably because a fun-run was going by. Now a crowd of 90 would be a cause for disappointment and emergency boardroom meetings; meetings which would be a lot easier to arrange if the Kleanwell Stadium actually had a boardroom.

In the National League South it turns out that our matchday income, which I'm pleased to say is well above the league average of £50,000 a year, is fine to keep us ticking over, but nowhere near enough to finance improvements on and off the pitch. Therefore, it has become essential to maximise other income sources. Having a clubhouse and bar that's open seven days a week is now a necessity. And handy for me.

It's cost us a lot of money and effort to make even the relatively small leap from being a glorified Sunday League team to a proper pyramid team. You'll remember that it cost us around £5000 to start the team off at the lowest level. It cost at least as much as that and more just to stay there, which was impossible to do on matchday income, even when we were not paying wages to players. So, right from the start we had to find other income sources, which meant we spent as much time fretting about selling beverages and burgers as we did about boots and balls – and we were constantly looking for ways to raise money in the community on the six days of the week we weren't playing football in the stadium. Trust me, if you want help selling raffle tickets then I'm your man. I can also provide you with ways to guilt-trip whoever wins the big prize into donating it back to the club.

Oh, well spotted, by the way. We are not playing at Whitestone Park any more. Or rather we are, but we made a tidy sum selling the naming rights. In fact, there was quite a bidding war between Kleanwell and Dryrite. The winners were Kleanwell, a well-established local company which by sheer coincidence is owned by an 'associate' of Kieran's Uncle Terry, who I believe he met when sharing a cell (for our American readers, that doesn't mean they used the same phone). Kleanwell are involved in the laundering business and, unusually for a friend of Uncle Terry, they actually launder clothes, not money, although when he negotiated the £20,000 naming rights Guy was slightly surprised to receive the sum in cash...

Now I know the Kleanwell Stadium is not a glamorous name, redolent of our several years of history and tradition, but we're not the only ones to have sold our soul for ready cash – sorry, leveraged the full market value of our currently limited assets. Cheltenham Town FC used to play at Whaddon Road, but then changed the name to the Jonny-Rocks stadium. It was still the same ground, it just sounded like a brand of condom. Even worse, for a short time it was the World of Smile stadium. Imagine walking away from the World of Smile stadium when you've just been relegated. Currently it's the Completely-Suzuki Stadium so thank God it hasn't got a silly name any more.

Saltergate, home of Chesterfield FC, is now the Technique Stadium, following a brief spell as the B2Net and ProAct Stadium, which I believe was named after the two robots who didn't make the cut in *Star Wars*. In Scotland, Livingston FC's poetic-sounding Almondvale first changed to the Energy Assets Arena and is now the Tony Macaroni Arena, although at least they can console themselves that it has acquired one of the best nicknames in football: the Spaghettihad.

WHEN THE FUN STOPS, STOP

We don't want to put you off starting your own football team, so let me stress that we are actually enjoying ourselves, it's just a little less fun than it used to be. And unlike that facile gamble-aware slogan above, it's very difficult to simply stop running a football club when you feel the pressure mounting.

It was after we reached the Southern Combination that things started to feel, well, a bit serious. A bit grown-up. And worse, a bit expensive. The thing is you do need money, proper money, even at that level. There may only be 90.7 people watching most games in the Southern Counties, but I'll tell you who else is watching: the FA, that's who. You might be a long way from the apex, but at that level you are on the same pyramid as Manchester City and Liverpool. And in the same FA Cup, even if your first game is played in the hot months when the back pages are dominated by tennis and cricket rather than a cup match played in front of the proverbial three men and a dog. Mental note: can we find a way to charge dogs to get in?

When we were promoted to the Southern Combination Premier League we discovered some of the real hidden costs of becoming a proper football team: taking part not only in the FA Cup but in the FA Vase and myriad other county level competitions. If we'd known how much it cost beforehand we may not have been so keen to get there so quickly – although, in our defence, not many teams have to get promoted quickly enough to meet the deadline for delivering a book.

In Division One and Two of the Southern Combination we were up against teams like Brighton Electricity (average attendance 26) and St Francis Rangers (23). In the Premier League we were competing with the likes of Newhaven (274), Eastbourne Town (224) and Eastbourne United (150). And for those who think that it's unsustainable for a small country like England to have around 120 professional football clubs, it's interesting that a town like Eastbourne, with a population of just over 100,000, has two teams in the same league. Crowd numbers of 274 may not seem a lot to most of you, but this is big boy and girl football now and that means big rules that you actually have to comply with.

For example, in case you don't know, and I'm guessing you don't, here are just some of the FA minimum ground requirements at Southern Combination level: National Grading Category H. You have to have a ground – so far so good – and you must provide 'security of tenure'. For football clubs, especially ambitious ones such as ours who may be applying for grants from the Football Foundation and other worthy bodies, that means documents to show either you own the freehold to the stadium or you have a leasehold rental agreement for at least five years and ideally ten. You also have to pinkie-swear that you are not sharing the ground with another club. That bit I am happy to do. The documents bit, less so. I'm hoping Guy knows where they are, because the last time I saw our freehold agreement I was doodling new away kits on the back of it.

Said ground must allow spectators to 'view the match, either standing or seated' for the full length of 'at least two sides of the playing arena'. Hang on, what about the ends? Does an end count as a side? Can you have a side and an end or does it have to be two ends or two sides? And, by the way, is there any football ground anywhere in the country that would have been built without allowing spectators to view the match unless the FA had suggested it? I pause here while fans of many clubs say, 'I wish I couldn't view the bloody match the way we're playing.' There is no minimum requirement for how many fans the sides/ends/side-ends should hold, but at least 50 of the fans should be under cover. So that sounds like a minimum requirement then and it's clearly 50. Although like all maths problems I may have to double-check that with Kieran.

Around the ground there has to be a perimeter fence of at least 1.83 metres and around the pitch there needs to be a fence at least 1.1 metres high and 1.83 metres away from the touchline. As 1.83 metres is the equivalent of six feet I can only assume these requirements were written in the 1930s when everyone was only 4'6" tall and therefore completely unable to invade a pitch without the aid of a ladder.

You need grass ('top quality'), which led to an amusing misunderstanding when Kieran's Uncle Terry said he could supply us, no problem, only to look very bemused when we asked for about 7000 square metres worth, as he measured it by the gram. Or you can opt for 3G artificial turf (an FA-registered brand) and you need floodlights with an average lux reading of 120. If I remember my Latin correctly* *lux* is the word for light, but Lord knows how bright that actually is or, if you prefer, *Dominus scit quam clara est.*

The artificial turf option is an expensive one, but several non-league clubs go for it because hiring out the pitch on non-match days can be a handy source of additional income. Maidstone United, in the National League, charge a minimum of £350 for a two-hour slot or, if you want to stage a mini-tournament, they will divide the pitch into four and charge you £600 for a six-hour slot. Oliver Ash, co-owner of the club, reckons that can bring in up to £400,000 extra revenue in a good year.

There are risks with artificial turf, though. The EFL don't allow 3G surfaces in their competitions so when Sutton United were promoted into League Two in 2021 it cost them £500,000 to remove it and replace it with grass. Promotion to the EFL obviously brings a lot of commercial activities which will help offset that cost, but for Sutton it also meant they had to find (and pay for) somewhere else for their academy, their women's and girls' teams, and their disability sides to play and train.

Whatever sort of pitch you choose, next to it, there must be two covered training boxes, clearly marked 'Home' and 'Away or visitors', that hold eight people each. Oh, so now the ground must be able to hold at least 66 people? No minimum requirement, my arse!

---

*I went to a Catholic Grammar School so Latin was compulsory. If you know a sailor who needs to tell someone in Rome he's scared of dogs, give me a shout.

What about player safety? That's covered. 'A stretcher must be provided' plus 'at least two trained first-aiders,' no doubt because long experience has shown that having just one first aider leads to a lot of problems carrying the stretcher.

Each team must have a separate dressing room with a minimum of four showerheads and a toilet cubicle. The matchday officials get their own room, of course, with at least one showerhead and a toilet that must be 'in a cubicle but need not necessarily be ensuite,' although imagine the bad reviews from refs on Tripadvisor if it's not.

The FA demands that fans also get toilets and, rather quaintly, the rules specify there must be separate facilities for men and women. I'd be intrigued to know when that regulation was introduced, because I went to a lot of games in the 1980s and I can't for the life of me remember seeing a ladies' toilet on any of the terraces I stood on. There must be at least two cubicles in each and there must be running water, although it's not clear whether that's in the toilet bowl or the sink, probably because to many male football fans there's no discernible difference.

My favourite regulation is that there must be an 'adequate' supply of toilet paper. Yeah, good luck with that. First, define 'adequate'. Second, has anyone ever turned up at a toilet in a football ground anywhere to find an adequate supply of toilet paper? And if there is, for some reason, most of it will be stuffed down the toilet bowl already.

That may be a slight exaggeration, but trust me, in general, if you have no reason to visit a male toilet in a football stadium then stay as far away as you can, preferably upwind. One of Kieran's many claims to fame is that he has never had a poo in a football ground toilet, such is his wariness of their cleanliness and hygiene. So if you ever see him doing the dirty penguin walk away from a game, it's not because Brighton have lost, but because anything is preferable to the unpredictable sit-down adventure in a stadium toilet.

Finally, to allow fans into the ground, there must be at least one revolving turnstile, although it doesn't have to be electronic. Well, that's handy because electronic ones are bloody expensive. Besides, if any of our fans are as bad with technology as I am, it will be half-time before they've managed to get their mobile phones the right way up to scan.

In fact, everything on that bloody list is expensive. Have you seen the price of stretchers these days? And I may not be certain what a lux is, but I do know that electricity prices are ruinous at the moment. Toilet paper doesn't come cheap either and we had to buy a tape measure to make sure those perimeter fences are the right height.

Actually, stretchers come in anywhere between £120 for one that is essentially a bit of canvas hung between bamboo sticks and £900 for one on wheels that looks like it may carry a fully-grown footballer without him falling through. '£900? Does it come with a chauffeur?' asked Guy when I showed him the catalogue.

It's those electricity prices that are currently (no pun intended) a huge problem for smaller clubs in particular. Forest Green Rovers are one of the most environmentally savvy clubs in the world and generate much of their own electricity using solar panels and wind turbines. Nevertheless, in the autumn of 2022, as the energy crisis really kicked in, their owner, Dale Vince, founder of energy supply company Ecotricity, said that their utilities bill had been around £90,000 the previous season and they were expecting that to triple in the months ahead, even though, presumably, he is charging himself mate's rates.

At around the same time, the Scottish FA announced it would allow clubs to kick-off early to cut down on the use of floodlights and heating, and the English FA said it was to do the same for clubs at Isthmian League level and below, and expected to extend that to at least League Two by midwinter. Meanwhile, Manchester City were criticised for turning on their floodlights 10 minutes into a 3pm kick-off against Crystal Palace on a bright sunny day in August.

Now we are in the National League, the regulations are even more extensive. And complicated. There are Harry Potter books shorter than the National League rulebook and it's clearly written by someone who loves words and semi-colons as much as Kieran loves numbers and decimal-points – and that's bordering on the semi-erotic. There are several pages alone on how to form a sub-committee – and wait until you find out the new toilet requirements.

The National League is within sniffing distance of the 92,* so the ground rules are getting tougher and much more specific. Which

*With a following wind…

means, of course, more expensive. And while bigger crowds mean bigger matchday income, they also mean more matchday staff, more matchday security, more matchday parking, more matchday media space and so on.

I don't think Kieran and Guy actually saw any of our first few home games. They were too busy sorting out the ticketing and catering issues that inevitably accompany a big step up. Luckily, they more or less agreed with me that too many cooks etc, so I was left to deal with the tricky problem of entertaining the away team's owners and directors. After all, we don't want people thinking West Park Rovers are the sort of club that serves red wine with fish.

At this level, Category D, the regulations start with a stern warning: 'The ground must give the overall appearance and impression of being a football ground suitable for the National League.' So, it mustn't look like a theatre, a tennis court or a bridge? Good advice. We could have wasted a lot of money there. And at this level, the FA not only tell you what it must look like, they tell you where it should be: 'The location of the ground, in so far as its relation to the conurbation whose name the club bears, or is traditionally associated with, must meet with the approval of the FA.'

OK, so the Kleanwell Stadium must not look like a theatre or be in Glasgow. Thank you for clarifying that. It does make you wonder, though, who at the FA nodded through Wimbledon's 2003 move to Milton Keynes, because the location of that ground to the conurbation whose name the club bore can be easily summarised as 'far away'.

The whole end/side thing is clearer too. I think. 'Spectators must be able to view the match from at least three sides of the playing area.' Correct me if I'm wrong, but it hasn't got three sides, has it? It's got two sides and two ends. As it happens, Kieran and Guy are less worried about the geometry and more about how we attract enough new spectators to fill those three sides and keep the money coming in. It's a fair point. If we don't get more fans, the ones we do have will be rattling about a bit, because there is now an actual specified minimum crowd capacity figure too. The ground must hold at least 1300 people, 'as calculated by a competent person'. Kieran loves counting, he can do that. And at least 300 of those people have to be under cover with a minimum of 150 seated. Excellent, more counting for Kieran.

Things are looking up hygiene-wise for our loyal fans as well. Toilets must now have waste-paper bins and 'a roof'. Can we afford both? Perhaps we could forgo the roof, let the waste-paper bins collect the rainwater and then we can irrigate the pitch with it? Also, did they have to specify the 'roof'? Were these rules written a long time ago by posh people who weren't sure whether ordinary folk preferred to urinate unmolested by the elements. Probably, yes. As it happens, back in the day, neither Fulham, QPR or Chelsea had a roof on the toilet in the away end. Perhaps it was a West London thing.

Ah, now this is the bit I do like: there must be 24 seats for directors, committee members and guests of the home club and 12 for the visitors, with hospitality and toilet facilities adjacent. Lovely! Somewhere warm where I can have a drink and a sandwich while Kieran is outside, counting up to 1300.

Of course, we don't resent in the slightest any expense incurred getting our growing number of fans safely into and out of the ground, especially as that means we have a growing number of fans in the ground who are ready and willing to show their undying support for our club by buying as much of our new range of merchandise as they can afford while we try to guilt-trip them into buying even more.

MAXIMISING NON-TICKET REVENUE
(AKA SELLING STUFF)

What? We have to make a living. Yes, Kieran, I know our loyal fans show their undying support by going to every game home and away, and, yes, I know that's expensive, but come on, who wants to break their child's heart by not buying them our new range of junior training kit and bobble-hats. Well, that seems to be the big clubs' attitude anyway and I for one can't wait until we have a merchandising hypermarket that's bigger than our actual ground. In fact, I've already designed the West Park Rovers garden gnomes – 11 of them. Show your love by buying the whole tiny team. At the moment our club 'shop' is a hatch occupied by Jean. She's not the friendliest lady, but she has a robust attitude to retailing that I admire. In fact, trying to sneak past Jean without buying a scarf is like trying to leave Disneyland without a giant pair of mouse ears and, more importantly, she is a volunteer.

We also have to provide press facilities now: at least two seats 'with lighting and writing facilities, and a clear view of the pitch'. I'm starting to get paranoid that the FA really do think we're idiots. Did they think that without that advice we'd have stuck the journos in a broom cupboard with a periscope so they can see the game through the window? Although, if they were reporting on some of our pre-season friendly defeats that might be a good idea. And sod providing writing facilities. They can bring their own pens.

Interestingly, this is quite a way up the pyramid, but the regulations still say 'There is no specific requirement for disabled spectators.' The regulations remind us of our obligations under the 1995 Disability Discrimination Act, but in a ground that holds a minimum of 1300 people we are not required to find room for disabled fans and yet the motto of the FA is 'For All'.

So, those are the FA regulations, what about those league rules that I mentioned? The Memorandum of Association of the Football Conference Ltd runs to 104 pages and would be several pages shorter if they just called it 'the rules' and didn't use words like 'hereinafter' and 'theretofore' so often. They also feel the need to define the meaning of words like 'year' and 'objection'. Why, I don't know.

Neither do I particularly need to know what the procedure is if the chairman is more than 15 minutes late for a meeting, but Kieran and Guy reckon it's probably for legal reasons and, unlike me, most club owners don't have the attention span of a toddler – and for the purposes of this book a toddler shall theretofore and hereinafter be deemed to refer to a young child who walks unsteadily with small uneven steps.

The National League also provides helpful back-up to those still befuddled by the FA's regulations: 'Ground' means 'the ground on which the club's first team plays'. Thank you. Any idea what 'grass pitch' means? 'Grass pitch' means 'a field of play that is natural grass or predominantly natural grass.' Much obliged. You can also get definitions of the words 'satisfied', 'team sheet', 'rules', 'work experience' and, believe it or not, 'FA'. If you need reminding that 'FA' stands for Football Association you may be in the wrong place.

There seems to be a rule, a regulation or a guideline for just about every aspect of running a football club. For example, you can't give an award for long service until a member of staff has been with you for at least 21 years and hasn't previously been given a long-service award by another club. A rule that can't be invoked very often, surely? That's going to come as a terrible shock to Old Ron who's only been hanging on long enough to get the second carriage clock of his career.

Speaking of hanging on. If your club reaches the 100th anniversary of its founding you shall receive 'a commemorative award'. What that award shall actually be the rules do not specify, which is odd because they specify just about everything else. Warm-ups, for example, if they are 'on the pitch' can last no more than 30 minutes and cannot commence until 45 minutes before kick-off.

Ever wondered how many games a season your National League club is allowed to offer free admission to or how many complimentary tickets you can give away for a play-off game? Three and 30. Kieran, being the accountant he is, had to lie down in a darkened room at the thought of three whole games without entrance money. Or rather at the thought of me drunkenly promising to let everyone in for free three times a season. Why would you give away 30 tickets to a play-off game, the one game of the season you are pretty much guaranteed to sell out? And, crucially, just how will those 30 freeloaders actually know who's won the game?

It's an important question. So important it makes you wonder why the answer is tucked away in Appendix C: in the event of extra-time in a play-off game, 'The team which has scored most goals will be declared the winner.' No shit, Sherlock. Aha, I hear you say, what if, after the end of extra-time, neither team has scored more goals than the other? A circumstance that we purists call a 'draw'. Don't worry. The rules are ahead of you. Should that be the case, the winners will be determined by the 'taking of kicks from the penalty mark'. So now you know.

While some of the rules initially appear to have been designed by a random word generator or seemed like a very good idea at the end of a drunken night out (to be fair, nearly all ideas seem very good at the end of a drunken night out, but those are best covered in another book), there is method in their potential madness.

The warming-up rule, for example, reduces wear and tear on the pitch for too long by one of the teams, and also ensures that the referee is on the premises to observe any untoward behaviour prior to kick-off. Imagine what would happen if two players had a fight on the pitch a couple of hours before the game and there were no match officials to put in a report to the local FA? My guess is that someone would film it and put it on Twitter so the match officials will see it anyway.

It seems to me, though, that the jubilation of each promotion is immediately followed by the financial equivalent of having a bucket of cold water thrown over you; a bucket that, it turns out, is also really expensive.

We are genuinely getting to the stage where it may be better financially if we don't get promoted again. At least not for a while. When we reach the National League itself our travel costs, for example, are going to shoot up, and not only are places like Gateshead and Maidenhead a long way away,* but if we get an evening fixture our pampered players are going to want to stay in a hotel. I'm not sure whether there's a Premier Inn near Gateshead, but if there is and I could persuade those same pampered players to share, I can't imagine they'd have a room for 15.

Incidentally, it may be a boon to skinflint club owners, but isn't it amazing that even at the very highest levels of football players are expected to share a bedroom on their travels? I presume it's a hangover from the early working-class days, when most players may never have slept in a single bed in their entire lives, sharing with siblings as a kid, and possibly other soldiers during a war or National Service, before being married off around the age of 21.

Historically they were often married off with the club's connivance or even the club's insistence. Brian Clough, for example, demanded that his players should be married, because it kept them grounded and sensible and he knew where they would be at night. He told them: 'I've tasted most things, but if there's owt better than family life then let me know.'

I think class may also be a factor in an issue we will have to address very soon. Many teams in the National League North are fully professional – and that's the level below the actual Conference. In contrast, only a handful of teams in the National League South

---

*Unless you live there, of course. A TV football commentator I know once spent several minutes complaining how long it took him to get to Selhurst Park on a wet Monday evening from his home in High Wycombe. I pointed out that it only took me 15 minutes to get to Selhurst Park from my home in South London.

are fully professional. I'm not sure why this should be, unless it's a sub-conscious hangover from the days when the posh chaps of the southern counties stubbornly clung to the notion of amateur football – 'Play up, play up and play the game'-type stuff – while those brash northerners were paying up to play the game and therefore winning most of the trophies.

It may be that even now, outside London, the owners of other non-league clubs in the south think it's financially impractical to pay full-time wages, because there just isn't room to grow their fanbase any further – which is odd because even the most cursory look at a map of the distribution of football clubs shows that the vast majority are situated north of Watford.

NEW REVENUE STREAMS

Whatever the reason, we can't afford to become a full-time professional club at the moment, but that will have to change when we get to the National League itself if we want to compete. As we will discover, many clubs there, the fifth division of English football remember, are paying wages higher than some Scottish Premier League clubs. So we need to find a way to boost our finances. Now, we could ask Jean to up her game a bit or we could go for Kieran and Guy's option: long-term and sensible investment with slow, steady and sustainable progress. But where's the fun in that? I vote we go for the quick fix.

When we started *The Price of Football* pod late in 2019, most of us had no idea what cryptocurrency actually was. Most of us still don't, but that hasn't stopped those people in football who definitely don't from trying to get a slice of the action.

Look closely at the sleeves of Premier League football teams and you will notice how many of them are sponsored by some kind of cryptobitcoinnftmagicbean provider. Or they were. It's quite possible that by the time you read this book the whole thing has collapsed and those same clubs have shamefacedly gone back to actual cash, having seen the bottom fall out of the magic bean market when none of the beans even produced a stalk to climb let alone a goose laying golden eggs at the top of it.

The basic definition of crypto is: 'A digital currency designed to work as a medium of exchange through a computer network that is not reliant on any central authority, such as a government or bank, to uphold or maintain it.' In other words, it doesn't really exist and it's unregulated. Even to a financial idiot like me that seems like a recipe for eventual disaster, yet the world's biggest clubs have been falling over themselves to join the revolution.

In March 2022 Paris St Germain paid Lionel Messi $20 million to endorse a crypto fan currency called Socios. Can you guess, however, at the currency in which he was paid? Yep, dollars! Just a few weeks later, a crypto start-up company called 3Key were revealed to be the masterminds behind a chain of alleged frauds worth over a billion pounds. This was a trifle embarrassing for Manchester City. Why? In November 2021 City had signed a deal with 3Key, announcing 3Key as an 'official retail partner in decentralised trading analysis'. However, City faced questions over the cryptocurrency firm's legitimacy when it emerged that its website provided no contact details, registered office or company number, and its named staff appeared to have no digital footprint.

To be fair to Manchester City, who are a well-run and hugely successful football club, they immediately suspended the deal themselves when they realised things were amiss, but also insisted that the club had entered the partnership only after conducting due diligence. It came as no surprise to me, though, that a company set up to trade a currency that didn't really exist didn't really exist itself.

If the lure of crypto is hard for normal fans (and at least one fictional club owner) to understand, the appeal of its cousin, the NFT, is even more baffling. NFTs are non-fungible tokens. That is, they don't actually exist either, but many clubs are still inviting you to buy them, preferably using a cryptocurrency which doesn't really exist either, which is where it gets really confusing.

Technically, a bitcoin, for example, does actually exist and is therefore 'fungible', whereas a token is a unique representation of something that only exists online and is therefore 'non-fungible'. I told you it was confusing and it doesn't help that 'Fungible' sounds like a Hobbit's middle-name. As Kieran has explained many times, NFTs are basically like digital Panini stickers that you collect, but only ever technically own and can only sell at a profit. But Panini stickers don't come with a health warning.

For example – and this may not un-confuse things – my club Crystal Palace has a fan-token scheme run by the aforementioned

Socios, using their in-app cryptocurrency Chiliz or $CHZ. The club website explains that 'Fan Tokens are digital assets – that means they're assets that can be owned and held, but only exist online.' It goes on to explain that owning $CPFC, or fan tokens (purchased with $CHZ), allows fans to access club-related benefits and merchandise that other fans cannot and gives fans a brand-new way to engage with the club and vote in polls. So, if I buy an online picture of Wilf Zaha scowling at a referee I may automatically get to vote on a new pie flavour and could be chosen as the first fan to taste it.

So far, so harmless. However, much of the excitable online announcement of the scheme consists of red flags, the first of which is worth quoting in full: 'Although we only promote $CPFC fan tokens as a tool to engage with the club, we recognise that a secondary market for trading does exist. As such, please note that (a) the value of cryptoassets is variable and can go down as well as up; (b) cryptoassets are unregulated in the UK; and (c) capital gains tax may be payable on any profits made on the sale of cryptoassets.' I love my club, but (c) really bothers me. You have to make a fair bit of profit before you pay capital gains tax, and, no doubt unintentionally, that implies to me that there is money to be made buying and selling these things.

The warnings don't stop there. The decision to open a cryptoasset exchange account 'requires careful thought and consideration.' Fans are advised to spend only what they can afford and seek independent financial advice if necessary and they should stay away if they do not fully understand the risks involved. The tokens are not suitable for children. And chillingly, buying or selling cryptoassets 'could result in a complete loss of funds.' A complete loss of funds! And possibly your house.

Having got those little details out of the way, the fun begins. The very next sentence reveals that buying fan tokens gives you the chance to watch the game from the Socios box at Selhurst Park and enjoy a 'VIP hospitality experience,' which may include that new pie you got to vote for.

Several other Premier League clubs currently have their own online magic beans and all of them carry the same warning on their website. Whether that is out of a sense of corporate responsibility or a sense of legally covering their arses, I leave you to decide. I'd love to be able to tell you exactly how much those clubs are making from NFTs alone, but, understandably, they don't want other clubs to know, so I can't. Anecdotal evidence would suggest, however, that fan resistance to them has been fierce. In other words, I don't know any Palace fan who has invested and there is a bloody big banner at every home game denouncing them.

The central premise of cryptocurrencies, NFTs and fan tokens does have some merit, though. There is a suspicion that the traditional banking industry, the one whose behaviour was a major contributor to the global recession between 2007 and 2009, partly due to selling 'magic bean'-style products of their own, cannot be trusted. Therefore, a decentralised money payment system such as cryptocurrencies, with a limited number of coins, is seen by some as a viable alternative.

Equally, some football clubs have huge fanbases. Manchester United claim to have 1.1 billion followers, yet their maximum revenues earned were £627 million. This works out as 57 pence per follower per season. Old Trafford only holds about 74,000 people too, so NFTs offer a genuine opportunity for a club to engage with the more than one billion fans who will never go there and monetise them, which is fine provided all parties know what is happening.

The downside of this whole sector is that it is also unregulated, highly volatile and easily manipulated.

The use of a football player to promote the NFT appears to be based on gaining interest, legitimacy and normalisation. This in turn potentially gives the NFT some semblance of inherent value and the use of the blockchain gives the 'owner' a digital receipt as proof of ownership, although anyone else can copy and download the image. As Kieran explained in splendidly non-official accounting terms: 'It's a bit like your mate being caught sleeping with his wife's sister, but then waving his wedding certificate as proof that his marriage is still sound.' Actually, his exact words were even more non-official, but children may be reading this.

With cryptocurrencies, NFTs and fan tokens being touted as investments by many self-titled 'traders' on social media, there is a blurring of the lines as to what exactly you are paying for.

You would, however, like to think that the footballing world would have some form of integrity in relation to these particular industries. An examination shows that 19 out of 20 clubs in the Premier League have signed up with some sort of crypto and tokens. Why? Because, as we will often discover, most club owners are blinded by the cheque, with some of the sponsor deals worth an estimated £20 million a year.

Having said all that, one thing I am not confused about is that some people are making a lot of money out of crypto and may be prepared to invest it at a level of football a step or two (or ten) down from PSG and City – Peter McCormack, for example, who was without doubt one of the most enthusiastic people we've ever interviewed on the podcast. So enthusiastic in fact, that it was less of an interview and more of an extended hymn of praise to his chosen passion. Regular listeners to the pod will know how enthusiastic Kieran's dog Finlay is when it's getting near Wonky Chomp time. You need to multiply that by 10 to even approach Peter's level of excitement.

And what is Peter's passion? Cryptocurrency and, in particular, bitcoin. He describes himself as a 'bitcoin businessman' and he hosts a hugely successful bitcoin podcast (1.3 million downloads plus half a million Twitter followers). In April 2022, not long after talking to us, he confirmed he had completed his planned takeover of Bedford FC, a club in Spartans South Midlands Division One, the 10th level of English football, which averages around 70 fans a game at McMullan Park.

So, not a big club then. Not even the biggest club in the town of Bedford,* a town you very rarely hear mentioned in the same sentence as 'hotbed of English football', but Peter not only bought them off the back of his bitcoin investment, he changed their name to Real Bedford and said out loud that his promise was to build a club 'with Bitcoin at its heart'. His ambition was clear: 'If we can separate money and state, we can get a football club into the Premier League.'

Sounds laudable, and to some perhaps a little bit laughable, but as I write this he's already attracted more than £250,000 of sponsorship, so who knows? He already has one promotion under his belt – I wonder if he has a fictional twin brother who might be interested in investing the same amount in West Park Rovers.

Some die-hard Bedford FC fans expressed their disappointment at the takeover ('It's a sad day for this club' was one tweet), but I

---

*Congratulations for those of you who knew it was Bedford Town.

suspect Peter McCormack is worried less about the small number of fans he has inherited and more about the huge numbers of new ones he hopes to attract.

Those disappointed Bedfordians will almost inevitably have sat in a pub lamenting the fact that they couldn't afford to compete with bitcoin millions by trying to buy the club themselves, but there are many who think fan-owned clubs are an achievable utopia, so fan investment is something we may have to explore in order to stay sustainable. But first, we have a very important task.

ALL WORK AND NO PLAY

It's an indication of just how unexpectedly difficult it is to start, maintain and grow a football club that I've barely mentioned the actual football team itself, which is a shame because now we're settling into this division they are playing some decent football in front of decent crowds. We are averaging around 700 a game and travelling to clubs like Chippenham Town FC, who get similar numbers, Eastbourne Borough (yep, turns out there are three clubs in the town), who play in front of 1000 at home, and Dulwich Hamlet, who average a very impressive 2100 a game and have very cannily tapped into a local hipster fanbase. Our matchday income, plus sponsorship and commercial revenue, mean that the ground is fit for purpose and we have the certificates to prove it. Plus we have had not one complaint about the quality of the toilet paper. Hopefully we can breathe out a little now, safe in the knowledge that we have established West Park Rovers as a proper football club with a sustainable future.

That means it's high time we faced our responsibilities away from the pitch and the stadium. Too often, I think, football clubs don't stop to consider what the word 'club' actually means. Basically, it's a group of people with a common purpose and it's time we expanded that group of people. As I said earlier, the community sustained us in the early days. Now it's time to think about how we can help the community in return – and we'll start with the biggest and most overlooked demographic of them all.

4

A WOMAN'S GAME

On 31 July 2022, at around 7.40pm, a BBC reporter is pitch-side at Wembley attempting to interview Chloe Kelly who, just 20 minutes earlier, has scored the winning goal for England in the final of the Women's Euros. It's clear that the young Lioness is still full of adrenalin and visibly distracted, but no one blames the broadcaster for wanting to talk to her, especially as, in a squad largely dominated by northern girls, Chloe was born and brought up just 10 minutes away from the famous stadium, so she's a double story.

Chloe, half-answers the first question, but then over the PA comes the opening bars of 'Sweet Caroline' and Chloe clearly doesn't even register what she is asked next. Her mind is in visible turmoil. The media-trained angel on one shoulder willing her to say something anodyne but friendly seems to be locked in a struggle with the little demon on the other shoulder whispering 'Sod this – let's go.' The demon wins. With a beaming smile she runs out of camera shot and is next seen bouncing up and down with her teammates singing 'So good, so good, so good' at the top of her voice, the BBC microphone she forgot to give back still visible in her hand as she punches the air.

It is a magical TV moment, one of pure joy, an image that would bring a smile to the face of a statue, and so far it represents the high watermark of women's football in England. A few minutes later, however, in the studio, Ian Wright is not happy. Ian, an ex-England player himself, is one of the most patriotic people I have ever met and a long-time supporter of the women's game, but in this particular moment of glory he has a scowl on his face.

Rather than celebrating, he warns that people and companies who had no previous interest in women's football will now be crawling out of corners to jump on the bandwagon. And without naming them, because 'they know who they are,' he mentions clubs that refused to host women's international matches at their grounds and, in particular, he is angry that a Women's Super League match between Arsenal and Manchester City at the start of the following season has already been rescheduled by Sky to a 7pm kick-off on a Sunday night.

How can we be saying that this win for England will hopefully give a much-needed boost to attendances at domestic Women's Super League games when we are already making it harder for people to get to them and scheduling them for the night before a school day? Ian's joy soon gets the better of him, but it's interesting that he chooses that moment to articulate his plea that the potential social and economic impact of this brilliant win for the women's game be managed properly.

Gabby Logan is one of the UK's finest sports presenters and broadcasters. If she had time to join your pub quiz team I guarantee you 10 out of 10 for any round about football. She hosted the BBC's coverage of the final and is, naturally, a big advocate for the women's game, but when I spoke to her afterwards she shared some of Ian Wright's concerns: 'Smart brands are getting in on it now... The smarter brands have been there since the beginning, but the ones entering the market now will be paying more, which is actually better for the game if that money helps grow it from the grassroots upwards.'

I asked Gabby about the inevitable comparisons to the men's game and the links to men's clubs. 'I have always felt the women's game has an opportunity to grow its own future and not copy a blueprint of the men. Its history is different, so its future can be too. Why not explore other models of ownership to build a sustainable league that is competitive and financially robust?' Agreed, but don't encourage the men to do the same. Especially as it would mean there'd be no need for our podcast any more.

Gabby gets most enthusiastic when she talks about the societal changes that the game can inspire: 'Successful sportswomen are wonderful and vital role models when it comes to health and wellbeing, and the camaraderie and love the Lionesses had for each other was another joyful positive. It's about seeing different types of role model, not just the unattainable Instagram influencers who look good in tights. We must keep young women playing sport and enjoying fitness for the health of the whole nation.'

It's vitally important, we think, that women's football bears Gabby's words about fun and fitness in mind as it continues to grow, and 2022 saw another significant development for the women's game. In June the Canadian national team went on strike and refused to play a friendly against Panama. They were demonstrating about World Cup prize money and unequal pay, with one of their main demands being 'an equitable structure for both teams'. The twist is that it was the men who withdrew their labour to demand the same rewards as their much better paid female counterparts. It was, ahem, a striking example of the astonishing global growth of women's football. And it's been a long time coming.

KNICKERBOCKER GLORY

We at West Park Rovers are passionate in our belief that football clubs occupy unique places in their communities. Sadly, though, we also have to acknowledge that for a century or more those football clubs have virtually ignored half of their communities. Sure, there would have been a few wives in the directors' box, a tea lady or two, and in that quaint 1930s newsreel footage of huge crowds at Wembley you may spot the occasional woman among the cloth caps and cigarette smoke; but for the most part the nation's game belonged to only half the nation.

The irony is, though, that one of the most successful sides in the early years of English football was a women's team. And even more ironically, it was that success that led to the demise of women's football for decades. The English FA's own history records 1895 as the date of the first official women's game, with The North beating The South 7–1, but there were definitely women's clubs before that, with one, probably called Crouch End, apparently drawing crowds of 10,000. I say 'probably' and 'apparently', because it's hard enough pinning down details of the history of men's football in the early years, but finding accurate reports of women's football, a game that was considered as somewhere between a charming novelty and an outrage against nature, is even more difficult.

In fact, even that official 'first' game is the result of conjecture, with some historians claiming that the game was actually between North London and South London. This seems unlikely considering the rematch was in Bury, but either way, 7–1 is still a shocking result for two South London lads like me and Kieran. Reports of that first game did not concentrate on the actual football either. The *Manchester Guardian* said, 'The costumes came in for a great deal of attention as one or two had added short skirts over their knickerbockers,' while according to a piece in another paper, this time from 'a lady correspondent', one girl was so much 'readier and active than the others the crowd decided he was a boy and called her Tommy throughout the game.'

Women in Scotland had their chance to play much earlier with a game played in Glasgow in 1881 between Mrs Graham's XI and a scratch team of English ladies. Many on both sides played under pseudonyms, including Mrs Graham herself (real name Helen Matthews), because they were unsure of the crowd's reaction – and with good reason. The *Nottinghamshire Guardian*, having first acknowledged that their 'costume was suitable' then reported that 5000 male Glaswegian fans were in initial good humour, exhorting the players with shouts of 'Go it, Fanny' and 'Well done, Nelly'. However, it seems they grew tired of this genteel banter and, encouraged by a 'crowd of roughs', they invaded the pitch, threatening the women to such an extent that they had to be escorted off under police protection.

There were further reports of near riots at women's games in Blackburn and Manchester, but I'm not entirely sure that necessarily represents a strength of anti-women feeling, because in those early days of organised football there was crowd trouble just about every Saturday. For most young men, newly released from the factory with money in their pocket and alcohol in their bloodstream, the idea of being legally allowed to gather with thousands like them to watch a game against local rivals was, I imagine, a novelty to be enjoyed, quite often with boots and fists.

By the way, to confuse matters even more, there are some historians who claim that the North team of 1895 was a pseudonym for a pseudonym and was actually Mrs Graham's XI who had moved to England because women's football had been banned in Scotland. One account says that Mrs Graham's assistant was the splendidly named Nellie Honeyball – and if there are any Honeyballs reading this, please get in touch.

Whatever the historical mystery, one thing is clear. The 1880s was just as dangerous a decade for watching football as the 1980s. So much so, that Preston North End were one of many clubs which decided that women would be allowed free entry to games in order to curb the loutish behaviour of the men. However, they soon changed their mind when more than 2000 women turned up for the next match! Instead they raised the admission fee for men in an attempt to price out poorer and therefore, as they saw it, rowdier fans.

TOO POPULAR

Whatever the attitude to female players was initially, the *Lancashire Evening Post* reported that just before 3pm on Boxing Day 1920, 53,000 fans were eagerly awaiting kick-off inside Goodison Park while the streets outside contained almost as many again who couldn't get in. It was the biggest crowd for a football match ever seen in the city of Liverpool and it was played between two women's teams.

One of them was St Helens Ladies, the other was that hugely successful team I mentioned earlier: Dick, Kerr Ladies. They were a team formed by girls from the Dick, Kerr Munitions Factory in Preston to play a charity game against girls from a local foundry on Christmas Day 1917.* A crowd of 10,000 turned up to Deepdale to watch and £600 was raised for wounded soldiers. Kieran tells me that's about £53,000 today. The 1920 Boxing Day game at Goodison Park raised over £3000 (just over £266,000 today) for ex-servicemen's charities, so they were clearly more than a novelty, as some men sniffily claimed.

So much so in fact, that by 1921 they were the unofficial England Ladies team† and, while still working full-time at the factory, they were playing two exhibition games a week across the country,

---

*During the Great War, with men's competitive football suspended, women's football became very popular.

†The FA has acknowledged their 2–0 defeat of a French XI in 1920 as the first women's international. The crowd was 25,000.

making so much money for ex-servicemen they were nicknamed 'the little goldmine'.

It was all too much for the FA who feared that fans going to see women play were therefore not going to see men play, which was quite a clever deduction by their standards and also, as it happens, a correct one. Not only that, but the Dick, Kerr Ladies, especially the glamorous, chain-smoking left winger Lily Parr, were inspiring many other women to start teams, providing even more competition for the men.

Initially the FA tried to claim they wanted to ban the women's game because of fears over their health and especially their ability to have babies. As the *British Medical Journal* said at the time, 'We can in no way sanction the reckless exposure to violence, of organs which the common experience of women has led them to protect,' but it was clearly the potential loss of revenue that was the concern. On 5 December 1921 the FA passed the following resolution: 'Complaints having been made as to football being played by women, the Council feel impelled to express their strong opinion that the game of football is quite unsuitable for females and ought not to be encouraged.'

Worse, they claimed that the Dick, Kerr Ladies were skimming money off the profits: 'We are of the opinion that an excessive proportion of the receipts are absorbed in expenses and an inadequate percentage devoted to charitable objects.' Note the use of the word 'opinion' there. They had no proof. Nevertheless, the FA ordered clubs to refuse permission for their grounds to be played on by women. That ban wasn't lifted until 1971. They did, in 1969, allow the formation of the Women's FA, although they drew the line at it being called the Ladies' FA, because 'ladies play golf', but it wasn't until 1994 that the women's game came fully back into the loving arms of the FA.

Now, England's Lionesses play in front of full houses at Wembley. We have a Women's Super League with its own separate broadcasting deal and a partnership with Barclays in the biggest brand investment ever in UK women's sport, and more than 3.5 million women and girls in this country participate in football.

At the men's World Cup Finals in 2022 there were women officials and globally the women's game appears to be getting bigger and bigger, although there are some cynics who say the only reason that FIFA have so enthusiastically backed the women's game in recent years is that they've run out of ways of making money from the men's game. Indeed, FIFA recently said that, 'Women's football is the single biggest growth opportunity for football today.'

DO THE RIGHT THING

So, of course, West Park Rovers needs to consider starting a women's team, because it's the right thing to do, but what if the right thing to do actually ends up costing us money? Because FIFA may be right behind it, but even they admit in a recent report that 70% of women's clubs across the world operate at a loss.

Sophia Axelsson, a player and part-owner of Clapton Community Football Club, told us about the harsh economic reality of the women's game in the Greater London Women's Football League, Tier 7 of the women's pyramid, far away from the bright lights of a sold-out Wembley, a place where things are so tight that 'harsh' would actually be a step up.

I asked her about Gabby Logan's notion that the women's game should grow its own future and not copy the men's blueprint. Sophia absolutely agreed, but added, 'It's too late. We're already there. Arsenal, Chelsea, Manchester City and Manchester United are the only teams who will be able to compete for anything for a very long time.'

Clare Balding is more optimistic. She told me that she thinks the women's game is still only in the early stages of its development and she expects teams like Liverpool and Aston Villa to be challenging for trophies very soon. And Clare thinks there is still plenty of time to make sure that the continued growth of women's football is properly managed to ensure that funds are distributed properly throughout the women's game so that 'the grassroots can flourish'. But she has a warning about the headlong rush to compete with the men's game. 'What do we want professionalism in women's football to look like? I want it to be fully rounded, where money is shared properly but where there is a genuine concern for the physical and mental welfare of all those playing the game at the highest level. I'd hate it to become just another product, like men's football'.

Clare thinks that with a global approach the women's game could be on the verge of great things, but she did have a couple of caveats: 'There still aren't nearly enough women working in football, and the lack of access to the game for many young girls has to be sorted out immediately'. And she calls for some perspective in the constant comparisons to the men's game when it comes to broadcasting fees, wages etc. 'We should be comparing it to the amount spent on men's rugby, athletics and cricket, not the amount spent on the most ludicrously overpriced league in the world'.

Claire and Sophia both fully endorsed Gabby's passionate belief that keeping young women in sport can benefit the whole of society, but Sophia wants to know where the funding is coming from. 'Sure, people want to invest more into women's football now, but it's not a generous gesture. They know it will boost their own brand perception, but they won't get any visibility investing in Tier 7. We train once a week on two-thirds of a pitch and it costs £11,000 for 40 weeks. If we weren't the club we are the players would have to pay that, at around £400 a year. People round here can't afford that and the risk is that even at this level women's football is becoming elitist.'

The 'club we are' is a very passionate, community-based club for men and women, attracting crowds of around 600 for both, and committed to a model of inclusivity. It's why, when Clapton CFC reached the third round of the Women's FA Cup in December 2021 and were drawn away to Plymouth Argyle, fans had to pay for the trip, because the cup prize money wasn't enough to cover the travel expenses. Six months later, Chelsea beat Manchester City 3–2 in the final in front of 49,000 people at Wembley, but along the way, one of the teams in one of the biggest tournaments in world women's football actually lost out financially by taking part. The 2023 Women's FA Cup Final, by the way, was completely sold out.

Very few men's teams will ever need to crowdfund an FA Cup trip. There will be more on FA Cup finances later, but for now I'm sure Sophia would like me to point out that for winning a first-round game a men's team receives £41,000, while for a women's team it's £6000. Win the final and the men get £2 million with £1 million for losing. Women get £100,000 and £50,000. In other words, the team that loses the men's final gets 10 times as much as the women who win theirs.

Doubtless the FA will argue that while the women's final may attract a huge Wembley crowd, games in the preceding rounds may not – but surely it's part of their remit to help build those numbers and if that involves subsidising the early rounds for the women then so be it. They can afford it. The Lionesses have already done their bit. Time for the FA to step up.

As we shall see, there are some big names who think that the women's game has gone as far as it can under the current regime and are calling for radical changes. In the meantime, anyone doubting that the FA take women's football seriously will be reassured to know that their guidelines for the women's pyramid are also bafflingly opaque, even though they must have been formulated much more recently.

There are just as many 'save as set out otherwise below' and 'as it considers appropriate and expedient' as there are in the men's rule book. In fact, one lengthy paragraph seems to be entirely formed of the words 'county', 'association' and 'league' with 'sanctioned' thrown in for occasional light relief.

The ground regulations are almost identical, including my favourite: 'The surface of any artificial turf must be of a green colour.' There must be separate dressing rooms for both male and female officials, which hopefully may one day be the norm in the men's game as well. It's interesting to note, however, that at the lowest level there is no requirement for separate changing rooms, but whatever the gender of the match officials, there must be 'an audible electronic warning device (bell or buzzer) linked to the players' dressing rooms.' Bad news for my mate who has just set up a klaxon business.

Equality-wise it seems like good news then that both games are treated the same in respect of ground criteria, or does it just indicate that the FA assume any women's football teams will simply share an existing men's ground? Although that would be a fair assumption. It's hard to imagine any women's team, no matter how successful, being able to build or develop their own ground from scratch and most of them do share a ground with men, although, from experience, I hope for their sake that the dressing rooms are fumigated if they're going in after the blokes.

GIRL POWER

The Women's Championship was formed as part of a restructure of the women's game in 2018 and 14 teams applied for a licence to join the new, and then part-time, second tier, with the top tier being re-branded as the Women's Super League (WSL), where teams are expected to be full-time professionals.

Crystal Palace Ladies (formed in 1992) had their bid for a licence rejected, despite finishing above Lewes FC Women and West Ham

United Ladies in the southern section of the existing second tier, both of whom were invited to join. Even worse, Manchester United were also granted a place in the new league, despite not actually having a women's team!

Mind you, it did indicate to many of us Palace fans that some sort of equality must be approaching if Man United's women were already getting the same preferential treatment as the men, despite the technicality of not actually existing. The following year – now called Crystal Palace Women – they were promoted (*by right*, Manchester United) to the Championship, where they still are.

They are a full-time squad, playing in front of 200-plus at Hayes Lane, the ground of National League side Bromley FC, although they draw crowds of around 1000 when they occasionally play at Selhurst Park, and they have their own academy and youth sides.

But despite the men's team being (at time of writing) a relatively wealthy Premier League one, Crystal Palace Women generate so little money that they are classified as a 'micro' company. This means that they don't have to publish detailed accounts with figures such as income, wages and profits, which, in turn, results in Kieran sulking in front of his keyboard. Since being promoted to the Premier League in 2013, Palace men's team has generated over £1.1 billion in revenue and paid out over £900 million in wages. Some players in clubs in the Women's Championship are paid as little as £4000 a year.

Even in the WSL itself, revenues can be as low as £300,000 a season and the average wage is £27,000 a year, although there is growth potential in these figures as big brands are now keen to align themselves to the England Lionesses' success.

Durham Women's FC (AKA the Wildcats) were formed in 2014 and have played in the second tier of women's football ever since. They were an unusual amalgamation of the hugely successful local youth team South Durham and Cestria Girls with Durham University, and, also unusually, they are one of the few teams in the top tiers of women's football who are not affiliated to a local men's team. Nevertheless, they are a thriving club, playing at Maiden Castle, part of Durham University's sports complex, in front of an average crowd of around 600, rising to 1200 when the big teams are in town. Interesting to note, then, that their average attendance is three times that of Crystal Palace Women (AKA the Eagles), despite big promotional and advertising campaigns from the latter's parent club.

Adult tickets at Durham are £7, students £5 and children £3. Another £10 will get you a scarf and, if you're peckish, the club website advises that Fat Frank's Food Truck is on site for every home game, providing burgers, hot dogs, bratwurst and chips, with some speciality items such as donuts and waffles 'available for high-profile fixtures'. Car parking is free.

Even with my fingers and toes counting method I reckon that amounts to only around £5000 a time in matchday income and they can't be making a huge amount on merchandise either: apart from that £10 scarf, you can get a pen for £1, a hat for £6 or a shirt for £35. You can also buy a matchworn shirt for £20 and, nice touch this, shirt air freshener for £2.

Nevertheless, in June 2022 Durham were financially secure enough to announce they were to become fully professional. Now, top players like Sam Kerr at Chelsea are earning £300,000 a year and obviously won't be a transfer target for the Wildcats anytime soon, but, remember, the average WSL wage is £27,000 a year and even if Durham's is lower than that, say £15,000, then you're still looking at around £240,000 a year in wages, set against matchday income and merchandise, which, being generous, can only amount to £100,000 a year.

That's a potential shortfall of around £140,000, which is a huge sum for a club the size of West Park Rovers to find to subsidise a women's team, even if the decision to become professional may be a long way down the line. There is no doubt that our men's team will have to go full-time soon if we want to compete and progress, but so, it seems, will our women's team. Unless, of course, they become a completely separate entity, in which case they will find it even harder to get finance. What should be a simple decision is becoming a bit of a moral maze.

Meanwhile, back in Durham there's a potential problem on the horizon – if the horizon is 19 miles away, that is.

In May 2022, following the takeover of Newcastle United by the Saudi Public Investment Fund, their women's team played their first ever game at St James' Park, a friendly against Alnwick Town. More than 22,000 turned up. They may currently play in National League Division One North (the fourth tier of the women's game), but if the Saudis invest as much money in them as they are expected to put into the men's team then the WSL surely awaits, which is bad news for Durham WFC, because that part of the world is dominated by the Toon and they will be a big beast to compete with – especially as Newcastle United Women recently became the first club in the third tier of women's football to go fully professional.

Which brings us to a huge issue for a game that has made incredible progress on and off the pitch in a remarkably short time – unless you're counting from 1895 of course, in which case it's taken a shamefully long time.

Following a recent match that got a bit physical, there is currently an unlikely rivalry between the Wildcats and the Eagles.* The Durham and Palace players may not like each other much, but the clubs share a common commitment to growing their game and making it accessible to the community. As Gabby and Sophia so eloquently express, football can be a positive force in improving female health and fitness, and in bringing together girls from many different economic and ethnic backgrounds who may otherwise never get to meet. It is a force for good.

Despite the Palace team being part of a Premier League club, there doesn't seem to be that much of a difference between their respective finances, but is the gap bigger between the Eagles, the Wildcats and those teams who are becoming the powerhouses of the women's game? Yes. Yes it is. Oh girl, it is.

PROFESSIONAL APPROACH

In 2020, Chelsea were WSL champions, with Manchester City second, Arsenal third and Manchester United fourth. In 2021 the finishing order was exactly the same. In 2022, by way of a refreshing change, Chelsea won again with Man U fourth, but Arsenal and Man City swapped places. In 2023, guess what? Chelsea won but in a dramatic reshuffle Man Utd were second ahead of Arsenal and Man City. You don't exactly need a telescope to spot Aston Villa and Everton in fifth and sixth, but it will be a miracle if one of them breaks into that top four, let alone wins the title.

*Whereas, of course, the rivalry between Palace and Brighton men's teams is entirely explicable.

See the problem? Spurs, West Ham, Brighton and Leicester all have teams in the same league. They are all reasonably well resourced and supported, but my guess is that for the next five seasons at least the WSL table will be topped by some permutation of those same four sides, although Liverpool Women were promoted in 2022 and may decide that they should be challenging for that title as well.

Teams like Durham, London City, Lewes and, I'm afraid Crystal Palace Women, can turn professional in an effort to get promoted and compete with the big guns, but unless they, or the club they are affiliated to, are bought by mega-wealthy individuals or countries (hello Newcastle!) it simply won't happen. That top four will get more prize money, more broadcasting money, bigger sponsorship deals to buy the top-class players they need to maintain their position and effectively create a mini-league in the WSL. That way, their qualification for the Women's Champions League is guaranteed every season, bringing them even more income. Sounds familiar, doesn't it? And it sounds unfair.

Lewes Women, for example, are an equal part of another wonderful community club. Men and women players are paid the same. You can buy a season ticket for all men's and women's games for around £260 and for an extra fifty quid you can buy a share in the club, giving you the status of 'owner' and a vote on club matters. Let me quote Lucy from the club's website: 'I am a Lewes FC owner, because the club is disrupting football and demonstrating how the sport should be, everywhere. The model of the club is authentic, ethical and inclusive. A club of tomorrow, today!'

They are fan-owned, not-for-profit, people-powered. Wage-wise they were the first gender-equal club in the world and they have the best ground name in football: the Dripping Pan. In other words, they are a cool club and, we think, an important one, even though they will never ever be able to compete with those four clubs at the top of the WSL, who, I imagine, think they are actually the important ones.

I have nothing against those top four clubs being successful and we have happily acknowledged on the pod that they also do fantastic work in their communities, but that difference in wages is staggering. Does it matter? You could argue that in the real world there will always be some businesses that are more popular than others, some products that are easier to sell, and if the top clubs are also using some of that money for good local causes then so much the better.

Well, for the sake of the future of women's football, yes, we think it does matter. The game is at a crucial point. England international games tend to sell out; league games rarely do. There is already a huge disparity between an elite group of four or five clubs and the rest, and it's getting bigger not smaller. If nothing changes we will reach a situation where equality is achieved because the women's game is exactly the same as the men's – the top league will be impossible for most teams to win, broadcasting and matchday income will be unfairly distributed, and championship teams will be bankrupting themselves to get promoted to the promised land.

Some high-profile people in women's football, though, clearly believe that there is more money to be made and it needs a professional touch to make it. Emma Hayes is one of the best managers in the game. With extensive experience in America she took over at Chelsea in 2012 and, in the words of one of her players, 'She built everything there,' creating an infrastructure and a squad capable of winning the last four WSL titles in a row.

The day after the Lionesses won the Euros, Emma told the *Daily Telegraph* what should happen next: 'The Women's Super League should be taken out of the hands of the FA and handed over to a commercial operation with experience of growing the sport in both broadcasting terms and the product* around it.' She thanked the FA for everything they had done (like, you know, helping England's Women to their first ever trophy), but stressed that it should be no part of the future, while hoping that the Premier League could be 'part of that conversation' about who replaces it.

Emma spoke, too, about expanding the WSL to 14 teams playing in stadia holding at least 10,000 people and 'perhaps even playing all games at their men's stadiums.' Tough luck, Durham. And bad news for broadcasters who are rightly showing a lot of women's football, but who, behind closed doors (which is the only place they will admit it), tell us they don't really want to show matches where there may be only a couple of thousand people thinly spread around Villa Park or the Amex. Also, and quite rightly, Emma spoke of the huge disparities in prize money, the need for an integrated women's academy system and, crucially, equal access and opportunities across the country for

'I've always had an irrational dislike of the word 'product' being applied to football!

UNFIT AND IMPROPER PERSONS

girls to play football at grassroots and school level – it's scandalous that many schools still do not allow girls the chance to play football.

So there is much to like in Emma Hayes' blueprint for a brighter future, but it strikes us that the future will be much brighter for Chelsea than other clubs. The only mention of the money being made from the 'product' being shared equally throughout the league is when she says that parity in prize money would be helpful, 'because the trickle-down effect is so impactful for smaller clubs.' But that's it and – no disrespect Emma – that money will have to trickle a long bloody way down before it reaches the likes of Sophia Axelsson at Clapton. Sophia herself puts it more forcefully: 'In the women's game, trickle-down economics categorically does not work.'

However, it may not be too late to put the genie back in the bottle and Kieran is exploring new ways of distributing money in the women's game, using US sport as a model. Yep, America, poster boy for Western capitalism, is surprisingly democratic when it comes to handing out money in sport. In the NFL, for example, all merchandising income is put into a central pot and shared equally between the clubs, meaning smaller teams like the Green Bay Packers get as much as giants like, well, the New York Giants. And, of course, using the draft system, the worst team of the season gets first choice of the new players available for the next. It's done to ensure that all teams have a roughly equal chance of winning the Super Bowl, thus maintaining the interest of fans and, more importantly, broadcasters, who, unlike our very own Sky Sports, don't seem to think that having one of the same two teams winning every season is good for the future of the game, no matter how much you hype each successive one as the 'season of the century'.

My guess is that the teams already entrenched at the top of the women's game are unlikely to be enthusiastic about a system that sees Durham and Lewes get as much money each year as they do, but anything that could help Lewes get into the Women's Champions League is fine by us, if only to hear the manager of Bayern Munich say, 'Was? Wo zum Teufel ist die Dripping Pan?'

On the face of it then, the women's game in England is thriving at international level and beginning to flourish domestically, certainly for those teams at the top, and much has been made of them getting their own separate broadcasting deal. In principle that's a great step forward, but in practice? The Premier League is slightly coy about revealing precise figures, especially when it's Kieran doing the asking, but their latest TV deal is estimated at £10.5 billion over three years. For the same period the WSL deal is around £24 million. In other words, for every £100 earned by the men, the women get 23p.

Looks like we may have to re-define 'thriving'. It's certainly growing, though, and hopefully the women's game will keep getting bigger. We know plenty of people who prefer to take their families there rather than re-mortgage the house to take them to see the men play, so who knows, in 20 years' time maybe Goodison Park will once again be filled to capacity to watch women's football. And maybe the FA will once again be so frightened of the effect it may have on the men's game that they find another reason to ban it.

VIABLE PROPOSITION

So West Park Rovers has a decision to make.

We know from experience roughly how much money to start a new football team, but how much money could this new team actually make us? Well, we'd have to pay to get there first, but if we win the WSL we'll get a rather handy £100,000. If we come second it's £67,000. And if we finish last and get relegated? £6000. How much? £6000. What??? You can add as many question marks as you like, it's still £6000. And how much would we get for finishing last in the Premier League? £100 million plus parachute payments of around £90 million spread over the next three seasons. Fuck me, that's hardly equal is it? If that's how things were in 1921 the Dick, Kerr Ladies would still be alive and kicking, because they would be a threat to no man's finances.

There are issues other than finance to consider, too, and I'm ashamed to say that until they were pointed out to us in the course of this chapter, us three men were woefully unaware of them. For example, we discovered that there are huge issues with retaining girls in football between the age of 13 and 16.

Ady Dolan is chair of Ashridge Park FC, a community club in Berkshire with a number of girls' and women's teams, and he told us that the two main reasons that so many drop out are body image and periods. Many of the girls simply can't afford to buy tampons or sanitary towels. Nor can they afford sports bras and are very often self-conscious about wearing kits. So they asked the girls (and their mothers) to design a suitable new kit and the club now provide sports bras and period products – distributed, of course, by female staff. Sophia elaborated: 'Women's team kit design is still secondary for many manufacturers.' So at Clapton they also designed their own: 'No white shorts, no placement of print across the chest, looser fit shirts and a collar that works for someone wearing a hijab.' I'm fairly certain my wife loves me very much, but the withering look of pity she gave me when I told her what I'd learned about these things will live long in my mind. It transpires that, 'Yes,' she had been aware that 'these things may be a problem.'

As Sophia pointed out, there is also another problem: things are changing at the elite level, but at grassroots level the vast majority of coaches are still male. If a young woman feels that her body is changing and it is affecting her performance, is an older man the person she will feel comfortable speaking to about it? Probably not, so it's easier to come up with an excuse not to be there.

So it's clear that we are three men with a lot to learn and it's clear that there is still a huge economic gulf between the games, but it's also clear that we have a duty to do the right thing morally, even if it may be the wrong thing financially. Say hello to West Park Rovers WFC. All we have to do now is find a manager, players and some kit, and check whether Omino's Pizza want to extend their sponsorship deal to the women. Oh, and what's the other thing? Come on, it's on the tip of my tongue. Oh yes, tell Gerald, the world's grumpiest groundsman, that there are going to be twice as many games on his pitch next season. And as the world's grumpiest groundsman is like the world's screechiest seagull, it won't be me, Kieran or Guy that tells him. I'm getting Jean from the club shop to do it.

5

YOUTH POLICY

'You can't win anything with kids'

Of the three owners of West Park Rovers, I like to think I am the one most accessible to our fans or, as our website puts it, I like to be 'forward facing', whatever the bloody hell that means. This is partly because Kieran is normally too busy spreadsheeting to meet people and partly because Guy isn't great with the whole eye contact thing (thus adding to my suspicion that he is on a witness protection scheme), but mainly it's because most of our fans know what pub I drink in. Consequently, if they have a complaint, and they usually have more than one, it's me that gets it in the ear.

Not that I don't love our fans. Of course I do. Without them (and their money) we'd be nowhere, but every now and then it would be nice if they just came up and said hello or thank you, rather than having a go at me, because the coach to Ebbsfleet was too hot or the beer at Dulwich Hamlet was too expensive. Friday night is the worst, because every Friday morning Ken McDuff, chief (and only) sportswriter on the local newspaper, invariably posts another story about a brilliant 14-year-old kid from down the road who has just signed for a Premier League Academy, which leads to me being surrounded by fans in the White Lion demanding to know why we keep missing out on the next Mason Mount.

McDuff's definition of 'down the road' extends to about four counties in every direction, but even though he has got it in for us since we changed the biscuits in the press room from Hobnobs to plain Digestives, we do seem to have missed out on some potentially decent local talent.

So I called a board meeting to discuss the issue and asked Kieran whether it was because we weren't identifying these kids ourselves or weren't offering their parents some tasty inducements to persuade them to join us, a practice which is definitely not allowed, but nevertheless definitely happens. He explained that the actual reason we keep missing out on talented youngsters is because we have absolutely no youth development scheme of our own. Ah…

When you look at photos of football teams from previous decades it's sometimes impossible to believe that any of those players are actually young. Looking back at you are grim-faced men who are either bald or have so much oil in their hair they're a danger to sea birds. They are rarely smiling and many of them look like they have just done a 12-hour shift down a coal mine or are having flashbacks to the beaches of Normandy.

And whereas, up close, today's players smell of Armani and new phones,* you imagine that the only acceptable scent for the players in those black and white photos would have been tobacco and liniment with a hint of defeated Germany. However, a quick browse of a search engine tells us that most of those players, standing there with all the emotion of a police identity parade, were not only quite young they were usually quite local. Unless they were Scottish, of course. As a kid it always amazed me that Scotland managed to have teams of their own when so many of their players were earning a living down south.

For the grim-faced young men resolutely refusing to say 'cheese' in those old photos, the hierarchy of a football club was very simple. You had a first team, invariably managed by a man wearing a blazer and smoking a pipe, and you had a reserve team invariably trained by a man wearing a roll-neck jumper and smoking a roll-up, usually with a limp so bad there was a furrow in the dressing-room corridor.

---

*You'll have to take my word for it, but if you ever get a chance to sniff Jamie Redknapp you'll understand.

Some clubs also had proper youth teams (the first ever FA Youth Cup was held in 1953), but many clubs just seemed to have a few youngsters hanging around the place. They were called apprentices – yet another reflection of the working-class roots of the game – and according to most of the autobiographies of old footballers that I've read, the apprentices seemed to spend more time sweeping the terraces and polishing the senior players' boots than they did playing football. However, if they were lucky they were signed on as professionals to battle those same senior players for a place in the first team and wait for the glorious day when they would be the ones bunging a teenager 10 bob at Christmas for cleaning their footwear.

If you talk to any player of that generation (for argument's sake let's call them all Harry Redknapp) they will tell you the apprentice days were the happiest of their lives. They got to play keepy-uppy in the car park, cleaning the toilets apparently taught them respect, running up and down the terraces 10 times a day kept them fit and, along with the smell of liniment, they inhaled the sort of values that young players of today just don't have any more.

Of course, Harry was one of the fortunate ones, so his nostalgia glasses are a little more rose-tinted. He got a professional contract at West Ham and had a long and illustrious career in the game. The vast majority of his fellow apprentices were not so lucky and with a curt 'Sorry, son' and a handshake their dreams were shattered and they were shown the door, back to the local streets from whence they came.

Occasionally, as in the case of George Best, a nervous homesick boy would be shipped in from somewhere like Belfast and stuck in a stranger's house two bus rides away from the training ground, but for the most part the apprentices were local and apparently a source of cheap labour, as much as a pool of potential talent.

Sometimes, though, the local youngsters were a cause of once-in-a-generation delight. The 1950s saw Manchester United's Busby Babes winning titles with youthful elan before being cut off in their prime. In 1967, the legendary Lisbon Lions of Celtic won the European Cup with only one player, Bobby Lennox, who was born more than 11 miles from their ground (he came from 33 miles away – I'm amazed they could understand his accent). Crystal Palace had the 'team of the eighties', who briefly led the top flight of English football with a team that included seven teenagers, and Manchester United produced another crop of young stars, the Class of '92, who went on to dominate the rest of that decade, despite ex-Liverpool player Alan Hansen's infamous claim that 'You can't win anything with kids.'

BABIES ON BOARD

Youth recruitment is very different now. No more waiting until they leave school and no need to live in the same postcode any more. Clubs are signing kids into development centres from the age of five and trading them as commodities across the globe like some sort of fleshy cryptocurrency. Every Premier League club has an academy in an attempt to hoover up local talent or lure them away from other clubs, hoping they will save themselves a fortune in transfer fees by unearthing a 20-goal-a-season striker from their own backyard, and sometimes it works. Phil Foden at Manchester City and Wilfried Zaha at Crystal Palace could probably smell the matchday onions from their bedroom windows, but mostly it doesn't and, although clubs do it more gently these days, 99% of youngsters are still shown the door at the age of 16.

So why then have academies become such a huge and hugely expensive part of the game at the highest level when so few of them seem to be producing players for the first team, let alone the national side? And as West Park Rovers approach the Vanarama National League without a huge budget to buy better players, is it economical to try to breed homegrown talent of our own? The problem is that, geographically, we are surrounded by Premier League teams, all with Category One academies, so how do we encourage youngsters to the Kleanwell Stadium? And, more importantly, once we've developed them, how do we stop our promising young players being lured away by the predatory Premier League club down the road, especially when we can't afford to offer their parents a new car or a house the way they can? And yes, Kieran, I know that sort of thing 'definitely' doesn't happen any more.

The Premier League clubs it appears, have it both ways. They spend millions on their own academies and if that doesn't produce any gems they simply step in and spend thousands on snapping up any talented youngsters that we produce. And how do we develop them in the first place? Luckily, as we have seen, whether it's a guide to pitch sizes or how many free tickets you can have for play-offs, the beautiful game loves a chunky PDF filled with rules and regulations, but my guess is that the EFL's *Youth Development Academy Players and Parents Handbook* is the only one that contains the word 'holistic' – and in the very first sentence too.

The handbook is also very big on words like 'pathway', 'vision' and 'mission', and in general seems to be written by someone who has just come back from a course on making things sound new and relevant and, you know, down with the kids. A side note warns parents to ensure 'a young person does not feel defined by football performance or be solely identified as a professional footballer.' Yeah, good advice, Captain Buzzkill. Advice that I reckon is ignored by just about everyone who reads it, which is a shame, because to be fair to the EFL the handbook is shot through with concern for the mental wellbeing of the kids at academies and especially what will happen to those who don't make it. That's one thing we want you to bear in mind as we set about attracting youngsters to West Park Rovers – we are not talking about assets and commodities here; we're talking about kids, real human kids.

The Elite Player Performance Plan (from now on known as EPPP to save me wrist strain) was established in 2012 and, even though its website assures us it was the result of consultation between the EFL, the FA and 'other key stakeholders', it is still very much the Premier League's own long-term strategy to build a 'world class youth development system' to provide 'more and better homegrown players' for the top clubs and, by extension, for the national team.

The website also tells us that the EPPP 'promotes the empowerment of each individual player through a player-led approach,' which is interesting because the Foundation Phase of the plan works with under nines to under 11s and I'm not convinced kids of that age are able to articulate the particular approach they want you to take, nor, in my experience does a seven-year-old want to be empowered, especially if it means he has to cook his own dinner or clean out the hutch of that rabbit he begged Santa for last Christmas. In fact, even in the Youth Development Phase (U12 to U16) and the Professional Development Phase (U17 to U23) I think the young people would be happier playing football than workshopping their empowerment needs.

Most clubs in the Premier League and the EFL recruit and process their youngsters through the academy system, but before West Park Rovers make a decision about if, or when, we do the same, we need to see how it works. Each club academy is independently audited and put into a category from one to four, based on a number of criteria, such as funding, facilities and staff numbers.

The highest is Category One, which most Premier League clubs are or aspire to be. Category One is an 'elite environment' guaranteeing the highest quality of coaching and the 'potential' of full-time education from under the age of 12. Category One academies can also recruit nationally from the age of 14, providing they guarantee access to full-time education.

That ability to recruit nationally is one of the very many reasons clubs aspire to be Category One. There are over 20 clubs with a Category One academy and their running costs vary, but Aston Villa claimed in their most recent accounts that youth development cost nearly £14 million, and the average running costs are estimated at about £5–6 million a year. In reality, that ability to recruit nationally will mean a club can have development centres all over the country (and sometimes the world), making it very difficult for clubs like us to attract the talent that we would later hope to sell to those clubs to the mutual benefit of us all.

Category Two is 'an elite development environment where academy players are typically recruited locally' and get additional coaching and educational support. Category Three is the same, but without the 'elite' and the 'educational support', while Category Four academies focus only on providing coaching and educational support for U17 to U21.

Until recently, some clubs, like Crewe Alexandra, based their entire financial model on spotting and developing young talent then moving them on to bigger clubs for a transfer fee that would keep them solvent for another year, but as you can see, EPPP is making that increasingly difficult. Category Two academies are estimated to cost a minimum of £1.5 million annually to run and Category Three £500,000. Category Four is a late development model run by clubs such as Brentford and Huddersfield for players 17 years of age and older. Those two clubs have stopped running higher category academies, because they decided that trying to compete with some of the larger clubs close to them geographically was not worth the effort financially.

Category One clubs benefit from not having to comply with the '90-minute rule', which existed before EPPP. The rule was that clubs could not lure youngsters who lived more than a 90-minute journey away and was designed to prevent bigger clubs from recruiting young players from all over the country. The relaxation of this rule has allowed those clubs to cast their net wider and allow their scouts to watch young players at every other academy in the country. Chelsea, for example now have soccer schools not just in London, but also seven counties in England and one in Greece.

ENTITLED TO COMPENSATION

The system of compensation that operates under EPPP has caused resentment from some clubs, especially in the EFL. A club recruiting a young player from another academy has to pay a fixed amount of compensation linked to the length of time at the original academy. This compensation is £5000 a year for a player aged nine and varies between £7500 and 80,000 a year for ages 10 to 16.

This means that if a youngster who joined a Category Three academy aged nine moves to a Category One academy aged 14, his first club would receive £82,500 in compensation for developing the player for five years. If the academy player is one of the lucky few who goes on to have a professional career, then there are further fees payable:

Appearances	Premier League	Championship	League One	League Two
10	£150,000	£25,000	£10,000	£5000
20	£300,000	£50,000	£20,000	£10,000
30	£450,000	£75,000	£30,000	£15,000
40	£600,000	£100,000	£40,000	£20,000
50	£750,000	£125,000	£50,000	£25,000
60	£900,000	£150,000	£60,000	£30,000
70	£1,000,000	£175,000	£70,000	£35,000
80	£1,100,000	£200,000	£80,000	£40,000
90	£1,200,000	£225,000	£90,000	£45,000
100	£1,300,000	£250,000	£100,000	£50,000

Source: Kieran Maguire

If the player is sold before they reach the age of 23, then the clubs involved in the player's development receive a share of the transfer fee, but there are two reasons why some EFL clubs have been unhappy with the way that EPPP works. The first is that the compensation payments have not kept pace with overall football inflation. In 2012, when EPPP was introduced, the total revenue of Premier League clubs was £2.35 billion; by 2022 (the last year for which we have figures pre-Covid) this had increased 138% to £5.6 billion, but compensation payments have risen at a slower rate.

The second is that there was a sense of bullying in terms of the decision to introduce EPPP. The Premier League introduced 'solidarity' payments to EFL clubs after the creation of parachute payments. These payments were initially a flat sum, about £2.3 million for Championship clubs and £230,000 for those in League Two. When EPPP discussions between the two parties commenced, the Premier League let it be known that these payments were voluntary and could be withdrawn if there was opposition to their academy proposals. EFL clubs had by that time committed to long-term player contracts which would have been difficult to maintain had they lost solidarity payments and so, with some reluctance, they agreed to the proposals. The solidarity payments were linked to the overall size of the Premier League prize fund, so EFL clubs do benefit from new Premier League broadcast deals, but this has come at the price of losing talented young players for what many clubs consider to be a pittance compared to their real valuations.

Tapping-up or poaching of academy players is strictly prohibited by all the governing bodies in football, but is difficult if not impossible to police, and despite Kieran's claims (so innocent, God love him) it definitely does happen. Talk to agents and others in the game and they confirm it is rife. Academy youngsters are offered 'gifts' of boots or games consoles and their families can be offered jobs (either at the club or a related party) or even a new house. These are seen as a relatively low cost to the club, which is recruiting a player who could be worth millions in a few years.

As one agent told us, 'Many clubs do it and the repeat offenders fund it via agents. The club pays the agent a fee, the agent then buys or leases a car or whatever else the parents want. If you try and do it via the book and everyone else is breaking the rules it makes the job almost impossible.' It's an indication of how sensitive a subject it is that the agent who told us that insisted we don't use their name.

ACADEMIC QUESTION

So, Premier League clubs are spending an absolute fortune on amassing vast collections of young players, but is it working? Yes, Liverpool fans can drool over Trent Alexander-Arnold, Palace fans can sing the name of Tyrick Mitchell and City fans can get their hair cut like Phil Foden, but very few teams in the top flight are based around a whole group of homegrown players as they have been in the past. Very rarely do you see more than one or two academy players in a Premier League starting line-up and, with rare exceptions, every single club in that league is spending at least £30 million in every transfer window. So are those academies value for money?

Chelsea has one of the most successful academy systems in the country and while it is not possible to separate out academy sales from those of other players, the club has generated the most income from player sales in the last decade. Chelsea are normally associated with both big money and the occasional left-field signings (like Steve Sidwell, AKA the ginger Pirlo), but homegrown players such as Tammy Abraham, Fikayo Tomori, Marc Guéhi, Tariq Lamptey and Bertrand Traoré have generated almost £100 million in income. Even if they can't keep the likes of Mason Mount and Reece James at Stamford Bridge, the benefits of the academy still vastly outweigh the costs, especially if those two fetch a hundred million between them.

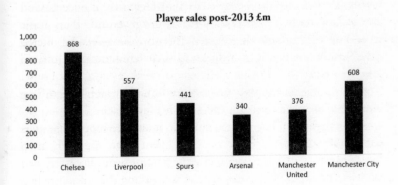

Player sales post-2013 £m

Source: Kieran Maguire

If you are reading this convinced that your five-year-old boy (and, hopefully, one day, girl) is the next Harry (or Harriet) Kane only two decades away from winning the World Cup for England and buying you a bigger house in the process,* how do you get him/her on to that path to glory in the first place? Well, one thing you should not do is browse the internet using any combination of the words 'academy', 'trial', 'better than Messi' or 'bigger house for mummy and daddy'. There are a lot of sites out there offering an array of soccer schools and seminars that will guarantee your infant prodigy ends up in a Premier League academy. Some are well-meaning, many are scams; all will cost you money.

As Manchester City's website starkly says: 'Do not trust any organisation that asks you for payment in return for a trial with a City Football Group club.' Basically, what you need to do is nothing. Sit back and watch your child play head-tennis with the cat, secure in the knowledge that if he is as good as you think then a big club will find him. This explanation of a Premier League club's scouting system comes from Tottenham Hotspur's official website, but it mirrors every other club in the league. Spurs explain that they have a network of scouts who work for the club on a local, national and international basis who are looking for players predominantly from under sevens to under 16s. And once they find your little genius? They are recommended to the academy recruitment department, which then decides whether to proceed.

Now, if at this stage you're worrying that perhaps your child is after all too young for this, then relax, because the higher up the age groups, the less likely they are to be offered a trial. In other words, their scouting system is so thorough that if they haven't already approached your boy by the age of seven he's more likely to end up at Southend than Spurs. There are no open trials by the way. Scouts watch players at local clubs or schools before inviting you for a trial.

And, unlike in my day when every Sunday League player was convinced that the suspicious looking old man lurking behind the tree was definitely a scout, there is no way of knowing that your

*Or being given one by a club desperate to sign the little goldmine.

child is being watched; the scouts are not always in club kit as the presence of a scout may put unnecessary pressure on the player, making them nervous or try much harder just because somebody is watching them. Frankly, if I was an ambitious parent I'd want the lazy little sod to try a lot harder if a Premier League scout was watching him. And if you're an ambitious parent, you won't be the first to get the good news, as clubs will always approach your kid's coach or manager before they contact you. Finally, and this may seem like an odd question, what are those scouts looking for? Quite simply, talent.

That's good, but after some detail about technical, tactical and physical attributes and so on, any 'target player', or if you prefer, 'target child', has to be assessed to see whether they have the potential to be better than the players the club already has registered. I'm not sure that bit is good. In other words, your talented child, at the age of five, is already in competition with kids from across the country and beyond, as well as kids already in the system.

As a club owner (fictional) and a parent (actual) I have no issue with the way kids are treated by elite football clubs. They all seem to show a level of care and safeguarding that goes way beyond the minimum requirements set by the authorities. It's just the whole concept that worries me slightly. Call me old-fashioned, but I think that five is an age when kids should be wondering what worms taste like or accidentally sticking their fingers together with glitter and glue rather than being thrown into the world of professional football. Yes, of course, it must be exciting for the kids getting to play football and wearing actual kit, but couldn't we just wait until they are a bit older, and give them a couple more years of running around pretending to be Harry Potter and annoying people at weddings?

To be fair, many clubs do stress the fun angle in the early years, and you may be proud and excited that your sprog has been approached, but in the first instance he will just be 'in development', learning ball skills and basic tactics and playing only non-competitive, eight-a-side games on small pitches. They can't actually sign for an academy until the age of nine, at which point they will be offered a schoolboy contract and, if they are still considered good enough at the age of 16, they will be offered a scholarship contract, allowing them to combine professional training with academic studies. They may even be offered wages and accommodation at this stage, too. Then, over the next three years, who knows, one of them may become a professional footballer, although it's statistically highly unlikely.

That statistical unlikelihood still doesn't stop tens of thousands of kids every year dreaming of glory and that brings a different peril. All clubs stress that their scouts will always approach potential recruits properly and that not only will the youngsters and their parents or guardians never be asked for any payment, the club will cover all costs of attending a trial. However, as mentioned earlier, clubs also recognise that the potential financial reward is so great, even for a five-year-old, that there are people willing to exploit children and their parents. Manchester City's website, in particular, offers extensive advice on how to spot bogus scouts who will normally ask for money in return for trials or even money to arrange for you to move house to be closer to the club.

It's good that clubs don't actually charge for your kid to be at their academy, but there are costs involved, both financial, as in travel and kit, and psychological, as in managing your kid's expectations. Such are the rewards on offer, though, that there are actually companies like La Liga Brokerage who cater for the number of young players moving countries to get a potentially better deal.

Apologies by the way that I always refer to the kids in the pipeline as 'he', although – and this is probably a good thing, equality wise – as women's football grows, clubs are beginning to take the development of 'she' seriously as well. The FA introduced the Women's Super League Dual-Career Academy programme in the 2018/19 season to provide elite female footballers with a pathway to the professional game, while also giving them the vocational education they may need to fall back on if they don't succeed. There is also a WSL Academy League for young women to gain experience in competitive football and many women's teams now have a successful youth system – Leah Williams, captain of the Euros-winning England team, was a product of Arsenal's, for example. However, the WSL Dual-Career Academy programme is for 16 to 21-year-olds and most women's academies don't enrol girls under the age of 16. It will be years before as much money, time and effort is spent identifying five-year-old girls as boys, so 'he' is just more accurate I'm afraid.

COME ALONG KIDDIEWINKS

I'm aware that I can sometimes make it sound as though the youth set-up in English football is like one giant version of the Child Catcher in *Chitty Chitty Bang Bang*. In reality that's clearly not the case, but there does seem to be a growing feeling in the game that the academy system is not only failing to produce enough quality players, it's also failing in a duty of care to those children who don't make it through.

Tony Pulis is a proper old-school manager – one who you would imagine has more sympathy with the character-building that came with cleaning boots and running up and down concrete steps than with the gentler methods of today – but in May 2022 he delivered a proposal to reform youth football to the Premier League and to the Professional Footballers' Association (PFA), based on a year researching the junior game. He starts with the shocking statistic we already know: at least 98% of boys in the academy system will not have a career in professional football. But he adds another that I didn't know: of those players who do turn professional at 18, 78% of them are no longer playing football three years later. Given that there are normally around 10,000 to 12,000 young people in the system at any one time that is a lot of disappointment.

And he claims those players are the fall-out of a deliberate policy of over-recruiting by academies: 'Young lads are used to service the system. Without the numbers, full on coaching sessions could not take place. Too many young men are being used as glorified cones with no chance of a professional career in the industry, in a games programme that incorporates 90% of all professional clubs, and [if that wasn't the case] the whole army of employed academy staff would be made redundant.' That's a pretty serious accusation. He's basically saying that academy coaches are willing to accept players they know won't make the grade in order to retain their jobs. And, of course, those players don't know they are not expected to make the grade right from the start, which makes it even worse, if, as Pulis claims, the boys given false hope are still not properly cared for when they are rejected and their hopes, along with their families' dreams, are shattered.

He argues that if football is going to demand the commitment of players and families, then football has to provide a safety net for those that fall – 'and the safety net is an education or a vocation.' Research suggests that academy players in the 9 to 11 age group are above the national average in terms of educational performance. By the time they reach 16 they are below the average. Pulis proposed to the Premier League and the PFA that the UK be divided into six regions, each with teams of mentors working with the youngsters. This should be part of a dual-scholarship programme with universities and colleges, because the current education programme for 16 to 19-year-olds is 'inadequate'. Pulis has a reputation for being hard-bitten and no-nonsense – as I say, old school – so if he thinks the academy system is failing our kids, then something is clearly wrong.

Right, we have a decision to make. Can we afford an academy and the staff it will need to give proper pastoral care? Will it be cost-effective or just be another potential source of players for the Premier League clubs up the road? The answer depends to a certain extent on geography. Part of the reason why Huddersfield Town decided to abandon their EPPP Category Two academy was that some claimed there were more Manchester City scouts in Huddersfield than their own. Apart from using a cattle prod to scare them away, little can be done to prevent the scouts from Category One clubs finding and recruiting the best players who are not already at their own clubs.

A little like the town of Springfield in *The Simpsons*, the exact location of West Park Rovers is not specified, but we do have a couple of Premier League clubs not too far away. It seems to us that if those clubs are hoovering up our local talent already, we may as well make it official, and if they want to poach kids from our academy rather than our local schools, then at least we may get some money out of it. Who knows, we may even progress a few into our first team, thus saving money on transfers. Yes, we're setting up a Category Three academy, because that's the only type we can afford for the moment.

It's exciting, though, isn't it? Our very own academy, although I still feel a little uneasy about ending this chapter by hoping we can make money out of children. So let's not end it that way. Because the good news is that if our academy doesn't produce good players fast, then we can just nip up to Scotland, the happyhunting ground, and nick some of their ready-grown and fully developed adult talent.

6

BUILDING BLOCKS

Vanarama ding-dong

To be fair to Kieran and Guy, I may be the forward-facing owner of West Park Rovers, but they are the forward-thinking ones. They have worked out (by skipping ahead a few chapters) that at our current rate of success we are going to be in the Premier League within five years and, let's face it, much as we love the old Kleanwell Stadium, at the moment it is most definitely not fit for purpose at the highest level.

So, we either start to look at local clubs whose ground we could ask to share or we plan ahead and build at least one new stand now, ready to welcome the fans of Liverpool and Manchester United and all those people who will suddenly claim they have been following West Park Rovers home and away forever and really need 10 tickets for the Chelsea game.

We also need a new manager: following our success in the National League South, Lars Cornelius has been offered a job by Fleetwood Town, so we have a vacancy on the bench. Despite his name, Lars was born and bred in Swindon and has been a great manager for us. He also likes a pint. I'll miss him. Still, we're in the Vanarama National League now, the fifth tier of the English pyramid. We are a club on the up and, even better, we are now a club with a broadcasting deal. I reckon we'll be a very attractive proposition for a manager looking for a new challenge. Anyone got a number for José Mourinho?

This will be our second season in a league sponsored by Vanarama, but I still have to remind myself who they actually are, which is a highly successful van leasing company. I didn't know that until last year, which must be slightly worrying for their marketing department considering they are the sponsors of what are essentially the fifth and sixth divisions in England's football pyramid.

Vanarama have been sponsoring the three National League divisions since 2014, because as their CEO Andy Alderton said when announcing the latest extension of the deal, 'These leagues are formed of real, honest clubs with real, honest fans and that resonates with us.' Turns out Vanarama pay an estimated £4 million for a three-year sponsorship deal with the National League. Apparently this works out at about £27,000 for a season for West Park Rovers. Thanks Kieran.

And with those decisions on a new stand and a new manager coming up, the good news is that we have a brand-new source of income to play with/invest wisely (depending on whether our fans are talking to me in the pub or reading our official website). BT Sport have been showing live football from the fifth tier since 2013 and will do so until at least the end of the 2023/24 season. At the moment it looks unlikely to extend beyond that as they have secured the rights to all European tournament games until 2027, but are looking to sell off their domestic rights and, while their Premier League package will attract the likes of Netflix and Amazon, those mega-corps don't seem desperate to broadcast the National League. In the meantime let's fill our boots, baby!

Sorry, that's pub talk. I meant let's discuss ways of maximising this temporary income stream. BT also show every goal from every game in a weekly highlights show, which they proudly boast is created with the help of students local to selected clubs, who receive on-the-job broadcast training. Which, of course, is all very laudable, but also makes me think that if they're using student staff then this broadcasting deal may not be as big as I was hoping. Let's ask Kieran: 'A National League North or South club only earns about £20,000 a year from the deal. Those in the National League itself earn double.' Only double?! A year? 40 measly grand a year? That's disappointing and also way less than I've been telling our fans. I may need to find a different pub.

This league is also quite good at taking money away from clubs. Nothing says you're climbing the pyramid more than the fines you now have to pay for doing something wrong. Gone are the days when you had to cough up a fiver because your corner flag was upside down. Misdemeanours at this level can do some serious damage to your bank account. This is just a selection:

Captain not wearing armband	£100	All leagues
Failure to wear official sleeve badge in a match	£500	Live TV match
	£200	National
	£100	North/South
Failure by home club to provide a full match video	£400	National
	£200	North/South
Failure of occupants of the technical area to wear corporate bench kit	£1000	Live TV match
	£400	National
	£200	North/South

Source: Kieran Maguire

Interestingly, those last two fines are doubled for each repeat offence, which suggests the National League take them very seriously. Interesting, too, that the corporate bench kit fine is so much higher for a live TV game, but that's because the manufacturer supplying all the kit worn by all the occupants of the coaching staff in the technical area will clearly take umbrage if any of them are not seen wearing it on TV. That's why we are quite often asked why a team is seen wearing a kit made by, for example, Puma when everyone else bar the players is in New Balance.

Still, it's going to be very exciting when we announce our first ever televised fixture. Let's hope it's against a team that's just been relegated from League Two, who also happen to bring 2000 lovely, if still angry, away fans with them, all eager to buy our beer and burgers in the hope of forgetting how badly things are going for them – because the National League, more so than any other I think, represents triumph or disaster in equal measure.

RELEGATIONS AND RE-ELECTIONS

Until the 1986/87 season it was almost impossible to be relegated out of the Football League. From 1921 to 1958, there was Division One,

Division Two and two Division Threes – north and south. The bottom two clubs in both Division Threes weren't relegated. Instead, they were invited to apply for re-election to the Football League. Almost every season, all four clubs were re-elected and those non-league clubs who had been asked to apply for election to the Football League were rejected. The people doing the actual electing were the other clubs in the bottom two divisions, but no one seems to know on what basis they cast their vote, although there were dark mutterings.

When the two regional divisions became the Third and Fourth Divisions in 1958, it was the bottom two in each division who applied for re-election and, again, almost every season all four were re-elected. Between 1924 and 1984 Hartlepools United* successfully applied for re-election 14 times. In fact, between 1958 and 1986 only four teams failed. Gateshead were replaced by Peterborough in 1960, Barrow by Hereford in 1972, Workington by Wimbledon in 1977 and Southport by Wigan in 1978. They were proper election campaigns as well, with hustings, presentations and meetings as the four clubs sought to persuade the other members of the Football League that they deserved to stay there. There was much cynicism about the process and the mysterious goings-on in cigar-fugged rooms – presumably the vote was one cough for yes and two for no. The Football League was pretty much a closed shop and no one was going to get in unless they could guarantee that they would bring more fans and more money to the party than the existing members (which Hereford and Wimbledon certainly could off the back of very high-profile, giant-killing FA Cup runs).

However it worked, it was almost inevitable that the outcome of a brief vote in those smoky committee rooms was the maintenance of the status quo. That changed in 1986 when it was decided that, subject to satisfactory financial and ground requirements, the champions of the Football Conference would be offered automatic promotion to Division Four and the bottom team in that league would be automatically relegated to take their place, with that being changed to two teams going down and up from 2002/03. The idea

---

*Not a spelling mistake. Hartlepools dropped the 's' in 1968.

was that in a decade of anti-trade union legislation it seemed unfair to have what was essentially a closed shop blocking the progress of those ambitious clubs at the top of non-league football. Although, as the estimable football fans' magazine *When Saturday Comes* said at the time, it was also a way of getting rid of some of the 'deadwood' in the fourth division.

Initially, though, it seemed like this relegation was going to be nothing but a temporary nuisance. Lincoln City, the first team to go, were back the following season, as were Darlington, with Colchester taking a season longer before they got back. Gradually, however, it became harder and harder to regain that precious place in the 92, which is why the Vanarama now is such a Jekyll and Hyde league.

For clubs like us, and Wealdstone, and FC Halifax, simply being in the National League is a major achievement. Now I know that some West Park Rovers fans reading this will say, 'Hang on, major achievement? You said this is only a stepping stone on the path to Premier League glory!' Of course, we did. There aren't many owners likely to say in public, 'We're done now, so say hello to 20 years in the same league and keep buying the merch, loyal fans.'

For clubs like Scunthorpe, however, out of the Football League for the first time ever, and Oldham, the first ex-Premier League side to be relegated to this level, simply being in the National League is an unmitigated disaster. They bring the number of ex-EFL teams in the Vanarama to 12 – that's 50% – and for Oldham and Scunthorpe it's a worrying reminder that this is now a bugger of a league to get out of, particularly with only one team going up automatically. Well, for the moment anyway. Talks are ongoing between the EFL and the National League about promotion between the two being three up and three down, with two automatic promotion places from the NL and one play-off. That does seem fairer if you are in the National League, but the response from League Two clubs is not likely to be enthusiastic, because no matter how much we talk about the Vanarama being the unofficial League Three, and no matter that most of the fans of those clubs will still go to games (and may even enjoy the novelty of visiting new grounds), it still represents a huge blow to the ego and the pocket.

And the honest truth is that the bigger the club relegated, the better the other clubs in this league like it. On a good day, by which I mean a Saturday afternoon, not a Tuesday night, we will take maybe 300 fans to Oldham or Scunthorpe. When they come to us they will bring around 1200 and, if it's late in the season with them challenging for promotion, it could be twice as many. That's more than a thousand extra people buying beer and pies in our ground. And who knows, we may even get to stock some of those half and half scarves we have optimistically been talking about for two seasons, although at £7 each with the minimum order a hundred, maybe not.

On the downside, we have trips to Gateshead and Torquay to pay for, but, in general, we are delighted to be here in a way that Oldham and Scunthorpe most certainly won't be. When clubs are relegated to the National League from League Two they get parachute payments for two seasons, 100% of the basic award (about £230,000) in the first season and half of that in the second. Clubs in League Two also benefit from solidarity payments from the Premier League, which are worth a further £450,000. Putting that all together, along with the EFL TV deal and more clubs with big followings, both home and away in League Two, it means that revenues in League Two are about double those of the National League clubs' average income of £2 million.

And there are no real savings on wages either, because the National League is now almost exclusively full-time in terms of player employment, although many National League clubs have contracts that expire on 30 April instead of 30 June to save clubs money once the season ends. Wages in the National League vary considerably, with some owners willing to subsidise their teams if it increases chances of promotion to the EFL. Some players are on as much as £5000 a week, although this is the exception rather than the norm.

While there is frequent talk about owners gambling with club futures in the EFL Championship, the same incentives to gamble exist in the National League, too. In 2018/19, the last season before Covid, only three National League clubs out of 24 made a profit and Salford City lost over £60,000 a week, although they were promoted via the play-offs.

STARSTRUCK

Actually, I can't wait for that away trip to Wrexham, but I must check what the boardroom etiquette is when it comes to the part-owner of one club asking the part-owner of another club to sign a pile of DVDs, for friends and family of course, definitely not for eBay.

Wrexham Association Football Club, or if you prefer, Clwb Pêl-droed Cymdeithas Wrecsam, is the oldest club in Wales and the third oldest professional team in the world.* They have won the Welsh Cup a record 23 times and for decades they competed with honour in European competitions, including a famous win over FC Porto in 1984. My guess, though, is that many of you will be more familiar with Wrexham's current owners than with their illustrious history.

In 2008 Wrexham's 87 years in the Football League ended with relegation into what was then known as the Football Conference. In 2011, after an extraordinary fund-raising campaign, the club was bought by the Supporters' Trust, beginning the long process of turning round years of financial mismanagement and getting back into the League. By 2020, both those ambitions were still a work in progress. Then something remarkable happened: Hollywood arrived in North Wales.

When British actor Humphrey Ker was filming a TV show called *Mythic Quest* out in Tinseltown, Rob McElhenney, star of the show, would occasionally join him to watch live Premier League football in his trailer. According to Ker, the star didn't really get the whole soccer thing, but was amazed by the passion he saw, both in the trailer and on the screen. And when Ker showed him the fly-on-the-wall documentary *Sunderland 'Til I Die*, McElhenney just had to have a team of his own and persuaded fellow Hollywood star Ryan Reynolds to join him in the quest to find a suitable candidate.

Ker was sent to the UK with a list of criteria that included facilities, fanbase, history, finance and, slightly more difficult to quantify, deservability. Wrexham scored the highest with 38 out of 50 and when Ker reported back that, 'Wrexham needs a break, the

---

*Depending on whether or not you believe Crystal Palace's claim that they were actually formed in 1861 and not 1905. I do, obviously.

fans need a break and the same goes for the town,' McElhenney and Reynolds had found the most unlikely of targets.

But would the Supporters' Trust want to sell? As they say in Hollywood, 'Hell, yes.' Of the 2000 members, 98.6% backed the deal and in February 2021 one of the oddest changes of ownership in English football was complete, made even odder because the club isn't even English. There were some dissenting voices. One local journalist asked, 'Are they buying a football club or making a documentary?'* but, in general, the new owners are very popular, although Humphrey Ker did give them a word of warning: 'I told them that at some point, you'll be at an airport or train station, and someone will call you a cunt.' Welcome to my world, boys.

You may wonder why I tell you this. It's partly because that's the sort of financial competition we are up against now in the Vanarama National League, but, more importantly, it's an indication that no matter how much proof there is that buying a football club is rarely a sensible idea, English (and Welsh) football is a hugely attractive global brand. Every club in the country is in the shop window and each successive promotion moves West Park Rovers closer and closer to the front of the window, and despite Kieran and Guy's misgivings, I am quite willing to jump up and down in the window waving my pants in the air if it helps to attract some of that lovely global money to our small corner of the world.

FROM THE FANDOM

It's also a quite stark illustration of the fact that even fans who own a club are aware that fan-owned clubs will eventually need outside help if they are to do anything but chug along quite nicely in the lower leagues. And, no, I'm not implying that there is more to life than chugging along quite nicely. Well, I am a bit, but let me state for the record that Kieran and Guy are not.

Those of you who have ever listened to the pod will probably assume that the fan-ownership model is the one we like the most. Well, yes and no. Of course, we are highly passionate about fan engagement.

*Both as it happens – *Welcome to Wrexham* aired on Disney Plus in autumn 2022.

Ultimately, a football club, as a concept, belongs to the fans – not to the owner, not to the players, not to the staff – the fans. The owner, the players, the staff may be brilliant, committed, and loyal, but they are ultimately transient, whereas fans are in for the long haul.

We believe fans should be consulted and offered a say in club decisions, especially where those decisions include a change in kit, badge or nickname. And that consultation should go way beyond the minimal involvement which comes with the purchase of a few NFTs. But, and it pains me to say this, until there is a fundamental root and branch change in the economics and governance of English football (i.e. the day after hell freezes over) then actual fan-ownership will only ever take a club so far.

Although, joy of joys, the government White Paper introduced in February 2023 following the fan-led review conducted by Tracey Crouch CBE MP does include plans to make consultation with fans on some off-field decisions compulsory. And as the White Paper will also be introducing an independent regulator for football you will definitely be hearing more about it in this book – if you can hear anything over the howls of indignation from some of the more reactionary club owners.

As of August 2022 there were 48 fan-owned clubs in the English football pyramid. Of those, only two, AFC Wimbledon (League Two) and Exeter City (League One) are currently in the EFL itself. Both clubs are well-run and passionate about their ownership model. Nick Hawker of the Exeter City Supporters' Trust told the BBC, 'We don't own Exeter City, it's in our safe-keeping. That's what some Premier League owners have to understand.' My guess is that Exeter City, fan-owned or not, will never be in a position to say that to Premier League owners in person. Does that matter? Well, you'll need to ask their fans I suppose.

As it happened, there were no Exeter fans on hand so I asked a celebrity Torquay United fan instead. Charlie Baker is a very fine musician and comedian and also a star presenter on talkSPORT. Torquay are now in the National League South so I asked Charlie if they had reached a level where he fancied buying the club: 'If I had enough money to be able to lose two million quid a year without it touching the sides, I would absolutely buy Torquay United. Then I'd give it to the fans to run'. Very laudable Charlie but would that model take Torquay to the Premier League? He didn't even have to think about the answer. 'I hope not. The Premier League is like the kids who went to private school and, yes, they have posh cars and holidays and 20 full-size pitches and fancy kit but would anyone really love them if Daddy went bankrupt and that all disappeared?'

As it happens, many teams in Germany's Bundesliga are sort of fan-owned, with the 50 plus 1 rule that so many English fans seem to admire so much, and it certainly hasn't limited their ambition. Introduced in 1999, partly to prevent the situation that seemed to be unrolling here with more and more clubs being acquired as business investments, the rule simply states that in theory no single investor can own more than 49% of the shares of a club. The other 51% are owned by fans, giving them majority voting rights on the board of directors.

What many English fans don't realise is that there are exceptions. Clubs who have been privately owned for more than 20 years are exempt: for example, Bayer Leverkusen, owned since 1904 by pharmaceutical company Bayer Ag; Wolfsburg, owned by Volkswagen since 1945; and Hoffenheim, where their majority owner, the software engineer Dietmar Hopp, has been an investor since 1990. Personally I'd have changed the club name to Hoppenheim, but Dietmar is clearly more mature than me.

Oh, there is one other exception, and it's arguably now the most hated club in Germany, which probably comes as a relief to Bayern Munich, whose trophy cabinet would be even more impressive if there was a cup awarded for unpopularity. In 2009, Red Bull, manufacturers of an energy drink for those who like their work meetings edgy, bought SSV Markranstadt, a tiny club in the fifth division of German football. First thing they did was change the name of the club to Rasenballsport Leipzig, shortened to RB Leipzig.

Honestly, it was just a coincidence that they were the same initials as Red Bull. A very handy coincidence, mind you, because clubs in Germany are not allowed to be directly named after their sponsor. Red Bull then changed the kit and the badge, pretty much erasing any memory of SSV Markranstadt, and very effective it was too, because, be honest, you'd never heard of them either, had you?

Fourteen years and hundreds of millions of euros later RB are one of the country's top clubs and have reached the semi-finals of Europe's two major competitions. It doesn't help that Red Bull are an Austrian company, but they are hated because they seem to openly flout every rule in German football without punishment. Worse, they seem to flout the very spirit of German football. Doesn't seem to bother Red Bull. They now own four football clubs around the world, as well as a hugely successful Formula One racing team, and have just received some very nice free publicity in this book.

Again, contradicting my own argument, Barcelona are fan-owned as well (again, sort of) and they are one of the most successful clubs ever. Closer to home, there are eight clubs in Scotland that are majority fan-owned, three of them in the Premiership, and when Hearts were taken over in 2021 they became the biggest fan-owned club in the UK. So why, then, is it so unlikely that we'll see a fan-owned club competing at that sort of level in England?

Anyone who has ever run any form of member-owned club, especially a sports one, will know there is a common management cycle. Initially everyone wants to be involved, but that enthusiasm quickly evaporates as people realise that committee meetings are 1% excitement and 99% tedium, and that their brilliant idea of partnering with the local micro-brewery does not have universal approval from fellow committee members.

The advantage of a fan-owned club is that fans do have an emotional connection and therefore want the club to be sustainable in the long term, if only because they like the thought of boring their grandchildren in years to come with tales of how they were involved in setting it up. There are, however, some downsides, too. Those involved in the running of the club may have enthusiasm and love, but don't have the expertise in HR, law, marketing and so on that is required to maximise revenues and control costs.

If the club is losing money, then someone has to fund those losses. If the club has a rich owner then they are in a position to transfer the money to cover those losses. In the case of a member-owned club, then things become more difficult as individual members are unlikely to have enough money to give to a club or, if they do, they might resent other members who refuse to pay in similar amounts.

This means, as far as English football is concerned, there is probably a natural ceiling to what can be achieved at a fan-owned club. In 2021/22 clubs in the Championship had operating losses averaging £476,000 a week – yes, a week. For established clubs with large fanbases that's a lot of money to find, especially in the current economic climate. For West Park Rovers, even if it grows to a core

UNFIT AND IMPROPER PERSONS

fanbase of 20,000, that means every single one of them has to find £24 a week for the club, which is a lot of money, especially if their fuel bill is due. And, given that some of those fans are children and pensioners with limited income, this is clearly unrealistic. Factor in those who simply think that the current centre forward is not worth the wages he is earning and they are paying, and it becomes almost impossible for such a club to survive financially.

In the case of technically fan-owned clubs such as Barcelona, their huge membership votes for a president every six years. In order to be successfully elected, telling people what they want to hear rather than talking about issues such as sustainability, governance and strategy, tends to be more successful. This probably explains why there have been so few accountants who have become prime ministers or presidents, as a three-word slogan from Kieran – something like 'Amortisation, amortisation, amortisation' – is unlikely to be as successful as, say, 'Take back control.' The price paid at Barcelona is that recent presidents have been elected on a platform of spending money on players, regardless of whether the club has the money to spend. This resulted in the club running up debts of over £1 billion.

When Joan LaPorta was elected Barcelona president in 2021, this was partially on a campaign to keep Lionel Messi, which would have been costly. In 2022 Barcelona was given a very restricted budget under La Liga's cost-control measures. LaPorta could have complied with this by cutting spending, but instead he kept to his populist message and pulled a series of what he called 'economic levers'. Even Kieran had to check what he meant by that and he's been an accountant since forever.* What he meant by that, though, was selling Barcelona's future income streams for up to 25 years in order to get cash now and sign players such as Raphinha and Lewandowski.

So he sold 49.9% of Barca licensing and merchandising for around €300 million to one investment group and 15% of their TV rights for €207 million to another. That's fine – unless you're the poor sod who's trying to balance the Barcelona books 10 years down the line and there is nothing left to sell. Especially as in the

---

*About the same time as he's been obsessed with Marmite and Abba.

118

2022/23 season Barca failed to even qualify for the last 16 of the Europa League.

Back to West Park Rovers, who are also technically a fan-owned club if you include owners who are fans of other clubs. If we were making a Wrexham-style documentary about our club, we'd have just reached one of those points of artificial tension that film-makers are so keen on. You know, the sort where a camera pans from tense face to tense face in the boardroom as an impassioned discussion goes on about what happens next, even though you know that in reality, whatever the decision is, it was made yesterday when the cameras weren't in the way.

Which is how we concluded that before kicking off in the Vanarama, we probably need to prioritise a new manager over a new stand. And as ever, when I say we, I mean I was outvoted. Of course we do need a new manager, but I was really looking forward to planning all those new executive boxes and the extended private bar next in the directors' lounge. Plus, of course, an improved matchday experience for our loyal fans, a brand-new family enclosure, more parking space, yadda-yadda.

That's the sort of stuff every club bungs on their website in the hope that fans will genuinely think building a new stand is not just an excuse to extend their appeal to the corporate market; those people that Roy Keane contemptuously dismissed as the 'prawn sandwich brigade'. We've all watched games on TV (and it's especially noticeable at Wembley and at Arsenal) where it's clear that in certain sections of the ground finishing the free nibbles and vino is more important than watching the start of the second half, like a proper supporter. The trouble is that those proper supporters are brilliant and they get through a fair few pints and pies at half-time, but pre-match they're lining the pockets of local pubs and cafés, so why shouldn't we try to make serious money out of slathering some prawns and mayonnaise between a couple of triangles of brown bread in an executive box full of people who don't know one end of a ball from another.

EXECUTIVE SEARCH

In the meantime, though, I have stopped doodling designs for the new stand on the back of old team sheets and am fully focussed on the hunt for a new manager. To be fair to Fleetwood they were absolutely above board in their approach for the old one. They contacted us for permission to speak to Lars, which we could hardly refuse when they told us how much they were willing to pay him and, more importantly, how much they were willing to pay us in compensation. That's not always the case:

While officially the football authorities thoroughly disapprove of any form of tapping-up of managers and players, in reality it is very common. In most other industries such behaviour would be called 'headhunting' and people would get paid for doing it, or it would be called 'executive recruitment' and people would be paid even more for doing it. In football, people still get paid for doing it, but via the modern-day equivalent of bunging someone a bag full of cash in the car park of a motorway service station. There is still an element of sleaze about modern football; only the methods of payment have changed.

One manager we spoke to advised us he knew a fellow manager was going to be sacked a fortnight into the season at an EFL club. The reason he knew this is that he had already been offered the job as a replacement. If a manager has signed a long-term contract, then anyone wishing to recruit him will have to come to a compensation agreement with his present employer. André Villas-Boas was appointed Porto manager on 2 June 2010. He won two domestic competitions and the Europa Cup in his first season, but mysteriously tendered his resignation on 21 June 2011. There's always a case for leaving when you're at the top of your game, as it were, but then a full 24 hours later he was confirmed as the manager of Chelsea.

Kieran never needs an excuse to ferret about in other people's numbers and he tells me that in Chelsea's accounts that year there is a line revealing 'compensation in relation to changes in the first team management' of £28 million. This was a combination of a £15 million pay-out to Carlo Ancelotti, who had been sacked an hour after the end of 2010/11 season for the heinous crime of finishing second in the Premier League, and £13 million to Porto for not kicking up a fuss in relation to the two remaining years of André's contract at the club.

In respect of our manager, while he doesn't have a specific compensation clause in his contract, Lars Cornelius also only had four months remaining on it when Fleetwood made their enquiry about recruiting him. We could have been awkward and made him sit out his notice period, but as he has some photos of the Christmas party that we would rather not be released into the public domain, we decided to accept Fleetwood's offer of £5000. As this sum is once again far less than I had envisaged, I have hastily deleted the social media posts claiming that Jack Grealish was seen looking intently at a window of a local estate agent last weekend.

The problem is that having publicly praised Fleetwood Town for the honesty of their approach to us, we can hardly sneak in and nick someone else's manager. That's good for our image and our karma, but it does limit our options somewhat. There are many candidates available out there and some of them are well-known names with a consistent record of success, but as fans of every club ever will say, they are available for a reason. In other words, they've just been sacked by another club so why are we even considering them? Similarly, our fans won't be impressed if we appoint a grizzled old pro who has just been 'released' by Blyth Spartans and nor will they want us to experiment by giving a young coach his first job.

Seriously, I'm beginning to regret some of the things I've said about the people who have owned Crystal Palace in the past. Running a football club would be much easier if there were no fans to please. Or Twitter. Luckily, the solution is right under our noses. Which makes a pleasant change from right up our nose, where he's been for the past couple of years. First-team captain Malky Porter has been with us from the start and from the start he has been telling everyone that he could make a better job of everything than we do. Despite being born and bred in Northampton, he is the most Scottish man I have ever known and approaches every conversation with us like a Highlander approaching a Redcoat at Culloden. He's 34 now and still a huge presence on the pitch, but his legs are going even if his mouth isn't.

He's been doing his coaching badges for a while and he's always telling us that he would make a better manager than anyone we've ever had, so maybe it's time to call his bluff? Or, as we will say when we put the idea to him, maybe it's time to utilise his extraordinary motivational skills to build a squad capable of taking us into an exciting future. Or, at least 'motivate' the players we already have to be better and save us spending money on new ones. The fans absolutely adore him, so they will completely forget he has absolutely no managerial experience and, hopefully, it will also save us a fortune in disciplinary fines every season.

The advantage of promoting someone from within the club to be manager is that he already knows the culture of the club and, from the point of view of Kieran and Guy, is cheaper than buying in. The downside of promoting someone from within the club to be manager is that he may know the culture of the club, but the fans will assume that his cheapness is the main reason we've hired him.

We can always tell them that taking such an approach allows us to increase the transfer budget. In the National League, 18 out of 24 clubs didn't spend anything when signing players in the most recent financial year. Therefore, we could spend £1000 on a player and tell fans that our budget is bigger than three-quarters of the league. It would be true, but I suspect that Guy would give me his trademark patient doleful look that means that telling the truth is not the same as telling the whole truth.

Right, that's settled. The new manager of West Park Rovers is Malky Porter and it's a measure of how grown-up we are now that it even merited an announcement on Sky Sports News, although I thought it was a bit cheeky when they said that if he can get as many points as he got red cards we should stay up comfortably. We've given him a bit of money to spend as well, and his first task is to replace himself, so I reckon a trip to Scotland may be in the offing.

ACTING UP

Now can we talk about the new stand? We can, but, hang on a second, I need to introduce you to another new addition to the West Park Rovers family. BT Sport present their matchday coverage from pitch-side, so it was imperative that we appoint a grown man to crowbar into a giant animal costume to cavort around them and make supporters laugh, although in my view anyone over the age of three who laughs at a football mascot needs help.

We could have gone for a cowboy, you know, as in 'Wild West' Park Rovers. We could have gone for a park-keeper, but they don't scream 'cuddly' as a rule. Instead we went for the obvious, so say hello to Rover the Dog. I presume he's a dog. It's not the most realistic costume and if it is a dog I reckon even a vet would struggle to say what breed it's meant to be, but to be honest the dog was also one of the cheaper options. A quick browse of the websites of the surprisingly numerous companies who make these costumes shows that even the most basic one starts at around £1600.

Nevertheless, the out-of-work actor inside him is taking the role very seriously, although he is still sulking a bit because Guy wouldn't pay his expenses for that research trip he made to Crufts. He's going to be even more cross when I tell him he's not allowed on the sofa, but the fans love him already and we can finally start charging grown-ups for the privilege of allowing their kiddiewinks to walk on the pitch holding the paw of a giant dog.

It's actually not a bad little earner that. Scunthorpe United charge £150 a kid and even though the package includes a kit and a ball I reckon if we charged the same we could turn a profit of a hundred quid a game, which is a decent bonus for giving a child the happiest day of their life. Four children if we're lucky. In the Premier League you're talking serious money. Liverpool, Arsenal, Chelsea and the two Manchester clubs don't charge for the privilege of being a mascot, which is great, but the downside is the waiting lists are so long your kid could be married by the time it's their go.

Other clubs, however, charge a lot. Everton are top of the list at a whopping £718, although it does include 'free' kit and two 'free' match tickets for your family. At West Ham United it's £700, but no kit. Leicester City charge £600, but you get a kit, four tickets and a hot meal. Honours are more or less even for Kieran and I. The top Palace package goes for £375, including three tickets and kit. At Brighton it's £350, including two tickets, a kit and all the quinoa you can eat.

STAND AND DELIVER

Finally, on to that bloody stand. The EFL's ground criteria states that by 1 May in its third season as a member, the club is required to have a minimum capacity of 5000, of which at least 2000 should be seats. So, if we are promoted from the Vanarama (spoiler alert, we will be), our ground is already fit for purpose. But we're thinking long term here, so what do we actually need to build and how much will it cost us?

Beyond that 5000/2000 figure, the EFL are surprisingly vague about stadium requirements. They stipulate how big the pitch should be and that the ground should be covered on four sides,* but beyond that, not much, although if you're looking for advice on what your club's insurance policy should cover then you're laughing. It starts with the usual: 'fire, lightning, explosion, earthquake' then throws in a few curve balls like 'strikes or political disturbances' and 'aircraft, articles dropped accidentally from.' That one's handy to know being underneath the flightpath of a major airport. And I wonder if you can be insured against being hit by a curve ball?

If the EFL can't help, let's check the trusty FA guidelines. They will surely stipulate all the unnecessary and expensive improvements we will need to make. Nope. Nothing. Turns out the FA Ground Grading Document stops at the Vanarama and merely says we must have the potential to upgrade the Kleanwell as required.

We know that the Premier League will require a lot of improvements when we get there, but in the meantime, even without clear EFL guidelines it makes sense for us to upgrade anyway, even if it's only to a capacity of around 12,000-plus, just to accommodate new fans and make lots of lovely new money. Trouble is, of course, it will cost lots of lovely old money and potentially lower our matchday income while the building work is going on. So is this the right time to do it, especially as labour and material costs have been going through the roof lately? Pun intended.

We have had a few construction companies around to give quotes. One was linked to Kieran's family, so was naturally keen on having cash payments instead of bank transfers. They also said that they were willing to work during the night on the project, which would be brilliant time-wise, but I suspect it's more to do with the fact it's easier to dispose of a body in the foundations during the hours of darkness.

When Accrington Stanley opened a new stand and hospitality venue in 2022, it cost £2.5 million. On the plus side, it did allow

---

*How many more times? There are two sides and two ends!

the club to generate additional revenue from the sale of wines, beers and 'traditional pies, peas and gravy', although I guess Kieran will insist that our peas are organic. If we're going to have to find the money for a new stand, it does need to generate money on more than the 25 or so home fixtures a season, so a hospitality and conferencing area is essential. Apparently, this will allow us to sweat the assets, something that also happens when Kieran's Uncle Terry appears in his weekly identity parade at the local police station.

The good news is that even if we do somehow manage to find the money for the stand, there should be help available. The Football Foundation offers grants to reduce the burden and if we install a 3G pitch then another contribution could come from the Football Stadia Improvement Fund. If we're building a new stand, it has to be future-proof and environmentally friendly, so we will initially commit to installing two EV charging points, but there will be ducting in place for up to 30 in the admittedly unlikely event that Elon Musk decides to take over the club and give all the staff Teslas.

There will be solar panels, air-sourced heat pumps and rainwater will be harvested to help with pitch irrigation. Whether these green credentials will impress those fans who are tucking into traditional pies, peas and gravy is open to question. There's no time like the present, though, so the decision is made. We are building the new stand. And, yes, I do realise that in this book time is a very fluid concept. I may have been watching too much *Doctor Who*.

Now all we have to do is raise the money. Here we have several options. We could sell the club to someone who can afford the necessary ground improvements, but that would slightly defeat the object, especially if we accidentally sold the club to someone who then sold the ground to a property developer and moved the club to a new site out of town. It would also mean this would be the last chapter of the book and I've already spent the advance, so that can't happen.

We could find a friendly benefactor who is prepared to fund or part-fund the project in return for the new stand's naming rights, although they would have to be a very friendly benefactor to spend that much money on a glorified vanity project. Although this is potentially the best option, because if we can bring on board someone who shares our values and buys into the long-term benefits then everyone wins.

We could issue shares. Some clubs, like Lincoln City, do that all the time and Kieran seems to approve. The only problem is that Lincoln usually issue shares to their very honourable and wealthy benefactor Clive Nates, and we tick neither the honourable nor wealthy boxes.

We could borrow the money from a bank. Strangely, this is probably the least likely option. The interest would be very high and banks are reluctant to lend to football teams in case they end up having to foreclose, a move not likely to be popular with local customers. Naturally, though, if you're a team the size of Spurs, banks will keep throwing you billions in loans, because they're happy to sit back and live on the interest for the next century or two. Realistically, this is not going to happen. The local manager has indicated that he doesn't fancy the West Park Rovers Ultras daubing his branch with 'Club killer' graffiti should we struggle to make the repayments and he does have to foreclose on the loan.

We could issue bonds. Basically that involves us becoming the Bank of West Park Rovers and asking fans to invest money on which we will pay very generous rates of interest. Clubs such as Norwich, QPR, Rangers and Peterborough have done this in the past, with a fair amount of success. I am not sure that West Park Rovers are big enough to make this work, though, unless we offer high rates of interest or a big bonus if we are promoted to League Two of the EFL. Then again, we could have a thousand pub quizzes, although there are a limited number of times we can ask the audience about which celebrities have dropped the 'C' bomb at me.

OK, we've sourced the money (don't worry how – Kieran had a word with someone), so these are exciting times for West Park Rovers. We're announcing a new manager and a new stand all in the same week, and the National League fixture list is out.

Until now we've been competing in regional leagues, which naturally keeps travelling costs down a bit, although there are some anomalies. Hereford v Gloucester City in the National League North is a tasty little trip for Boxing Day, Hereford v Darlington less so. And Chelmsford's trip to Taunton in National League South is hardly a cheap-day return, although, of course, the other side of that argument is that any away game for Taunton is going to be expensive in that league.

However, for the most part, away travel in a regional league is naturally going to be less expensive than a national one. In fact, there are some who argue that a return to regional leagues outside the Championship is a logical financial step for clubs like Carlisle and Plymouth Argyle, although ironically, Carlisle and Plymouth Argyle disagree. While travel and accommodation costs are certainly an argument for a return to regional divisions in the EFL, Plymouth are still a long way from Cambridge, Colchester and Walsall, although it's academic at the moment because Plymouth have just been promoted to the Championship. Regionalisation could also mean that some clubs who are close to each other geographically do not play each other, because they are on opposite sides of the North/South boundary. And as we shall see when Malky Porter drags us on our inevitable scouting trip to Scotland, travel is a very expensive proposition for many clubs in that beautiful but surprisingly big country.

Kieran has been crunching a few numbers on the costs and benefits of being in the National League. There is greater income from matchday sales, as the likes of Oldham, Chesterfield, Southend and so on do have a sizeable away following. The BT Sport deal is not huge at £20,000 to £40,000, but it assists a club in selling commercial packages as TV viewers are additional eyeballs. Revenues in the National League range from £1 million to £4 million. The downside is the costs of running a club with full-time player wages means that most clubs are losing money and those that break even are often grateful for some generous sponsor deals from owners.

So, while the Vanarama seems to represent a disaster for clubs like Oldham and Scunthorpe, whose only aim is to get out of it again as quickly as possible, for clubs like us it represents a bit of a dilemma. As I said, these are heady heights for clubs like West Park Rovers and Maidenhead, but what do we do now? Obviously, in terms of sheer glory, we want to keep going, but financially is it worthwhile? Will life in Leagues One and Two be so much more golden that we should throw the dice and go again with the risk of financial disaster? Or do we simply try to consolidate and get our fans used to mid-table finishes for a while as we find a way to properly finance the next leg of our journey? Median* annual income, wages and losses show the following:

	League One £ 000	League Two £ 000	National League £ 000
Income	6362	4166	2466
Wages	5702	3513	2083
Loss	(1626)	(667)	(360)

Source: Kieran Maguire

The clown car that is football finance in this country therefore shows, even in the lower divisions, that you get more money from being promoted, but your costs rise faster and so do your losses. In Kieran's admirable book, *The Price of Football* (which I cannot recommend here as it is not published by Bloomsbury), he says that there are four reasons for owning a football club: love, profit, vanity and insanity. From what I can make out, profit should probably be struck off that list.

*GCSE maths has finally been of some benefit.

7

FURTHER AFIELD

There's more to life than England

Sometimes things on the pitch are just beyond your control, which is an odd thing to admit about a fictional football team. As it happened, West Park Rovers didn't breeze through the Vanarama National League first time as you may have expected. We had a decent season, the home form was good, but we had to settle for eighth place in the end, just outside the play-offs.

By the way, though, our amazing rise so far is not entirely unprecedented. Wimbledon went from the Southern League to the old First Division in 10 seasons, and AFC Wimbledon had five promotions in nine years to go from the Combined Counties League to League Two, at one stage going unbeaten for 78 games in the process.* Dorking Wanderers managed to go from the Crawley and District League in 1999 to the National League in 2022, which is almost as quick as West Park Rovers, and even more difficult considering theirs were real rather than fictional promotions.

Anyway, Manager Malky Porter, as ever, remains bullish, 100% certain we will be promoted this year and suggests we gentle English folk stop worrying and leave everything to him. That's not exactly how he puts it, but you get the gist. Of course, Malky has decided that Scotland is a fertile recruitment ground for the 'two or three wee players' he needs to get the job done (Kieran and Guy are willing to

---

*Fun fact. AFC Wimbledon are the only team in the EFL formed in the 21st century.

bet that wee players still cost as much as tall ones). We've booked a little scouting trip, but because we're scared of him, none of us dare point out that all the players we're looking at seem to be at clubs within easy reach of his hometown. Apparently the fact that we're also going up there on the weekend of his mum's 70th birthday and they are having a barbecue is just an enormous coincidence, but we're welcome to come along for a dram or two if we think we can handle proper whisky. Challenge accepted.

West Park Rovers are part of the pyramid of English football, but while comparisons of wealth within that pyramid are useful it's also necessary to put that wealth into the context of football in the rest of the UK. The rest of the UK has had an enormous influence on the history and development of football across the world, but has recently become a victim of the enormous financial and gravitational pull of the Premier League, just as much as many clubs in England.

SCOTS WHA HAE

When Kieran and I were youngsters we knew nearly as much about Scottish football as we did English. Obviously, we very rarely saw highlights of their games on TV, but we knew all the teams and knew there was a fair chance some of their players would join the huge number of Scottish players at English clubs. Since then, I seem to have taken my eye off the Scottish ball: Cove Rangers, Kelty Hearts, Annan and Bonnyrigg Rose Athletic are nowhere near as familiar to me as names like Hamilton Academical and Queen of the South were growing up. As a football loving child I spent many hours crossing my fingers hoping that at around 4.50pm I would hear the magical score 'East Fife four, Forfar five' and I'm always glad to be in Scotland. However, I have heeded Malky's warning on the train that none of us should mention the World Cup, because apparently we are 'always bloody banging on about 1966.' That's a bit unfair considering *his* national anthem is about a battle that took place in 1314, but as we're approaching the border I have decided to let it go. I think he's still angry that our press officer made him tweet his congratulations when England Women won the Euros.

According to Sports Heritage Scotland, Stirling Castle is home to the oldest football in the world, dating from around 1540, and the

Argyll and Sutherland Highlanders Regimental Museum is home to the oldest football trophy in the world, a medal won way back in 1851. Scotland is certainly responsible for the first international football match. In 1872 the Queen's Park Football Club arranged a fixture between Scotland and England, and the fact that every single one of the Scottish team played for the Queen's Park Football Club is neither here nor there.* It ended 0–0, a result the Scottish press, naturally, hailed as 'a moral victory' against their bigger and stronger opponents. In 1873 the Scottish FA was formed, the Scottish League followed in 1890 and the game in Scotland was professional by 1893.

Scottish football was a major influence on the game in England with many clubs flourishing under the leadership of Scotsmen like Aston Villa's William McGregor, who turned his team into the country's first football superpower and, of course, founded the English Football League. Once the game in England turned professional in 1888, many Scottish players, as yet unable to play for pay at home, moved south and changed the whole nature of the English game for the better.

In the early days of the English Football League, teams played a glorified version of the kick-and-rush game so favoured by the public schools, where the man who had the ball simply propelled it goalward protected, rugby-style, by the other players. Scottish players, however, had developed a much more sophisticated game based on actually passing the ball to each other, using every part of the pitch to move the ball forward and developing skills as well as muscle. Those so-called 'Scotch professors' who signed for English clubs changed the way football was played for ever, and Scottish immigrants also did much to establish the game in northern Europe and South America.

As in England, the early game in Scotland was dominated by public schools and enthusiastic amateurs like those who ran Queen's Park, but gradually the game took hold among the urban working classes. Rangers first appeared in Glasgow in 1872, with Hearts starting in Edinburgh two years later. In 1875, Hibernian had their

---

*There had been a series of games in London in 1870/71 between English players and Scottish players based down south, but they don't count.

application to join the Scottish FA rejected on the grounds that the association was for 'Scotchmen, not Irishmen', but the SFA relented and when Hibs won the 1887 Scottish Cup Final in Glasgow, the Irish population of the city were so overjoyed they started a team of their own, called, of course, Celtic. Thus was born one of the biggest rivalries in world football, one that has utterly dominated Scottish football ever since and one that is based on politics and national identity as much as football.

Legendary Scottish comedian Fred MacAulay is a St Johnstone FC fan and was only too happy to discuss the dominance of the Old Firm. Actually, he was quite reluctant to talk about it, because fans of both clubs can be quick to take umbrage, especially if they sense anyone is leaning towards the other team, but bless him, after a couple of pints he opened up about the realities of the Scottish game: 'Basically, for teams like St Johnstone, anything is possible – but not while the big two exist. We've finished third in the table and did the Cup double a couple of seasons ago. In the circumstances they are remarkable achievements.'

I asked Fred whether, as some have suggested, the Scottish game may actually be better off if Rangers and Celtic were to play elsewhere, but he told me, 'It's about as likely as the European Super League happening and it could be politically difficult as well as commercially. If Scotland became independent can you imagine the passport queues for Old Firm fans at the border?!'

Fred used to be an accountant (imagine that, a funny accountant), so I wanted to ask him whether he would like to put a figure on that likelihood of a European Super League happening, but by that time he was telling me about an incident in a Copenhagen night club in 1975 that led to lifetime bans for five Scotland players and that was much more entertaining than the statistical chances of a breakaway league. In fact, Fred is quite philosophical about life as a St Johnstone fan: 'Let's be honest, Kev, your team will never win the league either, will they?'

The UK's other funny accountant, Kieran Maguire, was only too happy to provide some actual figures about the comparative finances of the big two and the rest of Scotland, his natural joy at being knee-deep in a spreadsheet outweighing any worries about subsequent angry tweets from Glasgow and beyond. In 2018/19, the last pre-Covid season, Rangers and Celtic generated two-thirds of the total revenue of the SPFL, and had the same proportion of the wage bill. When it comes to buying players, the gap is even more pronounced. Clubs such as Ross County, Kilmarnock, Partick Thistle and Hamilton Academical had squads that cost precisely nothing, whereas Rangers' and Celtic's squads together cost £65 million, and this was before Steven Gerrard's regime significantly kicked in and spending increased at Ibrox, culminating in the club winning the Scottish Premiership in 2020/21.

Scottish fans will point out that the game in England is also currently dominated by a small group of elite teams, but, unlike in Scotland, that is a fairly recent development. Although, of course, the Old Firm's domination has not always been total, and Hearts, Hibs, Aberdeen and the two Dundee clubs have all taken turns to challenge both at home and in Europe. Scottish fans are also right to point out that for the first hundred years of the game, Scottish and English football was closely matched, both in their leagues and at national level.

The year 1966 may not have been a great one for Scottish football fans, but 1967 brought compensation. Not only did those young and very local Lisbon Lions become the first British team to win the European Cup, but the national team beat the 'Auld Enemy' 3–2 at Wembley, crowning themselves 'unofficial World Champions' by doing so. It was the match in which midfield maestro Jim Baxter made himself a hero in the mould of Robert the Bruce and William Wallace when he taunted floundering England players by sitting on the ball.[*] Afterwards, Bobby Charlton said he knew Scotland were taking it seriously, because Denis Law had worn shin pads for the first time.

Denis Law was just one of many Scottish players who lit up the game down south. The likes of Dave Mackay, Billy Bremner, Kenny Dalglish, Gary McAllister and Andrew Robertson are just a few names of many. However, it is not only the players who have improved the English game. Some of the best managers in the English game have been Scottish, especially Matt Busby, Bill Shankly and Alex Ferguson, all from similarly tough working-class backgrounds.

[*]There seems to be no actual pictorial evidence, but try telling Malky Porter that.

It may seem strange to younger English fans, but not that long ago the Scottish Lion was the big beast in British football. In the early 1990s, the top clubs in Scotland were positively rolling in money and talent compared to their counterparts south of the border. The benefits of the English Premier League broadcasting deal were yet to kick in and matchday income in Scotland was such that they could compete with nearly any club on the continent for player wages. This meant English legends like Paul Gascoigne and Terry Butcher joined continental stars like Brian Laudrup and Henrik Larsson to ply their trade in a flourishing Scottish league.

MIND THE GAP

Those days are long gone, with Scottish football, arguably just as much as half of English football, falling victim to the huge amounts of money pumped into the Premier League from broadcasting deals and massive overseas investments. In fact, looking at the finances of Scottish football now, I wonder whether West Park Rovers may not have been better off starting a team there, rather than here. I mean, the rewards are probably smaller, but the risks are definitely fewer, especially at the highest level. Relegation from the Scottish Premier League is nowhere near the disaster that falling from the English version is. As Kieran says, the gap between the top leagues in Scotland is a gentle slope; in England it's a precipice.

In 2020/21 Sheffield United earned £97.6 million from Premier League central payments, which is the broadcasting and central sponsor monies generated by the organisation. They also finished bottom of the Premier League with just 23 points. One of the clubs that subsequently replaced Sheffield United was Brentford, who earned £8.4 million in broadcast income in 2020/21. The gap encourages Championship clubs to spend large sums to try to get promoted. Overall in 2020/21, which was admittedly impacted by Covid, wages in England were £120 for every £100 of income. In the previous decade wages exceeded income nine times. Rangers won the Scottish Premiership that season, earning about £3.3 million, and Hamilton Academical finished bottom, with £1.1 million. Hearts, who were the Championship winners, earned half that sum. The financial gap for Hearts was therefore just over half a million pounds, compared to almost £90 million for Brentford.

The rewards for promotion are far lower in Scottish football, so the incentive to overspend on players is far lower too.

The 24 clubs in the EFL Championship lost £530 million between them from day-to-day trading in 2020/21, compared to a profit of almost £6 million in the Scottish Championship, with only one loss-making club in the division. Take away the lottery-winning levels of reward for promotion to the Premier League and Scottish clubs show that the focus is on sustainability, not financial lunacy.

Brexit has also had unforeseen knock-ons for those Scottish clubs without the financial clout of the Old Firm. As Alan Burrows, CEO of Motherwell, told the *New York Times*, they are being 'squeezed at both ends'. Because of the new points-based work permit system it has become much harder for teams like his to recruit talent from the traditional hunting grounds of Scandinavian and Baltic countries. But it's also become much more difficult for smaller teams in England to do the same, meaning there is more demand for domestic players and therefore an inflation in salaries, which English teams are more likely to be able to afford. Not only that, but EPL teams who, until Brexit, tended to scout Europe for teenage talent are now scouring Scotland and luring their kids away instead.

You only have to look at Aberdeen to realise the huge gulf in finances either side of the border. Aberdeen are a big Scottish club with a proud history – three times winners of the League in the 1980s and European Cup Winners' Cup winners in 1983.* They are virtually ever-present in the Premier League and get average crowds of around 14,000. Yet they have a wage budget that isn't that much higher than ours and it's quite possible that West Park Rovers could outbid them if they also happen to be interested in one of the players we are here to look at. In 2020/21 Aberdeen finished fourth in the Scottish Premiership, as well as competing in the UEFA Europa Cup, where they were knocked out by Sporting Lisbon in the third qualifying round. They did this with a squad that cost just £2.5 million and a £9 million wage bill, lower than any club in the EFL Championship, and with only Wycombe Wanderers having a squad that cost less.

The problem for Aberdeen, if it is one, is that despite having the third highest level of income in Scottish football, they cannot

---

*Spellcheck does not like the phrase 'European Cup Winners' Cup'!

compete with Celtic and Rangers financially. The huge fanbases of those clubs, and their regular forays into UEFA competition group stages and beyond, mean they generate three to four times the revenue of Aberdeen as a minimum. Aberdeen's strategy is, if you can't beat them don't try to join them as it will bankrupt the club.

The downside of this is that Scottish football has only had two winners of the top division since 1984/85, when Alex Ferguson's Dons team were worthy champions. In addition, Aberdeen see their best players depart as they are unable to pay competitive wages. This is not just with Rangers, Celtic and the Premier League – non-league Salford City signed striker Adam Rooney from Aberdeen and paid him £5000 a week. The upside is that Aberdeen broadly live within their means and fans can be relatively relaxed that they will have a club in existence for the foreseeable future.

YOU TAKE THE HIGH ROAD

Much as I love the place, if you think I moan about how much we spend travelling to games now, imagine how much I'd moan at the travel costs if West Park Rovers did up sticks and move to Scotland. The town of Wick is 321 miles north of Glasgow and is on a line of latitude well to the north of Moscow. Their football club, Wick Academy, plays in the Highland League and, like many clubs in that league, their ground is fully compliant with Scottish FA regulations, which means that if they were ever to navigate the play-off system that leads to the SPFL, their place would be guaranteed. But would they want to take it? Even with much improved road links to the far north, their away travel budget could be ruinous.

It wasn't until 1994 that Inverness Caledonian Thistle became the first Highland League team to join the (then) Scottish Football League and, even now, partly dictated by economics, only three others have joined them. Norway has a similar problem. There could be up to 2000 kilometres between the most northerly and the most southerly clubs in their top division (the Eliteserien), and many of their lower-league clubs are based on one of the hundreds of islands dotted around the coast and the fjords. Norway also has a solution. Every club puts money into a central pot, which is then used to subsidise the travel costs of the faraway clubs.

Compare that to FC Isle of Man, who compete in the North West Counties League Premier Division, the ninth tier of English football. They not only have to pay their own travel costs to the mainland for away games, they have to pay for the away teams to come to the Isle of Man and their fans were furious when they raised ticket prices to help them continue to do so.

There is no doubt that Scottish football does team names better than we do in England. I reckon only Crystal Palace, Port Vale and Forest Green Rovers have names poetic enough to belong in the company of Heart of Midlothian, Queen of the South, Hamilton Academical and my new favourite, Bonnyrigg Rose Athletic. You'll also have to go a long way to beat their glorious nickname, the Rosey Posey.

As it happens, the team that has to travel furthest in Scotland is not actually in Scotland. It's that handy answer to a lot of quiz questions, Berwick Rangers, although if the quizmaster also asks which British town is still technically at war with Russia, the answer isn't Berwick. That's an urban myth based on a misreading of the treaty that ended the Crimean War. You're welcome. Berwick is a beautiful little town about 4 kilometres south of the Anglo-Scottish border. And because that border was long fought over, the town changed hands at least 13 times in the Middle Ages. Their football team did originally play in the Northumberland League before making the switch to Scotland in 1905. Looking at a map, it's obvious to see why: Berwick is closer to Edinburgh than it is to Newcastle and in 1905 even getting to Newcastle would have been a schlep, let alone Exeter or Torquay. They have a lovely orange and black kit and very passionate fans, but there is one drawback to being Berwick Rangers. My friend Fraser is Berwick born and bred, and explained that the team may be officially nicknamed the Borderers, but to every club in the League their nickname is the 'English bastards'. Fraser reckons it should be embroidered on the shirt.

LECHYD DA*

Wales has a similar issue, but the other way round. With Wrexham's blockbuster journey ending in promotion, four clubs from the

---

*Which is 'Cheers!' for you non-fluent Welsh speakers.

principality now play in the English Football League. Their promotion is fitting because the early years of football in Wales were entirely dominated by teams from the north, with the rugby-loving south resisting the charms of the round ball for way too long in my opinion.

The big question that's always asked by outsiders, AKA baffled English fans, is why some of their clubs play in England and some don't. It's a touchy subject, but the simple answer is that when those clubs were founded there was no Welsh league to play in.

For a hundred years and more there had been a Welsh FA (FAW) and a Welsh national team, but no Welsh league. It was an anomaly that FIFA never liked and there were mutterings that a country without its own league wasn't actually a proper country. The critics from other countries wonder why Wales has a national team (and therefore a separate vote on FIFA matters) instead of being subsumed into the English national team, a bit like the Borg in *Star Trek*. Hopefully you guessed it was Kieran who came up with that analogy!

So the League of Wales was formed in 1992 and, when Cardiff, Swansea and Wrexham were invited to join, they politely declined. A quick glance at the figures may explain why. Between them, Swansea City and Cardiff City have played in the English Premier League for a total of nine seasons. They have earned over £1.2 billion in broadcast money and parachute payments during that period. Even Wrexham, when in the National League, had revenues of over £4 million in that division and that was before Hollywood royalty took an interest in the club.

On the other hand, Colwyn Bay FC/CPD Bae Colwyn, who I am pre-disposed to dislike because their nickname is the Seagulls, had a 2021/22 average home attendance of 626 in Cymru North, which is the regionalised second tier of Welsh football. That was 41 better than the best average home attendance in the Welsh Premier League/Cymru Premier (WPL/CP), making them the best-supported team in the entire league, with an average attendance nearly five times lower than West Park Rovers. The second highest average attendance in Cymru North was Llandudno on 283, which was still higher than at least one WPL/CP club. Colwyn Bay are a bit of a problem child for the FAW, having a tendency to flit across the border and back on a regular basis. They were in England's

Conference North until 2015, but moved back to Wales, because their chairman revealed it would cost £100,000 a year to stay competitive in England.

The WPL/CP argument is that if Cardiff, Swansea, Newport and Wrexham did re-join the Welsh pyramid, they would automatically raise the standard of the game and attendances would be much bigger. They would also have a good chance of annual qualification into at least one of the European tournaments. The counter-argument is that attendances would only be higher for games against each other, and that the eventual rewards for reaching the English Premier League are too big to ignore, especially as two of those clubs (Swansea and Cardiff) are currently among the rest of the basket cases in the Championship spending money they haven't got trying to reach the promised land.

Welsh teams in English leagues did once take part in the Welsh Cup, because it was a potential route into Europe, but a UEFA ruling put a stop to that, giving those teams even less incentive to take any part in Welsh football. Until 2011, those Welsh teams in the English League were still under the jurisdiction of the FAW, but another ruling put an end to that anomaly – almost. Cardiff, Swansea and Newport may be enfolded in the loving bureaucratic arms of the English FA, but Wrexham, when they were outside the top four English leagues, were still part of the FAW. Pardon? Of course Reynolds and McElhenney knew all about that when they bought the club.

If you want to know how the FAW feel about those clubs playing in exile then their historic relationship with Newport County will give you a clue. In 1989, after a 77-year history, Newport County, laden with debt, were liquidated following relegation from the English Football League. Their fans formed a new team, AFC Newport, who were not liable for debts incurred by the old club. In that case, said the FAW, they had no claim to actually *be* the old club and it denied them the right to play football in Newport or anywhere else in Wales. Offered a place very low down the English pyramid, they found a home 85 miles away in Gloucestershire and did very well for themselves. So well, that the FAW relented and allowed them back to their old home – until 1992, when AFC Newport declined the offer to join the new Welsh league, whereupon permission to play in Wales was once more withdrawn.

Seven other clubs also initially declined the offer, which they saw as more of an order, and it took legal action before the FAW relented, presumably because the judge pointed out that Cardiff and Swansea had also declined to join the new league and they hadn't been sent packing across the border. In other words, having their four biggest clubs play football in England is a very touchy subject for the FAW.

FISHY TALES

One of my Irish uncles once told me he used to play for Derry City. I didn't believe him because he also claimed to have had breakfast with a banshee and been rescued by mermaids when he fell off a boat during a drunken fishing trip. Turns out he did play for Derry City, but he certainly didn't score the winning goal for them in a European Cup game against Manchester United in front of 37,000 fans and a couple of mermaids who'd only rescued him on the promise of match tickets. For a start, they've never played Man United in the European Cup, the Brandywell Stadium only holds 7700 and women of any sort would have been unusual at a Derry game in the 1950s, let alone two who were half-fish.

There's a theme developing here, by the way, because Derry City are the only team from Northern Ireland who play in the League of Ireland in the Republic. In their case, however, the reason has nothing to do with finances. During the turbulent years of 'the Troubles', the Brandywell, a ground in the middle of a Nationalist area in a mainly Nationalist city, was deemed to be too much of a safety risk, especially against teams with a traditionally Unionist following. Derry were forced to share a ground with Coleraine which, ironically, was one of those teams with a traditionally Unionist following. That situation was unsustainable and Derry withdrew from the league, turning almost overnight into a glorified Sunday league team, with successive applications to re-join the Northern Irish League being turned down. Eventually, with the blessing of FIFA, they were given permission instead to join the League of Ireland, across the border, where they still happily compete now. They left behind them a league that is now in a surprisingly decent situation financially, especially, as the *Belfast Telegraph* said recently, when 'it's not being unfairly compared to the more lucrative English and Scottish leagues.' Mind you, as discussed, the Scottish league is not *that* lucrative for all but two clubs, so that may be slightly misleading.

For example, in 2019, Crusaders FC, a club based in north Belfast, had the highest wage bill in the league at just over £1.1 million. That seems quite high, but while the club wouldn't reveal details of individual players' wages, it did admit that 40% of those wages actually went to non-footballing staff, many of whom were working in their brand-new, giant bar, Harry D's, which, the newspaper publishing those figures handily reminded its readers, is now open seven days a week. Even my rudimentary maths skills can work out that leaves a wage bill for players of around £650,000 a year. The wages of a National League team average about £2 million and we at West Park Rovers are more than an average team, so our wage bill in the fifth tier is around four times that of a team in the Northern Irish first tier.

The lowest wage bill in that league in 2019 was Carrick Rangers, with just £62,500. They are semi-professional, but even if that figure doesn't include bar staff, it's not a lot for a team in the top division. In fact, we have a couple of players who are getting that each, so maybe the *Belfast Telegraph* was being optimistic after all. It's also slightly worrying that the Northern Ireland Football League said that at the very least their players would be earning minimum wage – a whopping £9.50 an hour. These figures come from information provided to Sport NI, who demanded a full audit of all their clubs before they allocated money to help them through Covid, the biggest crisis football faced outside two World Wars.*

Since the pandemic, however, football in Northern Ireland is doing OK. They have a lucrative sponsorship deal with Danske Bank. Well, lucrative by local standards. The deal is estimated to be worth £75,000 over three years, which is reasonable for a league in which average attendances in the top league are around 1400, although that figure is skewed a bit by Linfield, whose average is around 2900, which is very impressive given the size of the country – the giant who built the causeway could probably cross it in just a

---

* I was tempted to add 'and one World Cup' to that, just to annoy Malky.

few strides. When it comes to league football then, it may be a while before players stop crossing the Irish Sea to earn bigger money, but Northern Ireland's national teams are both punching above their weight, the women especially, as in 2022 they qualified for the Euros for the very first time.

The Irish FA generated £16 million in 2021. That puts it at about the same level as a Championship club such as Blackburn. Admittedly the figure was much higher when Northern Ireland and their superb fans graced the Euro 2016 finals in France. This money, however, quickly goes – the wages are relatively low, but the commitment to grassroots, women's and youth development means that overall a breakeven goal is the main one.

On the face of it then, comparing Scotland, Wales and Northern Ireland to English football makes it look like those countries are having serious financial struggles, but comparing English football to France, Italy and Spain makes it look like those three are having serious financial struggles as well. In fact, Scotland has the highest per capita match attendance in Europe, at 21.3 out of every 1000 people – almost twice as many as England on 11.4 – and the game in Wales and Northern Ireland is actually as popular as ever. The lack of money there is not a reflection of a game in crisis, it's a reflection of the real anomaly: the stupid amounts of money floating around in England.

Right, time to get back to our trip to Scotland. We have players to look at and Malky's mum's barbecue to go to. I really hope she likes the West Park Rovers away shirt we've bought her as a present.

8

A PROUD MEMBER OF THE 92

Grandad, what was Division Four?

Well, that was definitely a productive visit to Scotland, and, I have to say, one of the best barbecues I have ever been to. The sight of Malky's mum doing that Elvis impression in her fishpond wearing nothing but our new away kit will live long in the memory. Not only that but the three players we picked up for very little north of the border helped Malky Porter to fulfil his promise of getting us into the EFL. Yep, a man more Scottish than Billy Connolly has taken us into the actual English Football League. West Park Rovers started their first season carrying crossbars on to a municipal pitch. We will start our next as the 92nd best team in England. And if they weren't called AFC Wimbledon, we'd be 91st. Damn you, alphabet!

In the end we did it via the play-offs, which meant extra matchday income, extra broadcasting money and a bafflingly unnecessary trip to the London Stadium, home of West Ham, where the final was played. If it was baffling to us, it was even more so for Gateshead and their fans, who had to shell out all that money for a trip to London and didn't even get a game at Wembley as compensation. And those fans who did not bring opera glasses with them may have been better off staying in Gateshead and watching on telly given the distance between the stands and the pitch. Nevertheless, it was a great day and a great experience for our players, who, let's face it, much as I love them all like family, probably won't be around when we are one day travelling to play West Ham in the Premier League.

For now, let's just enjoy the moment. It's a cliché that being promoted via the play-offs is the best way to go up. It would be if you knew beforehand that you were definitely going to get through them, but while they're actually happening they are a gut-wrenching nightmare – although I did quite enjoy the media attention, me being the public face of the club and all, and Kieran and Guy being too busy actually doing the important stuff like organising tickets and travel and tossing the coin for dressing rooms.

UP FOR A PROMOTION

In fact, I've never been so popular, especially with complete strangers who claim they are our biggest fans and ask if there's any chance of getting 10 tickets together for them and their mates? On those occasions I have to find a polite way of saying there is every chance and their best bet is a trip to our ticket-office. The London Stadium holds 55,000 people and West Park Rovers and Gateshead have an average attendance of around 7000 between us, so tickets were never going to be exactly gold dust.[*]

FA guidelines may helpfully tell you how to determine the winner of a play-off match, but what they don't mention is how much of a kick, bollock, scramble it is when you win the last game of the season and find yourself preparing for more matches, particularly as the play-off format in the Vanarama has an extra round: the champions go straight up, the teams in second and third go straight to the semi-final and the teams in fourth, fifth (that's us) sixth and seventh play in the Eliminators[†] to decide who makes up the other teams in the semi-final.

Unlike the EFL, however, each play-off fixture is a one-off match, rather than over two legs, with home advantage going to the team who finished highest in the league. Not only is each fixture a one-off match, but the National League rules also specifically state that 'games must be decided on the day,' which is good to know, especially if you're invited to a wedding the day after. It is a slightly odd format, but it keeps half the league involved right up until the

[*] Note to self: by the time we are playing Liverpool at home in the Premier League I should perhaps start drinking in a different pub. Preferably in a different town.
[†] I'm fairly certain I saw the Eliminators support the Specials in 1981.

end of the season and, more importantly, as the official Vanarama website breathlessly states, it brings 'five season-defining games – shown exclusively live by BT Sport.' Oddly enough, the phrase 'BT Sport' appears much more often on the Vanarama site than the word 'Vanarama' appears on the BT Sport site.

The play-offs can be lucrative, though. Clubs such as Wrexham, Stockport and Notts County can generate big attendances home or away, and after expenses are deducted the monies from the play-off matches are split between the two competing clubs equally. This means that a club could earn £100,000 just for being in the play-offs.

When it comes to the final, the financial outcomes are more volatile. It costs the National League a large sum to rent Wembley or the London Stadium for a day and this cost, along with all the others of hosting the final, is deducted before the gate receipts are shared. When Notts County played Chesterfield in May 2023, the attendance exceeded 38,000, so both clubs made some money. When Salford City played AFC Fylde in 2019 there were only 8,000 at the match and both clubs were out of pocket as a result.

But here we are, a member of the oldest football league in the world. One of the 92: hallowed ground. Mind you, if the architects of Project Big Picture, the attempt to concentrate control and money in the hands of half a dozen 'big' clubs had succeeded, there would only be 90 clubs, as the Premier League would have been reduced to 18 and other divisions maintained at 24 clubs each. 'Architects' is my word by the way. Kieran had a range of other words that I discarded on the grounds of taste and decency. 'Lickspittles' and 'greedy bastards' were some of the milder ones.

Luckily, Project Big Picture was quietly shelved, so there is no need to spend much time on it, except as yet another example of the naked greed for power and money of some Premier League club owners. Basically, PBP (as no one called it) was a proposal inspired by Manchester United and Liverpool, and presented to the world in the autumn of 2020. The idea was to reduce the Premier League to 18 clubs to free up extra dates for European games and lucrative friendlies. The one club, one vote principle would be abolished, as would the rule that 14 out of 20 clubs (or 12 out of 18 presumably) in the Premier League had to agree on any policy change. Instead, any major decisions would only have to be approved by the nine teams that had been in the Premier

League the longest and only six of them had to vote for major change for it to be accepted. In other words, the traditional big six would now control the Premier League.

The EFL, as compensation for the fact that two of its members would have to be booted into the National League, was to be offered a one-off payment of £250 million plus an annual 25% of Premier League revenue, up from 4%.

The proponents of PBP presented it as a show of financial solidarity to the 72 EFL clubs still suffering from the effects of the pandemic, but in truth it was a naked power-grab by the big six who had conveniently left it until the small print to mention the notion that each Premier League club would eventually control their own broadcasting rights by showing games exclusively on their own digital platforms. Also in the small print was the suggestion that there should be more games between the reduced number of clubs each season and, hey, why don't we play a couple of them in other countries?

The EFL, naturally, were tempted by the proposals, but they were met with horror by most football fans and even the UK government, which is not normally known for its fierce opposition to a bit of financial flexibility here and there, was shocked. A statement from the Department for Digital, Culture, Media and Sport said they were 'surprised and disappointed' that, 'There appear to be backroom deals being cooked up that would create a closed shop at the very top of the game.' As Kieran said at the time, 'They may have been disappointed, but they surely can't have been surprised.' Expletive deleted!

But enough of what might have been. Let's get back to us, proud member of the 92. But hang on a second. How do we actually become a member? I've been celebrating a lot since the final so I may have missed the email. Do we have to apply? Will it cost us any money? Kieran? Guy? Where are you?

CLUB OF CLUBS

The EFL, or The Football League Ltd as it is officially known, is ultimately a members' club and each club owns a share in the EFL, which gives it benefits such as voting on regulations and, of course, playing in the EFL itself. Under agreements between the EFL, the Premier League and the National League, these shares are transferred when clubs are promoted or relegated, usually in the first week of June. One day I'd like to see a relegated club refuse to transfer their share just to see what happens, but any day now Guy will be running through the car park waving our brand-new share certificate like we've won a golden ticket to Willy Wonka's Wonderland. Which in a way we have.

Speaking of hallowed ground, by the way, I have to say the Kleanwell is looking pretty sweet as we approach the first day of the season. It may have been very noisy in the office while they were building it, but the new Stewart Lee Stand is a thing of beauty, which is the very least you'd expect for the money we paid. However, the financial contribution of Mr Lee in both helping us to build it and buying the naming rights was very welcome, as was all the lovely stuff we got cost-price from the Lee-land Furniture Warehouse. Sadly, after a feasibility study, it has not proved practical to erect the statue of Stewart that he requested in front of the new stand, but we hope the stand itself serves as a fitting tribute to his generosity. Right up to the time we can put the naming rights out to tender again.

Fans don't seem to mind too much if a stand gets a new name, because most of them simply refer to it as the South Stand or the Main Stand, just as they always have. Naming rights for a whole ground are much more thorny. It's not too bad if you're moving to a new stadium: Arsenal's Emirates Stadium was never going to be called New Highbury, especially with Emirates paying an estimated £150 million for a ground-naming and shirt-sponsorship deal. Interestingly, UEFA regulations on sponsorship mean that for European games the ground is called the Arsenal Stadium.

Trying to change the name of one of football's most historic grounds is a different matter, as Mike Ashley found when he changed the name of Newcastle United's St James' Park to the Sports Direct Stadium, which did bring much publicity for his retail chain, all of it bad. Geordie fans, predictably and rightly, were apoplectic at this latest proof of Ashley's blatant disregard for the heritage of their club. The new owners of Chelsea have announced they plan to search for naming-rights partners for Stamford Bridge and it will be interesting to see how their fans react, the problem being that fans get no benefit from the name change. Would they be more favourable if the deal funded a reduction in season ticket prices? Of course not, because that wouldn't happen.

From the sponsor's point of view it's very difficult to quantify what they gain from paying all that money, apart from free seats in the best box in the house. Of course, they have to trust that the media will constantly name-check the new stadium name. Bolton are currently playing at the Toughsheet Stadium, which is admittedly funny enough to get the name-checks required, but if the Lancashire building company of that name discover that in future most fans are still referring to the ground as the Reebok they will have wasted a lot of money.

And speaking of names, I must say it sounds a lot better being in League Two than being in Division Four. As Kieran's favourite guitarist, Nigel Tufnell from Spinal Tap, might say, 'Well, two, it sounds two better than four.'

In 1958, with the country's economy and its transport system fully recovered from their wartime battering, the Football League decided there were no longer any real financial benefits to having a Third Division North and a Third Division South, so the top half of each were placed into the new Division Three and the bottom half were chucked into the new Division Four. No prizes for guessing which one Palace ended up in, but it's testimony to the huge popularity of football at the time that their average attendance in the 1960/61 season was 19,092, including one crowd of 37,774 for a derby against Millwall. In 1992, with the re-shaping of the rest of football following the creation of the Premier League, Division Four was re-branded as the Football League Third Division and in 2004 it went up another level to become League Two. Or, to give it its full title, English Football League Two or, as they would prefer us to call it, Sky Bet League Two.

To be fair to Bradford City, in the 2021/22 season they weren't far behind that astonishing Palace average with 15,000-plus trooping into Valley Parade for every home game (they regularly had attendances bigger than Burnley and Brentford in the Premier League). The rest of the division, however, gets by on an average of somewhere between 2500 and 6500, so the big question is, has it all been worthwhile getting here?

We were getting around 5000 in the Vanarama. Is that going to suddenly improve? Will we be getting more away fans on a matchday? How much better is the broadcasting deal? Can we charge more to sponsors now? What about hiking up the price of the prawn sandwiches in our lovely new executive boxes, in which, may I say, the Lee-land Warehouse tables are rock-solid, smooth and level. No need to worry about your glass sliding off any more. (Is that OK, Stewart?) In other words, can we rest a while making money in Leagues One and Two or do we have to wait for the Championship and the Premier League until we can make the big bucks?

IN THE MONEY?

We will, of course, be getting into those leagues in due course, but it would be nice to take a breath and sit back to enjoy the view for at least a couple of seasons. Jason Stockwood is chairman of Grimsby Town, who were promoted back to League Two in 2022 after just one season away. He told us that the benefits were not just financial, they also get to retain their academy status, which is otherwise lost after two years in the National League. There were intangible reasons for his obvious excitement, too, apart from the 'sheer thrill' of being in the EFL again: 'Everything just seems a bit more professional and grown-up.' We really liked Jason, but not enough to stop me hoping we stuff Grimsby when we play them.

Producer Guy, of course, is far more interested in the all-too tangible reasons for being in League Two. At last we're going to see some proper money and I swear I will do my best not to spaff it all on more shit furniture. West Park Rovers will receive £50,000 from the EFL in mid-June as our share of the broadcast deal and then similar amounts every month thereafter. In addition, we receive two payments from the Premier League of £225,000 in August and January. These are the so-called 'solidarity payments', part of their commitment to the funding of lower league clubs, which, of course, they are only too happy to share and only too happy to let the world know they are doing it: 'Hey everybody, look, we're being philanthropic.' Pardon? Yes, I imagine our view may change when we are in the Premier League. At the moment, as a League Two club we also get money for being part of the Elite Player Performance Plan.

For some reason I thought there would be a lovely unity between clubs at the lower end of the EFL, all united in their dismay at the unfair distribution of money from the top and with a sort of one-for-all and all-for-one sense of togetherness and cooperation. It seems I may be a bit too romantic. Max Rushden is a very popular presenter on talkSPORT radio and the host of the hugely successful *Guardian* football podcast. Despite the fact that he keeps beating our pod at awards ceremonies I really like him. He supports Cambridge United and is more realistic about life at this level: 'The Premier League has no genuine interest whatsoever in distributing money fairly, but no one in the game really cares about helping anyone below them. Altruism isn't very football'. I asked if he had a solution to that: 'Nope. Maybe the independent regulator will encourage more sharing. And I don't want nation states owning football teams or rogue businessmen gutting lower league clubs so maybe the regulator will help stop that as well?' I half-jokingly asked Max what he would do in the unlikely event that a small dictatorship somewhere decided to buy his beloved Cambridge United. He said, 'I'd walk away. Football should be about family, not winning at all costs.' Nice to know I'm not the only romantic one.

In the Premier League, the highest ever earnings made by a club in a single season was Manchester United's £627 million in 2018/19. In Leagues One and Two things are a lot different. The average income for a League One club is around £6 million and in League Two it is £3.5 million. This is because, with no disrespect to West Park Rovers playing Morecambe or Crawley Town on a Tuesday night, the clubs in these divisions do not attract global audiences, big brands, national media commentary or sold-out stadia. The broadcast deal organised by the EFL is stacked against clubs in the lower two divisions. For every £10 made from broadcasting rights by clubs in the Championship, a League One club gets just £1.50 and in League Two it is a mere £1. Therefore, West Park Rovers can expect to earn about £1 million in League Two from a combination of Premier League solidarity payments and the EFL's own £119 million a year broadcast deal. If we are promoted to League One this figure will be about £1.5 million.

If we draw a Premier League team at home in one of the cup competitions and the match is shown live then we could make some more money from broadcasting. Whether there will still be two senior cup competitions in which we could face Premier League opposition is open to question. There have been rumours for some time that the Carabao Cup may be culled to ease the fixture congestion for those of our clubs in Europe. In other words, a tournament that helps smaller clubs make money will be scrapped to help bigger clubs make even more money.

While it may be useful in a pub quiz tie-breaker or as a topic to bring up during an awkward lull on a first date, relatively few people have heard of sponsors like Strata (Hartlepool), JF Hornby Accountants (Barrow) and Angel Plastics (Sutton United). This will be reflected in the sums offered for a front-of-shirt deal and, sadly, when it comes to sponsors and commercial deals, while Kieran may be famous as the sexy accountant and is clearly catnip to pension managers of a certain age, it's fair to say our club profile is more Cricklewood than Hollywood. Ryan Reynolds, when he became an owner of Wrexham with Rob McElhenney, was able to leverage his fame and arrange shirt deals with brands such as TikTok, Expedia and Aviation American Gin. West Park Rovers, even with the benefit of being seen more often on Sky Sports and the EFL highlights package, are not going to be subject to a multi-episode series on Disney Plus, unless Producer Guy's flying car is used for the remake of *Chitty Chitty Bang Bang*. (I really must stop mentioning that film.)

Therefore, matchday income is vital and if we can capitalise on our new status as an EFL club, it is likely to be somewhere in the region of £1.5 to £2 million per season... pause while fans of Premier League clubs rub their eyes in disbelief at 'per season'. It is essential that we try our best at home matches to get fans to stay as long as possible on the premises, as that way they eat more, drink more and spend more. I am more than happy to chat to fans in the bars after matches and suggest they may like to buy one more celebration/commiseration/a draw's not bad round of drinks. Admittedly it can be a chore drinking for hours after a game, but I see it as part of my duty, even if Kieran and Guy do point out it's not actually mentioned in my job description.

League One has recently contained big clubs such as Sunderland, Forest, Leeds, Southampton and Derby. Big clubs mean big fanbases, with big away followings and big paydays for us when we play them at home in that league. If they come to West Park Rovers it is a chance to earn additional money, but here we face a dilemma. It doesn't take much to get our fans annoyed at the best of times, so they won't be happy if we suggest moving some of them from their usual corner when those big dogs come to town. However, that could mean we fit in an extra thousand away fans, which is an extra £20,000 in gate receipts, net of VAT. Add to that food and drink sales and we could easily boost our income by £3–400,000 over the course of the season. The average salary for a player in League One is about £120,000, so that would be a significant contribution to our annual wage bill. By the way, I always assumed that if fans paid cash for tickets at the turnstiles there was no VAT, but when I mentioned that to Kieran and Guy they both had to lie down for an hour.

Of course, it's easier for a club of our current size to kick back, relax a little, make a couple of quid and enjoy our time in League Two. But other clubs at this level, like Swindon Town and Bradford City, were in the Premier League not so long ago, and League One has five ex-Premier League clubs: Barnsley, Bolton Wanderers, Charlton Athletic, Derby County and Portsmouth. For teams like them, every season out of the Championship let alone the Premier League makes it that little bit harder for them to get back there.

Kieran has crunched some numbers (I can say that anytime of the day or night secure in the knowledge that Kieran will be crunching numbers on something – or that is certainly what he tells his wife when she wakes up at 3am to find him staring at a computer screen) to show what we gain from being in League One and what a club the size of Ipswich Town would lose. Might as well look at a club that's exactly the size of Ipswich Town then.

By the way, observant reader, yes, you are right. In this chapter we are in League Two and League One. I could lie and say this is a clever post-modern take on the tyranny of linear narrative in books about the finances of fictional football clubs, but it's basically because the finances in both divisions are so similar it was pointless separating them into their own chapters.

The EFL distribution model means that for every £100 of the TV and sponsor deal, £80 goes to the Championship, £12 to League One and £8 to League Two. The benefit to us overall is about £2 to £2.5 million in the form of higher gates when a club such as Wednesday or Derby come to the Kleanwell, with more chance of being chosen for one of Sky Sports' EFL matches and a 50% higher share of the broadcast deal than when we were in League Two.

For Ipswich, relegation to League One in 2019 was much more of a financial hit than the benefit of promotion to it for West Park Rovers. While the 2019/20 season in League One was impacted in the last couple of months by Covid, fans had already paid for their season tickets and sponsors for their front-of-shirt deals. Ipswich ended up with an overall £7.5 million decrease in income, which was over 40% of their total.

Of course, just as with Oldham and Scunthorpe in the Vanarama, we were one of many teams in League One who selfishly hoped for Ipswich to stay there, because they have a huge away following and it would have been a great place for our fans to visit. But I wonder how they feel about being such a big fish in that particular pond, especially when every season the expectation of *their* fans is that a combination of money and prestige should see them automatically promoted? Out of spite, as much as superb management and on-field achievement, Ipswich were promoted from League One in 2023 shortly after I'd finished writing this section of the book.

ACRIMONIOUS ANDY

Not everyone feels sorry for the big clubs stuck in Leagues One and Two. Andy Holt is the owner of Accrington Stanley, who are doing an amazing job of staying in the EFL on a wage-bill of around £1.8 million a year. Full disclosure alert, Andy is a friend of ours and was a very hospitable host when we did a live version of the pod in 2022. The show was in their brand spanking new Coley's Bar, which cost around £2.5 million to build, but was already making its money back in matchday corporate entertainment and midweek events like boxing and, the night after us, a gig by 70s legends Showaddywaddy (only one of whom was actually in Showaddywaddy in the 70s, but that didn't stop them selling even more tickets than we did).

My only regret about that night is that we can't repeat most of what Andy said about the bigger clubs at that end of the league – partly for legal reasons and partly because he uses a lot of words that my mother-in-law would refer to as 'unnecessary' and a Sky football commentator would refer to as 'industrial'. Quite simply, he swears like a docker's parrot, but he thinks he has a lot to swear about when it comes to competing with those clubs whose budgets and fanbase he can only dream of, especially as he is relatively new to ownership (he bought the club in 2015) and so doesn't accept that because those clubs have had a better deal historically, they should continue to do so now.

One recent target of Andy's ire is something that concerns West Park Rovers now that we are in the big league – live streaming rights and revenue. Older readers may remember a glorious time when you could buy video-recordings of your away matches. If you couldn't make the game yourself, you'd simply bowl up to the club shop a few days later and buy a VHS cassette with a hand-written label on the front. The quality was terrible, because it was a one-camera shoot and for Palace that camera was operated by the press officer who you could clearly hear dealing with requests for a lift home as he also tried to commentate on the game. Young people will be shaking their heads in disbelief, but in those days the only way to see the goals from an away game was to actually travel to the away game. So, shonky or not, we thought the future had arrived and jet-packs were surely just around the corner.

Live streaming is the (slightly) more sophisticated modern version of those VHS cassettes. As the EFL said, initially, live streaming was simply 'an added option for those fans who can't make the game in person', but it stressed they 'were very aware of protecting the live matchday experience.' Which they were, to a point. And for Andy Holt and Accrington Stanley that point was a September weekend in 2018.

The live screening of EFL and PL games was forbidden between 2.45pm and 5.15pm on a Saturday, partly to comply with the much loved UEFA Article 48, which states that each member country must have a period at the weekend when no matches can be screened live, and partly to protect matchday revenue, because there was once a romantic notion in the football industry that protecting smaller clubs, who are more reliant upon gate receipts, via a blackout was in the best interests of the game. Certainly that is true for a club such as Tranmere Rovers, who under the ownership of Mark and Nicola Palios have been a focal point of the community. For them, trying to attract fans to Prenton Park at 3pm on a Saturday if Everton or Liverpool had a match being streamed live at the same time would really hit attendances.

But the ban didn't apply during international breaks, so on that weekend the EFL decided that Saturday games in League One and Two could be live streamed. Including Accrington's home game at the Wham Stadium* against Burton Albion. Andy Holt objected, saying, 'This kills our income and destroys atmosphere.' Personally I

---

*No, it's not called that because Andrew Ridgeley bought the naming rights.

like to think that very few genuine fans would choose the streaming option over the actually being there option, but he has a point. As he does when he highlighted that there had been no consultation with the clubs before the EFL made the decision.

For Andy, it was the thin end of the wedge. The streaming service had originally been intended only for overseas fans to watch games, then midweek games were added for the domestic audience and now Saturday afternoons were being allowed, albeit on a limited basis. He asked a simple rhetorical question: 'Has the genie been let out of the bottle?' The EFL, who I reckon probably have a full-time member of staff just to monitor Andy's Twitter account, promised to review any future Saturday screenings and also promised that clubs would be consulted.

The iFollow service really came into its own when the pandemic prevented anyone travelling to home games, let alone away ones. The quality still wasn't brilliant (normally one fixed camera), but for fans of those clubs whose every game wasn't being shown on TV it did provide at least some semblance of matchday experience. During that time clubs sold passes for £10 each (so minus VAT they got £8.33 per pass),[*] which was a handy source of income during a time of economic turmoil. For example, if Accrington were hosting Sunderland and the Black Cats sold 10,000 passes, Andy Holt would get around a third of that, because in normal circumstances Sunderland would take 3000 actual fans to the game. So, assuming Accrington sold 1000 passes themselves, they'd be getting £40,000 – a massive and welcome injection of cash. Well, £33,320 after VAT, but still welcome.

In the summer of 2021, however, even with Covid passing (sort of), the EFL clubs voted by a large majority to make it compulsory to stream all matches *not* kicking off at 3pm on a Saturday. That vote also changed the way the money was distributed and the financial benefit for smaller clubs all but disappeared. If Derby County were to sell 6000 passes for a game at Accrington, then Derby County would get the money for all of them. Accrington refused to join the new scheme, but as Andy Holt said, 'The EFL board threatened my club with loss of income if we didn't join its

---

[*] Don't talk to me about VAT. Talk to Kieran. I hate it and don't understand it.

project. It was coercion at a time when the club was just recovering from near bankruptcy.' He called it a 'deliberately flawed concept' and argued that all streaming proceeds should be shared equally between EFL clubs in the same way as TV revenue.

Accrington want to set up their own streaming service so they can sell direct to away fans, but EFL regulations don't allow that. Neither do EFL regulations allow you to have no streaming service at all. West Park Rovers can either sign up to iFollow or we can set up our own stream, but like Accrington we will only get the money from our own fans who buy passes. When Portsmouth come to the Kleanwell, all the money they get from selling passes to their many fans across the UK and globally will go into Portsmouth's bank account, even though the game is at our ground. That doesn't seem fair. I want that money in my pocket. Sorry, our pocket. The big clubs in the EFL will now get more money from the broadcasting deal *and* from the streaming deal. That's the same big clubs who, along with the EFL, argue that the money from the Premier League's broadcasting deal should be shared more equally among all 92 clubs. Kieran is more philosophical about that sort of behaviour than I am. I call it hypocrisy; he calls it self-interest.

Every single football club owner wants to safeguard the financial future of their club and if that has an impact on the financial future of other clubs, well, tough, basically. Self-interest exists in all aspects of life and business. Given a choice, most people would rather earn more money, pay less tax, work fewer hours and retire at a younger age. But if everyone did this then society and the economy would be a mess, unlike the thriving, dynamic Britain in which we happily live in today.

In most industries, the aim is to have as big a market share as possible and if your competitors go out of business then that's great, because it means more customers for your organisation. Football is not like that, though. A match consists of two teams and if they are of a roughly equal standard (there will always be imbalances caused by financial disparities) then the audience has greater engagement, from both those attending and armchair fans. Part of the reason why football is popular is that, unlike internet porn, football has an uncertain finish – and it's not always a happy one.

In a 92-club professional structure, this allows clubs such as Bournemouth, Wigan, Swansea and (reluctantly I have to admit)

Brighton to come from the lowest level of the game to the Premier League. It also means fewer dead matches, which are little more than exhibition affairs, and in doing so helps clubs to survive as fans attend matches in hope, if not always in expectation, of a result. Increasing the financial imbalance between clubs in a division reduces the chances of an upset. Good for Goliath, but David might as well tuck his slingshot away and hide behind a rock. By giving 100% of the streaming rights to the seller of the pass, the bigger clubs, which already have a financial advantage, have this amplified. This results in a more predictable, less romantic sport. For a club such as Accrington Stanley, which is punching way above its weight by being smart, it makes a tough job almost impossible.

TO CAP IT ALL

Speaking to other owners in League One and Two (in real life, not fiction) it's clear that Andy is for the most part a popular member of the gang, albeit considered an occasional noisy nuisance. One owner, though, has proper beef with him – and it's because Andy Holt has always been vociferous in his claim that it's not always big clubs who provide unfair competition in these lower leagues. Sometimes it's clubs that are even smaller than Accrington Stanley, but just happen to be owned by erstwhile superstars who have access to a lot of money and a lot of followers on social media. Step forward Salford City and a long-running and very public feud between Andy Holt and Gary Neville.

As mentioned earlier, Salford made losses of £92,000 a week in 2020/21, ironic for a club controlled by a company called Project 92 Ltd. These losses, if you're a regular listener to the podcast, won't sound a lot in comparison to many other clubs, but is a huge amount for one in League Two with an average crowd of 2274. Salford made the biggest losses in League Two in both 2019/20 and 2020/21, despite the additional revenues and attention from the *Class of '92* documentary shown on Sky. While this caused some envy and resentment from other clubs and their fans in the lower leagues, it should be remembered that Salford did not breach any EFL financial control regulations.

There can't be many football clubs that were founded in 1940 with the blitz in full swing, but Salford Central were one. They became Salford Amateurs in 1963 and their success in local football was such that their nickname is still the 'Ammies, even though they became Salford City in 1989, by which time they had reached the lower level of the pyramid proper. And that's where they probably would have stayed had it not been for Gary Neville and the rest of the Class of '92 who acquired them in 2013, hoping 'to put something back' to an area that meant so much to them. A steady and well-funded rise up the leagues followed, as did that dispute between Andy Holt and Gary Neville.

It started in 2018 (Andy seems to have been particularly grumpy that year) with Salford, promoted to the Vanarama for the first time, signing striker Adam Rooney from Aberdeen on a reported wage of £4000 a week (some sources say £5000 – I hope our players won't read this). Andy Holt revealed that Accrington's entire budget for their upcoming League One campaign was then just £1.1 million and called for 'an absolute cap on squad spending', adding for good measure that Salford were trying to 'steal' a place in the EFL.

Gary Neville, who has replaced professional football with professional bristling, responded that, yes, they had invested millions in a bid to build a stadium and a successful team in a city they love, what of it? His parting shot being to imply that Holt wanted to pull the ladder up now Accrington were in the EFL themselves: 'You seem to want a franchise league where the established can't be challenged.' Holt hit back: 'What's your budget Gary? You're buying your way in, that's the word on the street.' Back came Gary: 'We put a lot of money in and aren't embarrassed.' They have continued to have a pop at each other ever since, with one memorable bout taking place in early 2021.

A vote at the start of the 2020/21 season approved salary caps, with League One clubs not permitted to spend more than £2.5 million per year on wages and League Two capped at £1.5 million. Andy Holt was cock-a-hoop until the cap was ended, as it was deemed to be in breach of the Professional Negotiating and Consultative Committee constitution. No, me neither. Andy was now whatever the opposite of cock-a-hoop is: 'Salford City can now spend £50 million on player expenditure if they so choose. It's wrong.' Gary Neville's response was succinct and included the words 'pipe down'. As it happened, Salford had actually voted for the salary cap. Awkward.

As you can tell, we love Andy Holt, but that doesn't mean we always agree with him. As a fictional club owner I fully understand his crusade against the unfairness of the finances of football, but I don't get his obsession with Salford City. If they were lucky enough to get new owners who are prepared to fund their bid for success, then good luck to them. It should also be acknowledged that Gary Neville, in his excellent book *The People's Game,* gives a lot of credit to Andy Holt and concludes that they essentially want the same thing in terms of governance, sustainability and a regulator.

In the absence of a major shake-up in the distribution of money in English football (which we will discuss later and which will never happen) then the playing ground simply isn't level and the most football can do is ensure clubs are at least competitive enough to actually stay in business. Let's face it, in real life, Kieran, Guy and I couldn't afford to own a football team. And if we did, the only way we could have got it into League One would have been to sell it to somebody much richer than ourselves and hope the new owners kept us on as directors or, more likely in my case, a programme-seller. A quick glance at the tables shows that Salford may have been able to 'steal' a place in the EFL, but they are still a whole league behind Accrington Stanley (until 2023/24), because sometimes money alone isn't the answer. And speaking of tables and money, have I mentioned what good value the new dining room sets are at Lee-land Warehouse?

Accrington and Salford may have been in agreement about the salary cap, but those two simple words have been the source of much heated debate in football recently, lagging just behind 'parachute payments' in the list of two-word phrases often used but rarely actually understood. The most basic definition of a salary cap is an upper limit to the combined salary of an entire team, but within those simple words lies a whole range of possibilities.

As we know, the distribution of money in American sport is surprisingly equal for a country where capital is king, and a salary cap is enforced there to ensure no team can outspend their rivals to lure all the best players and create an unbeatable team. The idea is that American football, basketball, ice hockey etc will only be of interest to fans and, more importantly, broadcasters, if every team has at least some sort of chance of winning the league.

So in 2022 the NFL salary cap was $208 million and, whether that alone is the reason, you can't argue with the outcome. The

Super Bowl has been won by 12 different teams in the last 15 years, unlike the same two or three teams we see in the English Premier League, the same two teams in Scotland and Spain, or, increasingly, the same one team in France or Germany. (We'll be looking at European football in some depth later, but it's interesting that all those English fans who insist the Bundesliga is financially the fairest conveniently overlook the fact that Bayern Munich, the richest club in the country, wins the title nine years out of ten).

The mere idea of a salary cap seems to raise the hackles of most English club owners, and even when it is suggested, no one seems to agree what form it would take. So, on a long away trip to a Papa Johns Trophy game I asked Kieran for his thoughts on the whole salary cap thing and whether West Park Rovers should be arguing for one. Those of you who know me will understand how bored I must have been on that train journey to even contemplate asking that question, but, hey, at least I may finally get to find out what the bloody hell the Professional Negotiating and Consultative Committee is. The gist of what he said follows.

A salary cap can be of use, but before that you have to consider what objective you're seeking. If it is to have a more competitive competition, then a hard cap, as seen in the NFL, is great. But a hard cap only works if there are few alternatives for players to earn their salaries elsewhere. In the case of the NFL, this is not an issue. American football has no significant professional markets outside America itself and therefore the players, while still earning substantial sums (the average annual salary is $2.7 million, but some positions, especially quarterbacks, can earn $40 to $50 million), know that they cannot offer their services anywhere else.

In football things are different. If a player has their salary capped in the EFL, then there are many leagues, in Europe and further afield, that may offer a more lucrative alternative. In 2019/20 EFL owners did vote for a hard cap of £2.5 million for clubs in League One and £1.5 million for League Two. This was quickly quashed when the Professional Footballers' Association (the PFA), using the skills of renowned sports lawyer Nick De Marco KC, won an appeal against the rule.

If the £2.5 million cap had been immediately introduced, then clubs such as Sunderland and Ipswich, which ultimately reported wage totals of £16.3 million and £12.9 million, would have made huge profits that season – great news for the owners of the clubs, but the players would have been worse off and so would the fans of those clubs.

An alternative is a soft cap, set at a percentage of revenue. Here the benefit is that it does bring in an element of financial control, but means that if there are existing differences between wealthy and less wealthy clubs, these become institutionalised. The best players will be signed by the clubs with the existing revenue advantages, which increases their chances of success, generating more revenue and so signing more of the best talent. Critics of a soft cap system see it as a way of creating a closed shop in football and reducing competitive uncertainty.

LACK OF COLOUR

Thanks Kieran. I think even a bear of small financial brain like me can understand that, but it occurs to me that so far life's all been a bit grown-up since we got into the EFL. It's all broadcasting rights, live streaming disputes, salary caps. That's not what we got into football for. *This* is what we got into football for:

Credit: John Devlin/True Colours

Thing of beauty ain't it? And you should see our away kit. And our brand new and arguably completely unnecessary third kit. Of course, for some of our older fans the idea of a third kit is an exploitative disgrace. For some of our even older fans the idea of a second kit is still one they are getting used to and if we had any fans of around 200 years old they would be baffled by the idea of an actual *first* kit.

In the early days players wore what they wanted to play football and often turned out in cricket whites with either a sash round the arm or a cap to tell the two teams apart. In fact, the first ever mention of any sort of club colours comes from the rules of Sheffield FC in 1857, which required each player to 'provide himself with one red and one dark blue cap' to be worn depending on which side they played for – because, of course, the disadvantage of being the world's oldest football club was that they had to play among themselves until somebody else came along.

Kits as such, didn't appear until the FA Cup came along in 1871, because as one infuriated newspaper reporter of the time pointed out: 'It is most essential that the members of one team should be distinguished from those of the other and to have a distinct uniform... The diversity of dress displayed yesterday not only confused the members of the team but the spectators were quite unable to say whether a man belonged to one team or the other'.

I suppose they could have embroidered their names on the back of the shirt, but considering the idea of fans recognising a player by a number was still decades away, having them all wear the same kit was an important step in the right direction. Having said that, the gentlemen who played the game in mid-Victorian England tended to buy their own shirt from their own tailor, so in many of the old photographs you will see that if a club wore stripes they were often of a different width on each shirt!

It was the advent of the Football League that saw the need for a second kit. If fans were being asked to pay actual money to watch professional football then they were entitled to tell which team they needed to boo. The story goes that Wolves travelled to Sunderland in 1890 with their natty new red-and-white-striped kit exactly matching that of the home team. So in 1892 it became a requirement that each club should have a set of white shirts in case of a colour clash.* So, every away kit was white, except it wasn't,

---

* This, or so the story goes, is why Wolves decided they wanted a unique kit and chose 'old gold' as a colour.

because the convention was that the home team would wear white in the event of a clash and if there was any dispute the team that had been in the league the longest got to choose who wore what. In 1921 it was finally decided that the away team should change colours in the event of a clash, and by the time Kieran and I started going to games in the 70s you still had the situation where most clubs' away kit was a plain shirt, normally yellow, worn with the usual home shorts and shirts.

Unlike today, clubs seemed reluctant to wear the away kit unless it was absolutely necessary. If there was no colour clash, both teams played in their first-choice colours, yet somehow the games managed to go ahead and apart from the occasional game on black and white TV where you had no way of telling who was who, there was no clamour for clubs to have an away kit you could buy the kids for Christmas, let alone a third kit to be purchased for their birthday.

That began to change for two reasons: the first was Leeds United, a club who will always be known to my generation as 'Dirty Leeds', but whose legendary manager Don Revie had a shrewd eye for innovation. In 1973, Leeds signed a deal with a new kit manufacturer called Admiral. They would not only supply the first-team kit but would also supply a number of replica kits to be sold to fans, with the club getting a cut of each one purchased. Admiral also had the clever idea of creating a completely new second kit (all yellow with a blue trim) that Leeds would wear for *every* away game regardless of whether they were playing the white-shirted Derby County or the blue-shirted Everton. And, of course, that doubled the number of replica shirts on sale in the club shop.

Then, in 1978, white-shirted Derby County landed the first ever shirt sponsorship deal, with Saab, the twist being the FA allowed them to only wear those shirts for the pre-season photograph and not actual games! A year later they relented and Liverpool kicked off an actual game with 'Hitachi' emblazoned across the front of those famous red shirts. Broadcasters continued to resist and if clubs featured on BBC or ITV highlights they had to wear plain shirts, until 1983 when, with history's greediest decade in full swing, the TV companies finally gave in, and clubs and sponsors suddenly became very aware of the value of a deal that enabled their product to be shown on TV every Saturday night.

SHIRT-PULLING

And here's an idea lads, what if we make shirts that were smart/ casual enough to be worn on a Saturday night out? That way thousands of fans will be paying us to advertise a product that we make in the Far East for fuck-all. So it was that sponsors helped drive the multi-million pound replica business we have today, a business that in the most supreme of ironies has not only created a nostalgia market for old kits, but for kits with old sponsor names as well.

Now, that potted history lesson may make it sound as though I disapprove of clubs constantly tinkering with their kit. Well, as a fan, I do, a bit, but as an owner, sod that, I'm all for it. My only regret is that we don't have a long enough history to fully exploit our fans with a range of those 'traditional' kits. Lacking that, let's milk this promotion for all it's worth with the release of the brand-new kits, then let's find a reason to launch another three brand-new ones next year, while at the same time hoping that not many other clubs follow the example of Forest Green Rovers, and recently Brentford, by announcing that they will retain new kits for two years. The former has done it mainly for environmental reasons; the latter in recognition of the current financial hardship fans are facing. All very laudable, of course, but don't worry – we'll make a contribution to Greenpeace and do a two-for-one offer on away shorts as soon as Christmas is over, so our conscience is clear as well.

Joking aside, there are still big issues around the conditions in which football kits are made, mainly in South-East Asia and Bangladesh. Manufacturers claim that sweatshops are a thing of the past, but there is no doubt that they prefer to have their shirts produced in countries where labour is cheap and employment law is not stringent. There is definitely a discussion to be had on the environmental impact of transporting football kits all over the world and I promise you we *will* have that once we're in the Premier League, and have the influence and money to make kit manufacturers listen.

In the meantime, my guess is that despite the many happy hours we have spent doodling those new kit ideas, Leopard, our latest kit supply partner, will be rather more keen on their Premier League partners' bespoke designs than the off-the-peg number we will be getting. So how does our deal work, how important will we actually be as a client, what will we be spending and – the question we will be asking Leopard first – how much can we make out of this?

While in the Premier League manufacturers fall over themselves to sign up the big clubs who have global fanbases with lucrative, long-term shirt deals, in Leagues One and Two their attitude is a bit more 'meh'. A club such as West Park Rovers, with an average attendance of 6000, could reasonably hope to sell about 3000 shirts a season. That's far more units than the collector's edition *Price of Football* shirt launched in 2022, but equally it's not going to move the dial in terms of income a huge amount. On a £45 shirt, the VAT man takes £7.50 (except on youth sizes) and our margin from the manufacturer is 40% of the net. So that works out as £15 a shirt for the club, so £45,000 for the season. Still enough for a good night out, but not enough to propel the club forwards financially.

The major kit manufacturers will supply clubs at this level, but they won't design for them. While Chelsea's latest variation of royal blue for next season has probably been worked on since last season, we would simply be offered an off-the-peg template design in a limited range that may be identical to another club, but with a different badge sewn on.

However, we did put our foot down on one thing: the home shirt will stay as our traditional green and black stripes, because it always has been, right from Chapter 1. We can't mess with that sort of history. I don't reckon we need an away kit, because no one else, except Plymouth Argyle, at a push, wears similar colours to ours, but we have to have one so we've gone for white with a green and black diagonal stripe. We definitely don't need a third kit but, come on, if York City and Crawley have got one we can't be left behind. Perhaps we could have a fan vote? On the other hand, perhaps not. I doubt if Leopard have the machinery to turn us out a kit with 'bollocks' or 'sell out' woven into the fabric. Let's just see what Leopard have lying around, bung our commemorative badge on it and get it in the club shop. Alright, they've just been on the phone. Yellow it is. By the way, the commemorative badge is exactly the same as the old one, but with the words 'League One 2022' added.

As Kieran points out, though, there is a certain section of our fanbase for whom the kit colour discussion is academic. If you're the same age as us and can recall those far-off days of football highlights with Jimmy Hill saying, 'Now, it's Everton versus Manchester United, and for those of you watching in black and white, Everton are wearing the slightly darker collar' then bear in mind that many people still have the same problem. Statistically, around 8% of male football fans (and, of course, players) are colour blind, which means they find it very difficult to identify team colours both at the ground and especially on TV, where the ludicrous range of pastel shades that constitute most away kits make distinguishing colours particularly difficult. Kieran is colour blind and to my shame I have never really taken it seriously. I mean, he's not going to qualify for a parking space because of it, is he? But he told me and Guy what it's actually like.

Colour blindness to most people is something they may have encountered at school when a teacher or health visitor put a series of cards containing circles of different colours and size in front of them. They were then asked what they could see, usually a number. To someone who is not colour blind, this is an easy task and the test is over in a minute or two. For the colour-blind person it's like looking at a tin of baked beans.* Most of the circles look very similar and no numbers form as a bigger picture. When you're then told you are colour blind the first reaction is to shrug, but then when you're told you can never be a train driver, which in 1968, aged six, was Kieran's career ambition, it is a crushing blow and one from which he has never quite recovered.

Colour blindness is best thought of as seeing things on a grey scale, in terms of light and dark. So blue and yellow, or black and orange, are very easy to distinguish. Red and green, however, are a big issue. Both colours are broadly the same when it comes to darkness and so telling them apart is difficult. In terms of the impact on football, it is challenging. Many kit manufacturers these days produce shirts that are aimed at the fashion or athleisure (dreadful word) market. This means they may be playing in colours that are not 'traditional' and have to be suitably different to those of the previous season to

* I haven't had the heart to tell Kieran that's how baked beans look to most of us.

persuade fans to buy them. That also means that being able to tell the teams apart via the kits they are wearing is of secondary importance, and makes the job of the fan, player and referee difficult.

Kieran's university football career was, apparently, brief. His team were playing in green and white stripes, the opposition in red and black stripes, and being a first-year student he was already unfamiliar with the rest of the team in terms of names and faces. By his own admission he was never a good player, but he describes it as the worst 45 minutes of his football life and was substituted at half-time, which was particularly embarrassing as they didn't even have a substitute to replace him. As a result he abandoned football and spent hours of his undergraduate life and all his student grant trying to score highly on the Student Union Space Invaders machine and lose his virginity. He concedes that in hindsight perhaps these two goals were mutually exclusive.

Many of you may say that football has much bigger social problems to address first, but if nearly one in 10 of our fans buying season tickets or broadcast subscriptions can't actually tell the teams apart in many of the games they watch then that's really not fair. Especially when it's a problem that could so easily be resolved by the kit person from each club phoning ahead and bringing a kit that won't look identical on TV. Perhaps that could become the only justifiable reason for having a third kit and, like I say, if many fans are colour blind then so are many players. We spoke to Kathryn Albany-Ward from Colour Blind Awareness who told us that players were reluctant to admit they were colour blind in case it jeopardised a move to a bigger club whose kit they may struggle to pick out on the pitch.

So that's the actual kit sorted, just boots and goalkeeper gloves to go and we're ready for the group stage of the Papa Johns Trophy. Boots and gloves won't take long, because it's one of the few costs in football that isn't actually our problem. Leopard will provide shirts, shorts and socks, plus training kit and travel wear, but it's up to the goalies to sort out their own deal for gloves and caps, and for all the players to sort out their own deal for boots. Or, if the worst comes to the worst, actually buy their own.

Obviously that's not a problem for Premier League players, many of whom wear a fresh pair of boots for each game. I was at Crystal Palace's training ground once (by invite, I wasn't lurking) when a delivery turned up for striker Christian Benteke. It was a basket the size of a small skip full of his boots for that week. He dived in like a kid in a soft-play area, emerged with a few pairs he liked and wandered off whistling a happy tune. I asked the kit-man what happened to the rest of the boots and he said they get shared among the academy players. Apparently that process happened every week to some degree for every player. Still, it solves the conundrum of why young footballers all buy their cousins football boots for Christmas. And their dads and their nans too.

Those of us looking for parity between the men and women's game will probably have been delighted at the uproar over prices for Lioness replica shirts during Euro 22, with top-end items going for the best part of £115. West Park Rovers Women are also doing well, so will Leopard also be supplying kit to them? And do we need to get separate replica shirts for the club shop? After all, they play in the same colours and have the same sponsor as us. Presumably Leopard are unlikely to design different shirts for different genders when the prevailing view seems to be that most are bought by or for younger children.

We have already seen that elite women footballers are demanding non-white shorts and there is now a greater clamour for kits that are more specifically designed for women, especially boots. Research indicates that having to wear men's boots is causing foot injuries, deformations and stress fractures for women players, although it remains to be seen whether kit manufacturers who unite in their praise for the women's game will think it economically viable enough to actually design and manufacture bespoke kit for them.

Speaking of sponsors, I am pleased to announce that our new one is ... drum roll please ... Montague Insurance. As the press release said: 'All of us here at West Park Rovers would like to take this opportunity to thank Omino's Pizza for their continued support during our formative years. We are proud to have been associated with such a prestigious and popular local brand, but we both feel it's time to move on and explore other commercial initiatives.'

Which is a fancy way of saying that we thought we should get more money from Omino's now that we are in the league and they disagreed. Let's face it, that long-running legal battle with Domino's Pizza hasn't left them with a lot of spare cash and apparently the cost of mozzarella has gone through the roof since Brexit.

And get this – Montague Insurance have company, because we have back-of-shirt sponsorship now as well. Yep, just below the player's name and just above the number, in quite small lettering I admit, you will see that the back of the shirt is sponsored by Feliway, who, as I'm sure you know, are there for all your cat care needs. Yes, I know we're called Rovers, but we couldn't find a dog care needs provider that were interested.

As a kid I used to get *so* excited when a new team reached the football league. I got just as excited recently when Sutton United, just down the road from me, reached League Two. I hope other fans are just as pleased and bemused by our achievement. The football pyramid in this country is a fine thing and we were proud to be part of it, but to be part of the 92? Wow. We have come a long way. Now the real work begins as we head onwards and upwards to the Championship, arguably the most exciting and most financially chaotic league in the world.

9

ONE OF THE BIGGEST LEAGUES IN THE WORLD

The basket case

On Friday 29 July, the 2022/23 Championship season began with Huddersfield Town at home to Burnley. As the game kicked off, the Sky Sports match commentator enthused: 'This is the league where anything is possible. The door to Premier League paradise is open and the journey starts here.' Well, we're all excited on the first day of the season, but I would question whether it was the league where *anything* is possible.

There may be a team that decides to experiment by using only their right foot for a whole game. A referee might strip off and dance a samba round the corner post and there could well be a pitch invasion by angry ducks complaining about the noise on a Tuesday night in Norwich but I'm not putting money on any of them.

Still, I get his point. Sky sell the Championship on three things: the big one is that it's the path to paradise, the highway to heaven, the bus lane to bliss and various other breathless metaphors for 'promotion to the Premier League'.

Then, after the Bundesliga and the PL, it's the third most-watched football league in the world – in the grounds that is, not necessarily on TV. Sometimes, depending on the commentator, it's 'the fourth most watched' or 'one of the most watched'. Either way I'm rarely convinced that I should be watching Hull City play Luton Town on Friday night telly just because the ground is quite full.

But by far the biggest selling point as far as Sky are concerned is its unpredictability. Seriously, they bang on about it so much that sometimes I'm frightened to look away from the screen in case I miss something: 'What, there were ducks on the pitch?!' If it wasn't for the pause button I would have to go through entire games without a visit to the toilet or the fridge.

Still, all the hype should mean that Montague Insurance and Feliway will be getting even more publicity from their sponsorship deal than they did last season when we won the Papa Johns Trophy, came second in the tightest promotion race League One had seen for years and went on an FA Cup run that was only stopped by Aston Villa after a penalty shootout in the quarter-finals.

CUP DREAMS

No disrespect by the way to Papa Johns, whose pizzas I am now free to say are infinitely more tasty and less likely to be lost on the way to your front door than the previous sponsors of our club, but getting to Wembley in the FA Cup would have been much more exciting than doing it for the EFL Trophy that bears their name.

It's a great tournament played between the teams in Leagues One and Two plus an additional 16 sides from Category One academies. In other words, there is an U21 side in each group of four. The prize money is not bad either. You get £20,000 just for taking part with £10,000 for each group win and £5000 for a draw. Winning the final gets you a hundred grand and you could win up to £260,000 in total.

I am chuffed we won it in front of 30,000 people at Wembley and the money was really handy, especially as we had to buy a trophy cabinet, but the competition was only established in 1983 and only a relatively small number of teams take part, so it hasn't yet got quite the cachet of the trophy everyone wants to lift.

The FA Cup has been with us since 1871 and virtually every club in the country takes part. If we'd won that, 90,000 would have seen us do it and we would have received £2 million. Even better, the name West Park Rovers would be engraved on the most famous piece of domestic silverware in the world. For me, even though there are many who argue that it has lost some of its lustre lately as it struggles to compete with the appeal of the Premier League – and those clubs in it who may not take the cup so seriously any more – it is still the one trophy I yearn to see being paraded around Croydon on an open-top bus and the third-round draw is my absolute favourite football moment of the year.

That's the stage of the tournament when Premier League and Championship clubs join in and those small clubs* still in the hat dream of a trip to Anfield or Stamford Bridge. And while the small clubs are dreaming of a 'plum tie' (copyright every sports presenter over the age of 50) fans of the bigger clubs are dreaming of an exotic trip to a new away ground where they can swan around patronising the locals.

The third-round draw takes place in December, but some clubs begin their FA Cup journey months earlier. When West Park Rovers were still pretty much a glorified Sunday League team we started in the extra preliminary round, a full 10 months before the final, and we would have needed to win seven more games after that before our ball was in the same bag as Arsenal and Manchester United.

Although the Football Association was formed in 1863, even the FA's official history recalls that as the 1870s dawned, teams were still 'playing in a patchwork of local friendlies, few venturing beyond the most parochial of boundaries to play games.' It wasn't just parochial boundaries: teams like the Old Etonians and Old Harrovians were extremely reluctant to face teams not of their social class.

One Old Harrovian, however, was more of a forward-thinker. Charles Alcock (Kieran, stop sniggering) was the Secretary of the FA and, drawing on memories of inter-house matches at his old school, decided that a national tournament was needed to unite all those disparate clubs, especially now the railways were reaching every nook and cranny of the country.

*I believe 'minnows' is the correct legal term.

The FA agreed, even if many clubs didn't. Only 15 of the 50 registered with them accepted the invitation to take part and following further withdrawals only 12 took part in the first tournament, which ended on 16 March 1872 with the Royal Engineers beating Wanderers FC in front of around 5000 people at the Kennington Oval in London. It didn't take long for the tournament to catch on, though, especially when the rapidly increasing numbers of clubs in the industrial midlands and the north joined in, although that also highlighted the fact that posh people were still reluctant to play the oiks.

In 1879 a team from the small Lancashire town of Darwen were drawn to play the Old Etonians at the Kennington Oval in the quarter-final. The ex-public schoolboys were one of the top teams in the land and were captained by Arthur, 11th Lord Kinnaird, considered to be the best and most sporting player ever, and described at the time by *Athletic News* as 'an exemplar of manly robust football'. The ex-public schoolboys weren't keen to play the game, however, because there were rumours that Darwen paid some of their players, something they considered to be an even bigger crime than being working class.

The FA insisted the game went ahead and despite Darwen being 5–1 down at half-time it ended 5–5. Lord Kinnaird, that great sportsman, declined the offer of extra-time, opting instead for a replay. However, he and his team point-blank refused to travel to smelly old Darwen to play it. Instead, the Lancashire lads had to travel back to London for a game which finished 2–2. Kinnaird again refused to play extra-time or to travel north so the Darwen players had to ask the people of the town to donate the train fare, so they could go down to London for a third time. That game finished 6–2 to the toffs, partly because Darwen were down to nine men very early after tackles from His Lordship. So, for 'exemplar of manly robust football' read 'dirty posh bastard'. Nevertheless, by the turn of the century with the growing professionalism of the game, the FA Cup was fully established as a national tournament and the amateur aristocrats of the game had been sidelined.

The FA Cup Final of 1938 between Preston North End and Huddersfield was the first domestic game ever to be shown live on the BBC and became famous not for the football but for commentator Thomas Woodroofe, who with one minute to play in extra-time and the score at 0–0, said, 'If there's a goal scored now, I'll eat my hat,' just moments before the ball hit the back of the net to win it for Preston. To his credit, he did eat a hat, but slightly less to his credit, it was one made of cake.

The enormous popularity of the FA Cup was only enhanced by the great giant-killings that every fan loves until they happen to his or her team: From 1949 on, non-league teams like Yeovil, Hereford, Wimbledon, and Sutton beating opposition from the top division of English football have become the stuff of legend.

There came a time, though, when the cup lost its shine and that time was 1992, with the formation of the Premier League. The huge amounts of money to be made in that league gradually meant the FA Cup became far less important to the clubs in it and, worse, to some of their fans as well. This was starkly illustrated in June 1999 when Manchester United, the holders, withdrew from the coming season's FA Cup so they could take part in the brand-new and money-spinning FIFA World Club Championship in South America in January 2000. Astonishingly, it was at the request of the FA!

David Davies, the FA executive director at the time, said that the World Club Cup was here to stay and it was essential that English clubs were part of it: 'We have to be leaders on the world stage.' That, however, was the smokiest of smoke screens as many conjectured at the time that the FA and the UK government were worried that a failure to send an English team to FIFA's new tournament would damage England's bid to host the 2006 World Cup. Whatever the circumstances, it was United who copped the flak for what looked like an arrogant and contemptuous attitude to the most famous cup competition in world football.

In recent years the top clubs have been accused of taking the trophy too lightly as the prize money is so insignificant compared to winning the title. It's an odd accusation, because West Ham in 1980 were the last team from outside the top flight to win the cup and of the 31 cup finals since the foundation of the Premier League, Arsenal, Chelsea, Liverpool, Man City and Man United have won 28 between them!

It's certainly true, though, that the prize money is not the reason those big clubs want to win the FA Cup. The £1125 the tiniest of teams receives for winning that extra preliminary round in the first week of August may come in handy and the £105,000 a non-league team gets for a giant-killing in the third round proper would be an added bonus to going down in football history, but, let's face it, for Liverpool, the £2 million they got for winning the cup in 2022 is simply loose change down the back of a sofa, even if, as we have seen, it's way more than the women get for winning their trophy.

My goodness those cup-runs were exciting. We were on telly more often than Romesh Ranganathan, Montague insured more unlicensed drivers than ever before and Feliway sold a record number of scratching posts which will help them pay us lots of lovely extra money as all those success clauses Guy negotiated in the original deals kicked in.

The romantics among us have sniffed a glimmer of hope recently that the FA Cup still retains some of its allure, particularly as the last eight of the 2023 tournament contained four teams from outside the Premier League, although none of them got to the final. But, still, my guess is that if you offered any team in the Championship the choice of winning the cup or winning automatic promotion, I know which one they would choose. In fact, offer West Park Rovers first time promotion from the Championship and we would bite your hand off.*

LEAGUE REALITY

Now we are only one step away from the real goal: the Premier League, where you get paid a fortune just for being in it and another one for being relegated out of it, but for the moment, exciting as it is to be in the Championship, according to Kieran this is arguably the most messed up league in the world, a place where sustainable financial plans come to die – and the longer we are here the more perilous it becomes. Why, you may well ask, have we half-bankrupted ourselves to get here then?

Sky Sports commentators may shriek that it's the third-most watched league in the world with the most unpredictable football in the universe, but they rarely mention the eye-watering amounts of money that clubs with very little actual money are prepared to

*It might be safer to offer your hand to Forest Green Rovers, as they're vegan.

spend to get to the first-most watched league in the world, where their one ambition will be to stay in it as long as possible to earn as much money as possible.

In fact, the Championship is less of a league and more of a mid-life crisis. Like that perfectly respectable and sensible chap you know in the pub who decides to have one last go at happiness and blows all his savings on new teeth and a Porsche, then ends up alone in a bedsit six months later.

In the last two decades, partly driven by broadcasters, a sort of folk-myth has taken hold that the Premier League is the goose that lays the most golden of eggs and once you get there, even if it's only for one season, then your club's money worries are over forever. So why bother about how much you spend to get there?

I could understand spending money you haven't got on the headlong rush to the Premier League if it was actually easier to get into. Technically, the same rules apply in the Championship as in League One and League Two. The top two teams go up automatically and a third joins them via the play-off final – or as Sky Sports call it, the richest football game in the world.

However, in reality only one team goes up, one *new* team, because nearly every season at least two of the teams relegated from the Premier League, fuelled by parachute payments, tend to go back up again, leaving only one place to be competed for by the rest of the clubs. History has shown us lately, though, that if you're not promoted back by the time your parachute money runs out, then you may be stuck in the Championship for a long time.

Fulham, Watford, Norwich City and West Bromwich Albion seem to exist in a semi-permanent state of drift between the Premier League and the Championship, caught in a biennial quandary. Do they spend, spend, spend in a desperate bid to get that second season in the Premier League, which may give them a base-camp to stay even longer, or, accepting financial logic, should they go down with a sheepish grin and spend, spend, spend the parachute payment in a bid to get back again?

Of the 24 clubs that started the 2022/23 season in the Championship, 19 had been in the Premier League, which proves that getting there may be difficult, but staying there is even harder. Of those 24, I reckon only one will accept that the Championship is a decent level to reach, so there's no point knackering yourself to go any further. In fact, there's no point even knackering yourself to stay in the Championship if it means jeopardising your actual existence by gambling money you haven't got.

That club is Rotherham United who have, ironically, become a yo-yo club between the Championship and League One. The last time they were in the higher league they had some players who were only getting £3000 a week in wages[*] – not very sexy but very sustainable. They still manage to compete, but they also accept there are worse things in life than relegation, like bankrupting your club, for example.

On the very first podcast we ever did, back in the days when I was still capable of being surprised by the finances of football, Kieran referred to the Championship as a 'basket case'. Here's why: UEFA have a red flag that suggests that in order for a club to be sustainable, for every £100 of income received it should be looking to spend no more than £70 of that on wages. In 2020/21, clubs in the Championship spent an average of £128 on wages for every £100 of income. It should be noted, however, that the figures exclude Derby County, because Mel Morris decided that compliance with company law was an unnecessary detail, so he didn't sanction the publication of any accounts after 2018. In addition, Wycombe Wanderers were deemed to be such a small club that they were not legally obliged to publish wage data.

Of the 22 clubs that did publish their accounts, many spent more than £128 and the winners of the overspend trophy that season were (cue another drum roll) Reading FC, who spent £243 in wages for every £100 in income. They finished seventh in the table, so did not even have the joy/misery of the play-offs to console themselves. Yes, 243% of their income went on wages. Even I'm aware that technically you can't have 243% of anything, but it focusses your attention, doesn't it?

[*] I agree. There aren't many of us who would complain about 'only' getting three grand a week, but to many football clubs that's spare change.

Championship Wages/Income 2021

Club	Percentage
Huddersfield	55%
Cardiff	61%
Bournemouth	75%
Barnsley	78%
Swansea	101%
Coventry	111%
Luton	111%
Rotherham	111%
Norwich	117%
Watford	119%
Stoke City	124%
QPR	166%
Millwall	167%
Middlesbrough	172%
Blackburn	177%
Preston	196%
Forest	202%
Sheff Wed	209%
Bristol City	212%
Birmingham	230%
Brentford	234%
Reading	243%

Source: Kieran Maguire

By spending more on wages than is generated in income, the club's future becomes precarious. There is no money to spend on mowing the grass, heating the changing rooms or even switching on the Christmas Tree lights outside the stadium in early November, which is heartbreaking for a middle-aged boy who loves Christmas like I do, so much so that I readily agreed to ceremonially switch on the festive lights in the Crystal Palace club shop one year – and it literally involved putting a plug in and flicking the swich.

Such a wage strategy means that the only way the club can break even is to either sell players at a profit, which means your squad will be less competitive, or rely on owners to fund the losses. That's a very risky approach if you want a club to be sustainable and means teams in the Championship were very vulnerable to economic shocks like Covid, the owner's personal circumstances deteriorating or new owners suddenly realising just how expensive it is to run a club (Au Yeung at Wigan put the club into administration within a month of acquiring it). Or as we are about to find out, some owners just lose interest and decide they do not want to subsidise the losses any more. So there are going to be a lot of things going on while we are in the Championship, but we have one simple mantra: £100 in, £100 out, £100 in, £100 out. Wish us luck.

TV REALITY

Despite what broadcasters would have us believe, there was actually football before Division One became the Premier League. It may not have been as good; the pitches may have been shit and that brand new foreign striker you'd bought was more likely to be from Scotland than Senegal, but there definitely was football. Kieran and I were there. We remember it. We also remember that being outside Division One was a nuisance, but it wasn't a disaster. Basically the only difference was that you were less likely to see highlights of your game on TV.

There were certainly no huge financial differences. Manchester United, Spurs, Villa and Newcastle all spent a season or more in the old Division Two and attendances barely changed, which meant matchday income wasn't seriously affected and broadcasting deals were tiny compared to now, so that income wasn't much missed either. In other words, there was no need for those clubs to go mad and panic-buy in order to get promoted back up again, especially as wages were low enough that dropping a division meant most of your players stayed anyway.

When Brighton were promoted from the second division to the top tier in 1979[*], their income increased from £950,000 to £1.2 million. A nice increase, but not a huge one. When they were promoted in 2017, their income went from £29 million to £139 million. The six preceding seasons in the Championship generated losses of £110 million or £354,000 a week. The introduction of the Premier League in 1992 changed everything – the broadcasting deal especially. Not only did you get paid for simply being in the Premier League, you got paid a shed-load for being seen on TV in the Premier League. In 1992, for one season in the Premier League, the broadcasting deal earned you on average £2.3 million; in 2002 it was £25.3 million; by 2012 it was £60.1 million; and by 2022 it had gone up to this:

[*]Palace were champions of Division Two that season. I thought you should know that.

£147.8 million. No wonder then that everyone seems to think it's worth betting the house in order to get a piece of that action.

Nottingham Forest and Derby County are bitter east Midland rivals united by just one thing: being led to unprecedented success by a legendary manager. Indeed, each time they play each other the winning team receives the Brian Clough Trophy – and in recent seasons they have played each other a lot. Both were long-time residents of the Championship until 2022, when they both left it, but in different directions and under very different circumstances.

Forest were formed in 1865 when a group of shinney players decided to form a football team. Shinney was a sort of violent, unregulated hockey, so obviously football was considered the safer bet, at least until ambulances were invented. They chose their kit in honour of the Italian 'Redshirt' freedom fighters and in 1868 one of their games saw the first ever use of a referee's whistle. Or, for you pedants out there, heard the very first use of a referee's whistle.

After that the usual stuff happened: a league title, an FA Cup win or two, some League Cups, plus they became the first club to buy a player for one million pounds. Oh, and in 1979 and 1980 they won the European Cup two seasons running. Unfortunately, after three short spells in the Premier League, in 2005 they became the first ever European Cup winners to be relegated to the third tier of their league. They returned to the Championship in 2008 and there they stayed until finally reaching the promised land of the Premier League in 2022.

Derbyshire County Football Club were founded in 1888 after Derbyshire County Cricket Club noticed that more people seemed to be watching football than cricket. The chaps who ran cricket at the time took exception to a football club in a working town having the same name as the nice middle-class cricket boys, so they became plain old Derby County and that same year were the youngest founder members of the Football League. Not quite as successful as Forest (sorry, Derby fans, please send your complaints to WestParkRovers.co.gb), they do have an FA Cup to their name and two league titles, one under Brian Clough in 1972, one under Dave Mackay in 1975. By 1984, though, they too were in the third tier of English football for the first time in their history.

In 2007 they had clawed their way back to the Premier League, but a disastrous season, with only one win and a record low of 18 points, saw them go straight back down, and despite a couple of flirtations with the play-offs they too stayed in the Championship until 2022, but unfortunately their trajectory was down not up.

So, two famous, traditional football clubs with an illustrious past. But their recent history couldn't be more different. Greek shipping owner Evangelos Marinakis (who also owns Greek club Olympiakos) acquired Nottingham Forest in 2017 and has ploughed a tanker full of money into reaching the Premier League. With a fortune estimated at around £510 million he will still only be the 17th wealthiest owner in the Premier League, but in the summer of 2022 he spent a fair chunk of that fortune as manager Steve Cooper bought in an entire new team of players, including Jesse Lingard on a free transfer, but on wages reported to be north of £120,000 a week. Forest were the fifth biggest-spending club in world football in summer 2022, laying out more money than even the luxury shoppers of Barcelona, Paris St Germain and Bayern Munich.

Marinakis appears to be a friendly, approachable and genial man, fully aware of the emotional and financial commitment it takes to escape the Championship. He also seems to have been willing to sign the weekly cheques for half a million quid that were needed to fund Forest over the last few years, until they were promoted.

Mel Morris on the other hand... Well, let's just say that without him the list of wrong'uns in Kieran's wallet would be a lot shorter. Yep, Guy's wallet bulges because of the bank notes and Kieran's bulges because he carries round an ever-growing list of unscrupulous club owners. Morris, a local businessman and self-proclaimed lifelong Derby County fan, took ownership of the club in 2015 and initially showed an enthusiastic willingness to splash the cash. The club transfer record was broken four times in three years and he managed to lure Wayne Rooney to the club as manager. Things were looking hopeful with three, albeit unsuccessful, play-off campaigns showing the club's potential for success.

But things didn't seem quite right and from the start of the pod, Derby County had Kieran's spidey senses tingling like a wind-chime in a breeze, so much so that he became the first ever snitch in the history of the Maguire family, when he reported on Morris's unusual accounting for players, which reduced the club's losses by £25 to £30 million over a three-year period. Uncle Terry would be spinning in his grave. Well, he would be if he was dead and we're fairly certain that body in the concrete under the flyover isn't actually him.

Then, it seems, Mel Morris just began to get bored with owning the football club he had apparently supported all his life, or perhaps he realised that the accounting techniques he used to keep losses low were about to unwind now that they had been exposed by super-grass Kieran. Morris first made an investment in Derby in 2014, shortly after the club had lost the play-off final to QPR. That season Derby had a wage bill of £16 million. By 2018, the last year Morris deigned to publish any accounts, the wage bill had increased to £47 million and the club had incurred operating losses of £110 million in the intervening period.

Morris also sacked managers. Paul Clement was dismissed for not following 'the Derby Way'. Steve McLaren was sacked by Morris in May 2015, reappointed in October 2016 and sacked again in March 2017. In addition, Morris dismissed Nigel Pearson, Gary Rowett and Philip Cocu, with the expensive appointment Frank Lampard leaving to join Chelsea through choice. In January 2020 Morris appointed Wayne Rooney manager and on 22 September 2021 he put the club into administration.

Morris also dismissed captain Richard Keogh for gross misconduct after he was a passenger (Keogh does not have a driving licence) in a car crash involving two other players, one of whom was the driver, after a team bonding evening. All three individuals had been drinking alcohol. The two other players, Tom Lawrence and Mason Bennett, who fled the scene of the accident, were not dismissed. Some say this was because they were much younger than Keogh and therefore had value in the transfer market. Keogh contested the claim and won damages of an estimated £2.3 million against the club. Whether his dismissal by Morris was another example of 'the Derby Way' was not confirmed.

If Kieran was suspicious of Mel Morris from the start, the rest of us understood why when Mel Morris sold Pride Park to a very willing buyer. Himself. This allowed the club to book a £40 million plus profit and successfully defend subsequent charges from the EFL in relation to potential breaches of their Profitability and Sustainability rules.

Covid hit Derby County, but it also hit every other EFL club as well. So the initial blaming of the pandemic for the appointment of administrators seemed a little strange. There was not a special variant in the East Midlands resulting in more financial distress there than anywhere else in the country. Morris claimed the club was losing about £1.5 million a month during the pandemic, but it had also been losing huge sums beforehand too. When he first became involved with Derby its wages were £81 for every £100 of income. Not great, but very modest by Championship standards. By 2018, wages, due to the contracts agreed and signed off by Morris, were £161 of every £100 of income.

Prior to administration, Morris also took advantage of a deliberately relaxed approach by HMRC to collecting money during Covid and ran up a total of almost £30 million in unpaid taxes. By not putting the Stadium Company, which he had set up to buy Pride Park, into administration as well as the football club, Morris was still in a strong position to have some influence over who could ultimately buy the club from the administrators. This may have explained why the club was not sold to Mike Ashley, who it is fair to say, has a chequered relationship with some former clubs. Just ask fans of Newcastle and Rangers.

Mel Morris did invest/lose many tens of millions from his dalliance with Derby. He was certainly unfortunate with Covid and also that at least two high-profile takeovers of the club failed to materialise after the buyers appeared to have signed up for an 'all fur coat and no knickers' competition and funds to buy the club never materialised. But whatever he and his cronies may claim, and whoever else they blame for the near collapse of Derby County, only one person was responsible and that was Mel Morris. And there is absolutely nothing to stop him buying your club and doing the same thing to you.

Forest and Derby are just two examples of the financial mayhem that is the Championship and it's telling that even the apparently sensible good guy in that story was, in 2021, still paying £202 in wages for every £100 in income at Nottingham Forest.

FAIR PLAY

What I have never been able to fully understand is how every club in the Championship can spend that recklessly when there are Financial Fair Play rules expressly designed to stop that behaviour.

To be fair, as it were, that's partly because I don't understand Financial Fair Play rules full stop. But seeing as how West Park Rovers are desperate to avoid falling into the same income/wages trap, perhaps I should do a bit of revision.

By the way, as Kieran and I are what the European Super League clubs contemptuously referred to as 'legacy fans', rather than 'fans of the future',* I shall continue to use the phrase Financial Fair Play rather than the correct expression, Profit and Sustainability Rules – partly because we legacy fans are naturally creatures of habit and partly because it's a handy reminder that the rules may be financial, but they don't always seem to be fair. It's also fair to say that the new rules encourage neither profit nor sustainability.

In fact, because we legacy fans are obviously all very old and therefore tire easily I'm not even going to type out the whole name every time, from now on it's just FFP. By the way, if you detect a certain annoyance about that phrase 'legacy fans' then you're correct. Well, to a degree. If you replace annoyed with absolutely fucking furious then you'd be bang on the money.

FFP is probably the topic we have discussed more than any other on the pod. In fact, so much so that I guarantee every football fan I meet will ask me the usual polite questions about the family before launching into a question about why their club seems to be the only one obeying the rules or suggesting a cunning scheme for their club to get out of obeying them.

UEFA introduced the concept in 2011 and the basic FFP idea is a sound one. It's simply to stop clubs from spending money they haven't got in order to win the title or get promoted. That should protect the financial future of the club and also mean, technically at least, that smaller clubs will have to earn the right to be able to compete for trophies. The downside of this is it's very difficult for a smaller club to compete with the established elite given the financial advantages that regular participation in the Champions League and being a big 'brand' bestow on the likes of Real Madrid, Liverpool, Bayern and PSG. The rules don't limit how much money you can spend, they limit how much money you can lose, assessed over a rolling three-year period.

---

*At our age we are also not big fans of the future either.

Some expenditure doesn't count for FFP purposes. For example, anything we spend on the academy, on the women's team or on charitable causes in the community is excluded. However, that aside, Championship clubs are currently allowed to lose around £13 million a season. That means, if, God forbid, West Park Rovers are stuck here for three seasons we will be able to lose £39 million, although obviously, as Producer Guy is quick to point out, we might 'be able to lose £39 million', but I shouldn't make it my bloody ambition. If we lose substantially more than that then the EFL have a range of sanctions they could use against us, starting with a telling-off and going through transfer embargoes, fines, points deductions and even demotion. Seems simple enough. Except it's not. Hidden in that brief explanation is a world of detail, contradiction, controversy, inconsistency and conspiracy theory.

The Premier League and EFL FFP rules are now completely aligned to avoid previous situations, such as Queens Park Rangers flagrantly ignoring the EFL rules to get promoted to the Premier League, which would then not impose sanctions because it wasn't their rules that had been broken. Leagues One and Two, though, have their own separate rules, and the major European leagues all have their own interpretation of FFP. They may all be under UEFA's jurisdiction, but UEFA seem to have a fairly loose idea of what that jurisdiction actually means and only focus on clubs who are playing in their own competitions. So West Park Rovers are free from their beady eye, because we are not in the Champions League... yet.

It's actually quite difficult, therefore, to keep track of who is behaving and who isn't, although Kieran normally has a fair idea. Salford City must be fed up with the sight of pointed fingers, supporters of 19 clubs in the Premier League are convinced that Everton's recent transfer outlay must put them in breach of the rules, and everyone in Europe is gobsmacked that Barcelona can be zillions of euros in debt yet still be allowed to spend God knows how much on new players without breaking every rule there is.

Truth is, of course, that every club, to a greater or lesser degree, knows how to play the system. So does Kieran. I keep telling him to give up the teaching and club-owning game and set himself up as a freelance FFP avoider, accounting's version of James Bond, ready and willing to abseil in and show your club how they can spend without sanction. And, of course, they can offset his fee against FFP.

Kieran is obviously too moral to do that, but in the meantime here is his handy guide to bending the rules.

UEFA's FFP rules focus on a profit and loss approach, as well as a wage cap, the principles of which we have previously discussed. Profit is revenues less costs, so if you want to be a bit creative, you either inflate revenues or deflate your costs. There is now a cottage industry set up to find ways to circumvent the rules, as well as numerous units to properly enforce them – it's like a continual game of accountancy whack-a-mole.

In terms of inflating revenues, the broadcast revenues are distributed by the likes of UEFA, the Premier League and the EFL, so are presently relatively easy to confirm. Whether this will still be the case if clubs are at some point able to sell their own streaming rights is open to question. An unscrupulous club could, in theory, sell huge numbers of streaming passes to parties or countries connected to the club owner and this would boost income.

Matchday revenues are also a challenge to manipulate, but a challenge is not the same as an impossibility. For example, Chelsea used to charge former owner Roman Abramovich £1 million a season for the right to look slightly sinister at Stamford Bridge each year. This was before his assets were frozen by the UK and other governments following the Russian invasion of Ukraine. If Chelsea can do it, other clubs can do the same. A series of boxes for the owner, one for his wife, one for the cat and so on, all at seven-figure sums, is feasible.

Clubs play matches in the domestic leagues and UEFA competitions, but also arrange pre-season tours. In theory there is nothing to stop a club from agreeing to participate in a four-team tournament which carries a £20 million first prize where the opposition is the local leading U12 team, some people who won a raffle and the chorus line of *Les Misérables*.

The biggest area of both opportunity and scrutiny comes with commercial income. Manchester City's deal with Etihad Airways was subject to a lot of comment in terms of the sums involved, resulting in an investigation by UEFA. City were given a part suspended £49 million fine and a squad restriction in 2014. In 2020, for similar issues, they were subject to a two-year competition ban, which the club successfully overturned.

In addition, there are stories of a Premier League investigation into City's commercial dealings that has been slowly meandering on for many years. No one is exactly sure what is happening, apart from that the lawyers are getting rich(er). And when I say no one, that includes Kieran, a man whose ear is usually so close to the ground a millipede couldn't limbo-dance underneath it. As it happens, while we were writing this, City were charged by the Premier League with committing more than 100 offences dating back to 2009. Again, the only certainty is that this has simply added another couple of years to the process, along with giving lots more lovely money to the legal industry.

The authorities have tried to counteract any skulduggery by setting up 'fair value' panels who give their opinions as to the true commercial value of sponsor contracts, but they have a problem. What exactly is the fair value of a front-of-shirt deal for a club? It's a bit like trying to value a painting by an up-and-coming artist or an unsigned copy of Kieran's first book – it's worth what someone is willing to pay for it.

When it comes to deflating costs, the aim is to shift them to someone else. Clubs outsource some activities, such as catering, security and HR. There is nothing in theory to prevent them from outsourcing these to a 'friendly' party, who then charges them a much lower fee for these services. This can also work if you are part of a multi-club ownership (MCO) group, where central costs are allocated to those parts of the MCO where there is no FFP to worry about, reducing the costs for the clubs under greater scrutiny.

In terms of the new UEFA rules in relation to soft wage caps, these only cover player wages, agent fees and net transfer costs. A club could therefore employ a relative/partner/associate of the player and pay them a large sum, either as a staff member or consultant, and these costs would be excluded from the wage cap calculations.

Another problem is that, perhaps understandably, leagues are reluctant to impose sanctions on a club that may lead to legal action or, even worse, may lead them to them having to impose sanctions on another club in future to avoid accusations of inconsistency.

Throughout the Mel Morris saga there were constant calls for the EFL to step in and sanction Derby County even further than the points they deducted. But the EFL is made up of the 72 clubs that are in it and those clubs are hardly likely to want to set a precedent that they then may suffer from in the future.

PANDEMONIUM

Covid complicated things even further. A global pandemic that seemed to threaten the future of football clubs across the planet was obviously very bad news for the game, but, as we have seen, not only did English football come through relatively unscathed, it now had a handy new weapon in the war against FFP. Income lost during the pandemic did not count in FFP calculations and, while clubs like Newcastle United and Crystal Palace claimed a shortfall of around £40 million, Everton claimed a whopping £170 million and didn't have to detail what those losses were.

Of course, and I want to be absolutely clear on this, there is no suggestion that Everton deliberately inflated that figure for FFP purposes, but it did give me a cracking idea. I suggested to Kieran and Guy that we could post a Covid loss of £300 million and then the EFL might actually owe us money. Unfortunately, that idea was frowned on, with the usual explanation when I asked why it was wrong: 'It just is.'

Barcelona also claimed their own Covid shortfall of €300 million in lost receipts and additional costs of testing, travel etc, but that still doesn't explain why they seem to be getting away with financial murder without any sanction from UEFA or La Liga – and it's the Spanish League's own salary restrictions that Barcelona seem to be flouting more than anything else.

Reluctance to take action against Barcelona, a club that is the symbol of an entire region and a global institution, is perhaps understandable, but UEFA have bared their teeth before. AC Milan were booted out of the Europa League in 2019/20 when even the finest accountants in Italy couldn't find a way to balance their books. However, a cynic might say, and remember Kieran is not a cynic, that Milan deliberately took a voluntary one-year hit from the Europa League as it was cheaper than fighting a case, losing it, and potentially facing a ban in another year when the club was in the Champions League. The Milanisti are proud fans and persuading them to watch their team face the second best club from Denmark on a Thursday night at the San Siro would not be an easy task.

Perhaps UEFA are wary because when they took on the really big clubs in Europe they came out licking their wounds. Manchester City and Paris St Germain are not only really big, they are seriously rich, so when UEFA sanctioned them for breach of the rules those clubs could afford much better lawyers and both won their case in the Court Of Arbitration for Sport.

WAVING THE WHITE PAPER

As for those people pointing the finger at Salford City... Well, say what you like about Gary Neville (nicely though, no swearing please), he's a feisty little bugger when it comes to defending his club. Following the publication of Tracey Crouch MP's fan-led review of football finance in 2022, the government decided to implement most of her findings into law, including the appointment of an independent regulator for football. We shall be looking at the report in detail when we discuss alternative models for football governance, but for now let's just say that Gary Neville was nearly as enthusiastic about the regulator idea as Kieran and, as pod listeners will know, Kieran likes the idea nearly as much as he likes Tracey Crouch.

When Gary tweeted his support for a regulator, he was challenged by Simon Jordan, once the owner of Crystal Palace (who went into administration on his watch and avoided liquidation only by a matter of minutes when new owners found the cash to pay debts) and now a bafflingly popular pundit on national radio station talkSPORT.

Jordan responded to Neville's tweet by saying that a regulator wouldn't deal with the real issue of financial redistribution, adding, 'Let's hope your club observes FFP – as I'm not sure it does'. Neville replied that a regulator was needed because football clubs couldn't be trusted to follow the rules of their own accord unlike Salford City who put their cash in upfront every season because, 'Cash upfront/bank guarantee should be in every league'. (The benefit of having cash upfront from the owner via a pre-season bank deposit is simple: if that owner goes bust/does a runner/gets bored halfway through the season and heads for Florida then at least the club has already received enough money to pay its contractual commitments until the end of the season).

Jordan came back with, 'Get your house in order with FFP – as huge losses at Salford is hypocrisy'. Both of these alpha-males wanted the last word. Neville called Jordan's analysis 'crass and incorrect'. Jordan told Neville to 'grow up' before Neville showed just how grown-up he already was by signing off with a laughing-face emoji. None of it was particularly big or clever, but it does indicate how emotional a subject FFP can be and how sensitive some club owners are to accusations that they are playing the system.

It's a particularly thorny one for Gary Neville as he was such an angry and public spokesman against the greed of those clubs who wanted to break away to form the European Super League, including Manchester United, a club he is passionate about, but he clearly feels Salford City are doing nothing wrong in their bid to buy success. In 2021 he told Sky Sports, 'We only spend money that we have. It's a lot of money to lose, but we've come from step eight and had to spend millions and millions of pounds on this stadium. We do one day long for sustainability at the club.' He added that the Class of '92 could have spent their money on fancy cars and people would still have complained. Fair point, but Salford City's wage bill has been increasing year on year and for every £100 of income they were paying £143 on salaries in 2020/21, which on that particular metric would make them a mid-table Championship side.

Just so you know, here are the FFP rules for League One and Two, home of Salford City (for now anyway – who knows where all that spending could take them). Leagues One and Two use the extravagantly named salary cost management control system. This means that clubs can spend 60% of their revenue in League One on player wages (50% in League Two), but there's a catch, too: EFL turnover rules for Leagues One and Two allow donations from the owners of the club as long as there is no expected repayment to the donor. Injections of equity also count as turnover. This allows the wealthier club owners, who don't need any donations to be repaid, to fund any losses, but as Gary Neville points out, if they do that in advance, is that a bad thing?

Again, I cannot stress enough that this is not a criticism of Salford City. West Park Rovers are very keen to remain well within the Profit and Sustainability (P&S) parameters, partly because Kieran and Guy are very moral, rule-abiding people, but mainly because we haven't got enough money to do otherwise. It seems to me that the Class of '92 are genuinely involved for the right reasons and they want success for the club, because it will represent success for the area. Yes, they may also enjoy swanning about in the directors' box drinking free champagne but, hey, so do I. And it's not actually free, they paid for it. Salford may have more money than most at their level, but compared to some owners they are the smallest of fry.

MONEY BAGS

Imagine owning a club in the Championship knowing that you are actually worth more than the Premier League is. Imagine having vast fortunes available at your fingertips to assemble a squad good enough to get you into that Premier League and then still having easily enough money to scrap that squad and buy another one that will get you into the Champions League. Then imagine how frustrating it must be that FFP regulations prevent you from doing that, even though you could afford to pay any financial penalty a million times over?

That is the predicament of Bet365, owners of Stoke City, once a fixture in the Premier League and now stuck firmly in the middle of the Championship. The *Sunday Times* Rich List is an annual update on the thousand wealthiest people or families resident in the UK. According to the 2022 list, the Coates family, owners of Bet365 and Stoke City, were worth £8.637 billion – £189 million up on the previous year. That made them the 17th richest in the country. By comparison, Roman Abramovich, at his wealthiest was worth around £10 billion.

The owners of Stoke City are wealthy beyond the dreams of most people, but they are not your archetypal evil capitalists. They support the Labour Party for one thing and invest widely in a number of community projects in their native Staffordshire and beyond, an area of economic deprivation for many. Yet they are not allowed to spend nearly as much as they could on the football team they own and support. Is that fair? Well, for me, yes it is. West Park Rovers arrived in the Championship in June with around £500,000 as a welcome from the EFL for our part of the broadcast deal to add to our bank account. How can we compete with people with more than £8 billion in theirs?

You may argue that it is just the nature of competition. The Coates family have worked incredibly hard to build up a multi-billion-pound business, so why shouldn't they be allowed to spend what they want on what is just another part of their empire? I would argue that is the way to kill football. If American sport recognises that unfettered capitalism will kill competitive sport then that seems to me to be the sensible approach to adopt here. Besides, Bet365 still have plenty of wriggle-room to spend freely within the FFP parameters and it hasn't bought them promotion back to the Premier League, which is exactly the point: you simply shouldn't be allowed to try and buy success, even if it very rarely works, *especially* because it very rarely works and you are risking the future of your club in the process. Sorry, the fans' club.

As it happens, the Coates family are careful and responsible club owners. On 28 May 2021 Stoke City sold the Bet365 stadium to… Bet365, for just over £70 million. This meant that Stoke's losses were reduced from £43 million to 'just' £9 million. By an amazing coincidence the EFL changed their rules on 1 July 2021 and prohibited stadium sales from being included in FFP/P&S calculations.

Nick Hancock is an actor/comedian and host of a very fine football podcast called *The Famous Sloping Pitch*. He is also a fanatical Stoke City fan, so much so that when he hosted the boisterous BBC panel show *They Think It's All Over* and Phil 'The Power' Taylor, then the world champion of darts, was a guest, Nick wouldn't talk to him directly because he was a Port Vale fan! I asked Nick about the Bet365 situation: 'It's frustrating to know that our owners want to spend money that they clearly have. But I understand that the system is there to protect clubs from the charlatans, adventurers and fantasists that have been all over football like a rash'. I was also very relieved to hear that he could live with not being in the Premier League but only because he hates VAR so much! Having said that, I'm slightly worried that in writing this book, the three of us fall very definitely into the 'charlatans, adventurers and fantasists' category. Well, one of us does.

We haven't heard the last of FFP but I think it's all getting a bit serious so let's move on, particularly as the F and the P keys on my laptop are starting to jam. Football is supposed to be fun, after all, even for club owners, so let's discuss a completely different and more light-hearted subject. Now then, what's next on the agenda? Oh bollocks.

PARACHUTE OR TRAMPOLINE?

If you think FFP is a difficult and controversial can of worms then parachute payments are a difficult and controversial can of worms that you're trying to open in a minefield during a thunder and lightning storm underneath a massive tree while waving a nine-iron over your head.

In every league we've been in it seems that we are competing with clubs that are, well, way out of our league financially. Normally, that's because they are simply richer than us, whether because they are big, traditional clubs who still retain a huge fanbase or small clubs whose owners had the foresight to make millions out of business (or out of being very good footballers), while Kieran, Guy and I wasted our time on teaching, the BBC and showbusiness in that order. I don't mind that, it's the way of the world: some clubs are richer than others, some girls' mothers are bigger than other girls' mothers.* What is a bit odd, though, is to arrive in a league where that financial unfairness is baked in.

Again, I used to think that, in principle, the idea of parachute payments was a fair one. But since part-owning a fictional football club I've come to realise that everyone hates parachute payments except those clubs in receipt of them. Of the 22 clubs that competed in the first ever Premier League season only seven have been in it ever since: City and United, Everton and Liverpool, Arsenal, Chelsea and Spurs. Of the other 15 clubs, four are currently back in the Premier League: Aston Villa, Crystal Palace, Nottingham Forest and Sheffield United. My guess is that all of those five, no matter how well-off or well-supported they are, will say that their first priority at the start of each season is still being there the following season, because while they were out of the Premier League, every single one of those five at one stage suffered financial crises so bad they threatened the very existence of the club.

Of the 10 other founder members of the Premier League back in 1992, six are in the Championship and two are in League One.

---

*You'd be amazed how much longer the pod would be each week if we kept in all the lyrics to Smiths' songs we bandy about.

Wimbledon are in League Two* and Oldham Athletic are now in the National League, the first ever ex-Premier League team to be relegated out of the 92. I tell you this just to show that for all but the traditional big six, relegation from the Premier League is a real possibility every season and that relegation could send every single one of them into free fall, which is exactly why parachute payments were introduced.

Before then, those relegated clubs lost a huge chunk of broadcast revenue, which meant offloading high-earning players to cut wage bills, which meant weaker teams, poorer results, smaller crowds and so on. As the Premier League broadcasting deal got ever huger, so did the financial costs of relegation and also, it seems, did the realisation that clubs weren't going to be sensible enough to prepare for those financial costs themselves. So in 2006 along came the parachute payment and with it the solidarity payment – money distributed to all the clubs in the EFL who *aren't* getting parachute payments in order to offset any criticisms that relegated clubs are getting an unfair advantage.

Gary Lineker told me that the parachute payment was a minor consolation when Leicester were relegated recently, but said a bigger problem for other clubs going down from the Premier League was a failure to prepare by putting relegation clauses in players' contracts. He also said there was actually a sense of relief in going down: 'We can go back to just being Leicester now, instead of ex-champions Leicester'.

At its most basic, the parachute payment means that you still get a slice of the Premier League broadcasting deal even if you're relegated. If you like, it's a slice of a slice, because it's based on a share of that part of the revenue that is distributed equally between the clubs. In their first season back in the Championship, each relegated club gets around 55% of what they would have received from the broadcasting pie if they were still in the Premier League. In the second season they get 45% and in the third, and last, season of parachute payments it's 20%. On recent figures that works out to around £40 million, £35 million and £15 million, so over three

---

*Assuming you count AFC Wimbledon as the original Wimbledon and not MK Dons, which you should because they are.

seasons a relegated club is around £90 million better off than other clubs in the Championship (except the other relegated ones obviously). There are a couple of exceptions. If you are relegated after only one season in the Premier League you only receive two years of parachute money and if you are promoted back after one season, your parachute payments are discontinued.

Critics of parachute payments say they reward failure, but is it failure for clubs such as Blackpool, Cardiff, Hull and Bournemouth to get to the Premier League in the first place? They certainly do give clubs a financial advantage in the battle to get promoted back again, but defenders of parachute payments point out that their original objective, of preventing relegated clubs from going into administration when relegated, has been achieved. They also observe that the existing system has resulted in 50 clubs competing in the Premier League since it started in 1992/93 and that for every Norwich or Watford there is a Sunderland or Wolves, who get relegated to League One despite being in receipt of parachute money. However, the sums involved are probably too generous and the parachute has become a trampoline, helping too many relegated clubs to quickly bounce back into the Premier League.

In the binary world that is the 21st century, most people are either very much for or against parachutes. The solution is, as is the case for many disputed topics, somewhere in between. Reducing both the size and duration of the parachute payments could ensure clubs can survive relegation while continuing to trade, and not have too much of a head start against the other Championship teams. So relegation isn't quite the licence to print money that we may have been led to believe, but it is a handy little mattress to fall back on.

Why then are so many clubs vehemently opposed to parachute payments, including one or two owners in the Premier League who you'd imagine would be only too happy to make that mattress even bigger just in case? Some dress it up as altruism. Parachute payments, they say, are anti-competitive. The Premier League should instead be offering the rest of football a fund of, ooh, say £200 million to be shared out sort-of equally, because that would be much more fair.

It's a good job Kieran and I are not cynical, because otherwise we might point out it could be seen as anti-competitive that, for example, were West Park Rovers to be relegated we would still have lots of lovely Premier League money in our bank account, while those clubs relegated in the past two seasons would now be getting far less money from the new 'much more fair' system than from parachute payments.

Several club owners in the Premier League are vehemently opposed to any potential change in the system and, surprise, surprise, they tend to be owners of clubs outside the traditional top six who seem well-enough established in the Premier League, but could, like Everton in 2022 and 2023, possibly be drawn into a relegation battle. We will discuss this in more detail later, but Aston Villa, Crystal Palace and West Ham were absolutely opposed to the suggestion in the Tracey Crouch fan-led review that parachute payments could be replaced. Karren Brady, West Ham's vice-chair, said that Tracey Crouch had 'fallen into a do-gooder trap' and clubs would go bankrupt without parachute payments.

The EFL, however, are 100% behind the removal of parachute payments because of their impact on the competitive balance of the Championship and on the financial sustainability of the clubs not in receipt of parachute money. They are currently in negotiation with the Premier League about a 'fairer' distribution of money but as one PL official told me recently (I promised not to name him), 'What have they got to negotiate with?'

Some of you may well be asking why West Park Rovers have waited until now to voice concerns about parachute payments. After all, clubs relegated from the Championship to League One, from League One to Two, and from League Two to the Vanarama get a parachute payment and that hasn't bothered us. Well for a start, what they actually get is a 'solidarity' payment – and the money, while no doubt very welcome, is nowhere near big enough to distort the finances in those leagues. However, the main reason is this. The Championship, remember, is the league where anything is possible, where you can see paradise through that open door. However, that open door already has a queue of clubs in front of us right from day one, because as many as nine of them could still be in receipt of parachute payments from previous relegations. What's more, most of the rest of them are wealthier than us, because they've been marooned in the Championship for seasons, earning more money than us in the process. All we can hope to do is manage fan expectations and hope that we can do a Luton and get to the play-offs on a tiny budget or, if it has to be, a Rotherham and go back to League One with our dignity and our finances intact.

The Premier League's solidarity payments are given as a percentage of parachute payments. It's not a big percentage, but it's worth about £4.5 million for a Championship club and £450,000 for a League Two club. Therefore, if the value of Premier League rights increase, so do the benefits for smaller clubs. When the Premier League initially introduced solidarity payments it was on a voluntary basis, which seemed very kind at the time. However, a few years later, by which time EFL clubs had become accustomed to both receiving and subsequently spending the solidarity payments, things became a bit more Machiavellian.

I NEED A P

The Premier League wanted to introduce the Elite Player Performance Plan (EPPP). The plan has some very good features, but some are bordering on malevolent. In brief, EPPP abolished the rule that prohibited a club signing a young footballer who lived more than 90 minutes from the club's academy. This allowed the elite clubs to pick up talented young players from other academies, including those from EFL clubs, at fixed, often low, fees.

The Premier League offer was that if EFL clubs accepted EPPP, at the same time solidarity payments would change from voluntary to mandatory. If they did not agree then the Premier League had the option, should it so choose, to terminate solidarity payments. The EFL clubs did have a vote on the matter, but by then they were so dependent upon solidarity payments that they had little realistic choice but to accept the Premier League offer.

Of course, the other thing we could do is lighten up a bit and discuss all the lovely money we can make in the Championship. Sheesh, come on, we've not kicked a ball in this league yet and we're already moaning about parachute payments like we've been here for years. Let's be positive, because I'll tell you one thing about the league where anything is possible: it's possible we could be on live telly even more than we have been recently.

Crowds will be going up, too. I reckon we're looking at an average of 14,000, so that's more beer and merch (I know I'm too old to be calling it merch, but the kids like it and they're the ones with pester power) and it's also more Chablis and canapés in the corporate lounges, not forgetting that extra screw we'll be getting from our sponsors, Montague Insurance and Feliway. Kieran, what does that all look like on paper?

	£m
Matchday	4.7
Broadcast	8.0
Commercial	5.3
Total income	18.1
Operating expenses	
Wages	21.7
Overheads	4.0
Player amortisation	3.7
Depreciation	0.4
Total expenses	29.8
Operating loss	(11.7)
Player sale profits	2.6
Pre tax loss	(9.1)

Source: jobs4football.com

Hang on a second. I'm just going to try and revive Producer Guy. I'm not sure that losses of £9 million a year are quite what he had envisaged. And how are we doing on the old income to wages ratio? It looks like we've spaffed £120 on wages for every £100 of income? Already? Shit.

This is a book about football finance, but any discussion about the Championship seems to involve way more finance than football. That's sad, because for all the breathless hyperbole of those Sky commentators it is a brilliantly mad and gloriously unpredictable league to be in. Regardless of what we can gain or lose off the pitch, on it we have two games a week to look forward to, in packed stadia against some of the biggest names in English football. Our green and black stripes and our brilliant fans will be seen and heard on TVs across the world. Bring it on!

10

THE PREMIER LEAGUE

The promised land

We all make decisions in life that we later come to regret. Sometimes they are big decisions, like ending a relationship, sometimes it's choosing a madras rather than your usual korma. I am beginning to really regret my choice of ringtone on my mobile phone. I adore Laurel and Hardy, so it made perfect sense to choose 'Dance of the Cuckoos', their unofficial theme tune, to announce when I had a call. It always brought a smile to my face when the phone rang, and to the faces of my fellow passengers on the train. But that was before we reached the Premier League. Now my blinking phone never stops ringing and the novelty is beginning to wear off.

Our CEO is of the opinion that it's not appropriate for the part-owner of a Premier League football club to have such a flippant ringtone, especially if it goes off during a tense contractual discussion we're having with Chelsea about loaning their fifth-choice striker for the season. It doesn't help either that Kieran's phone chirps out a jaunty version of 'California Uber Alles' by the Dead Kennedys and Guy's goes off to 'Goldfinger' as a tribute to his favourite Bond villain and mentor.

We got a taxi together the other day and the driver nearly had a theme-tune induced nervous breakdown, although he was still able to ask if he could have a couple of tickets for the Liverpool game, because his eldest is a huge fan of Jürgen Klopp. It's amazing how popular we have become with complete strangers since that magic moment at Wembley when the referee blew his whistle at the end of the 'richest game in world football' (© Sky Sports) and we were in the Premier League.

I have to say though that I have been surprised by how many football fans do not think the Premier League is the promised land. Comedian and TV legend Jo Brand told me recently she has fallen out of love with football because of the huge riches in just one league: 'Money is corrupting in most circumstances and local teams are being overlooked in favour of flash bastards,' she said. I asked how she would resolve the issue and her answer was surprisingly simple: 'find a group of kindly nuns and give them power of attorney over the money earned by the richest clubs'. Hmm, Jo may make a decent independent regulator.

I also asked Jo, who is a fellow Palace fan, whether she would be happy for Russia, Dubai, or Belgium (in that order) to buy our club if they promised to invest enough to guarantee we won the title: 'Absolutely not,' she said, 'but if Judi Dench wanted to do a Ryan Reynolds on us, absolutely yes!'

I wouldn't mind, but the whole mobile phone thing is just one of many unexpected irritations that promotion has brought. Still, there is one consolation. To use the technical accounting term, we are fucking rolling in money! And we've been paid a lot of it already. The Premier League gives clubs a big slice of their 'equal share' of the broadcast deal (the one that is not augmented by live appearances and final position in the table) in mid-June, so we are already looking at an extra £32 million in our bank account and there's plenty more where that came from.

Seriously, I can't stop looking at our bank statement. It's like the moment I first saw my new-born son and had that sense of wonder and that incredible pride of being able to say, 'I made him,' while my exhausted, sweat-soaked wife looked at me thinking, 'You made him?!' Mind you, I'm beginning to regret saying that the players were also part of my family, because I reckon I'm going to have to say goodbye to half of them and bring in the strangers we need to help us stay up.

Oh, where are my manners? Let me introduce you: our new CEO is called Miranda Nurse. We headhunted her from an energy company, which means she is not only very clever and very efficient; she is very imaginative when it comes to getting more money from our customers. And once she remembers to stop referring to our loyal fanbase as customers she will be practically perfect in every way.* As it is, Miranda is already worth her weight in gold. Well, certainly worth the £400,000 a year I reckon we must be paying her, which is a bargain because I know for a fact that there are CEOs in the Premier League earning £3 million a year.

She may have zero tolerance for Stan and Ollie, but Miranda has a laser focus on the problems ahead; little things like actually buying all those new players and the urgent upgrading work the stadium needs before we can even kick a ball in the top division. The upgrading requirements came as a bit of a surprise. The Kleanwell Stadium may only hold 18,000, but it's neat and tidy and all-seated, with that brand new funky electronic advertising board all-round the perimeter so we can have baffling messages in exotic foreign languages, like all the other clubs do. And if we follow the example of some of the other clubs we may even raise the height of those boards, so we can run more adverts at the same time and make even more lovely money. Trouble is that would mean removing the front row or three of seats, because punters wouldn't be able to see over them and that would cost us money. And a hell of a lot of bad PR. One for Miranda, I think.

As it happens, those expensive and urgent upgrades we need to make to be Premier League-ready will be largely invisible to our fans, no matter where they are sitting. The *Premier League Handbook* stretches to 338 pages and 37 of them are devoted to Section K and 'Stadium Criteria and Broadcast Requirements'. Holy Mary, it's complicated. Along with the other eight clubs who were in the play-off mix, we had a visit from the Premier League's broadcast department in February to assess whether our facilities would be up to scratch if we did get promoted. Turns out the answer was a resounding 'no', so we were already in a dilemma.

We could have gambled on going up and started to spend the money then, so we would be ready before we got promoted, but if we hadn't got promoted we could have been stuck with three-year contracts for, say, new floodlighting or IT, services that we didn't need in the Championship. So we decided to wait and see, but that

---

*She doesn't like me saying that – 'I'm not Mary bloody Poppins.'

has left us with just a few weeks to make the necessary adjustments and it's going to cost us around £5 million.*

As *The Athletic* said of Huddersfield Town's promotion to the Premier League in 2017, 'That minor miracle was matched by the heroics their stadium operations team achieved off the pitch as the John Smith's Stadium was converted from being a functional stage for football and rugby league into a film set for world-class live entertainment.' Because that's mainly what the Premier League wants – consistency of broadcast quality. Every single game can be watched in every single part of the world and every club taking part has to ensure that every single detail can be seen in full high-definition and every single post-match interview can be heard with full clarity.

Obviously, we still have to provide the usual dressing rooms, toilets etc, but now we also have to provide a drug-testing area as well. That's not too expensive I imagine, probably just a room with a couple of bottles and some litmus paper, but after that the costs really begin to ramp up.

We were able to get away with frost covers in the EFL, but undersoil heating is compulsory in the Premier League and very expensive. Realistically, we need to spend at least £500,000 on installation and then there are the running costs of about £5,000 a day in terms of having it on, so if there is a whole month of cold weather then that works out at £150,000. That will be even more if the energy crisis worsens, but at least we don't have to choose whether to heat or eat.

Incidentally, and this turns out to be one of many things I did not know, technically, 'You can only carry out remedial or repair work to the pitch at half-time' with the express consent of the referee. Turns out that ground-staff simply ignore that regulation based on the logical assumption that if you don't mention that you're going to be putting divots back, Anthony Taylor will not march on to the pitch and kick them up again. And I'm not sure the Premier League would like the sight of our grumpy groundsman twatting a referee to be broadcast in ultra-HD around the world.

---

*Both Brighton and Leeds revealed that's how much they allocated for the upgrades.

Speaking of Anthony Taylor, I imagine our fans are looking forward to booing in the flesh all those celebrity Premier League refs they have only seen preening themselves on TV. I'm afraid that even as a club owner, my admiration for how well the officials do their job doesn't prevent me from shouting at them for not doing it better than us. I don't know if Professional Game Match Officials Ltd (PGMOL) – the organisation that supplies everyone who spoils your fun – provide training in how to stop your lip trembling when 18,000 people are calling you a wanker, but that's because they are not big on giving out information on anything, especially how much those match officials are paid.

Referees have been professional now since 2001. Before that they were just paid expenses and the only thing we knew about them was where they lived, because for some bizarre reason matchday programmes always put their place of residence in brackets next to their name. To this day I still can't hear the name Graham Poll without automatically adding 'Tring, Herts' in my head. I presume the reasoning was that angry fans could console themselves with the knowledge that at least the referee wasn't so biased towards Liverpool because he was born there.

Today we know even less about referees, especially their income. It *seems* that the match fee is £1500 per game and the basic salary anywhere between £70,000 for a standard Premier League ref and £200,000 for those who are FIFA-qualified, but which referee gets what is not disclosed. Probably for the best. Assistant referees and video assistant referees are apparently on £40,000 as a basic salary, which, in the latter case, doesn't seem a lot for being among the most hated men in football.

Guess what? Female referees don't get paid as much. Sian Massey is one of the most respected assistant referees in the men's game. When she runs the line in a Premier League game her salary is topped up by a match fee of £500. For doing the same thing in a WSL game the fee is £60. A WSL referee (most of whom are now women) is paid an annual salary of around £4000 with an additional match fee of £120. WSL referees are not professional and in 2021 the FA announced there were no plans to make them so until at least 2025. This means that despite having to meet the same fitness levels as male officials in the EFL, they receive no sickness or childcare benefits. Can someone remind me what century this is?

West Park Rovers now have to provide the facilities to review VAR decisions, but we already have the goal-line technology we installed in the Championship (although we didn't do the actual installing and the handbook is very clear that 'for the avoidance of any doubt, ownership of the Goal Line Technology shall not belong to the club'). We have a big screen already, too, so that's fine, except the Premier League rules are quite fierce on what we can show on it: 'only action replays of positive incidents'.

Then it all gets a bit technical (and even more expensive), but I think it's worth sharing some of these costs, because they illustrate to fans just how seriously the Premier League takes its responsibilities to broadcasters and just how much we have to spend, especially considering the relatively few times our home games will be live on TV compared to the traditional top six. The Premier League's response to that complaint, by the way, is basically suck it up. You'll be getting a facility fee of around £1 million every time you are on TV if you appear more than 10 times, so this initial investment is a small price to pay for being in the world's most exclusive football gang.

As you can imagine, a modern, well-run club like West Park Rovers is, of course, wi-fi enabled, which is handy because the Premier League is encouraging all its clubs to move from paperless tickets as soon as possible (one of the many things our fans are unhappy about, despite the fact we've got them into the best league in world football*), but we now also have to provide 'internet connectivity with a bandwidth capacity of 750 megabits per second for the exclusive use of broadcasters, accredited members of the media and data partners'. I don't actually know what that means, but I've seen the projected costs and it is serious money, although on a lighter note everyone in the press room will get to hum along to Laurel and Hardy.

We also have to supply the same network access to the outside broadcast compound, which is about a hundred metres away and, according to our tech people, is going to need a router the size of a

---

*Actually, I don't blame them. There are many older fans without 'fancy' phones or who aren't tech-savvy and many younger ones like, ahem, me who want a paper reminder of games we've been to.

small horse (and no, they couldn't be more specific). That bloody outside compound is going to be there permanently, meaning we lose about 30 parking spaces for every game, which is something else for the fans to complain about.

We now need a TV gantry, hardwired, which has to be a minimum of 19 metres wide and 2 metres deep, with space for at least three domestic commentators and five cameras, and it mustn't face directly into the sun. Yes, God forbid Jonathan Pearce should have to shade his eyes occasionally during his commentary on our game, which will probably be last on *Match of the Day* when most viewers have already gone to bed. To be fair to the Premier League, they do state that clubs won't be penalised if stanchions are in the way because it's an old stadium, but we have to tell them that in advance, leading me to believe they are happy for Jonathan Pearce to have to peer round a stanchion, but he can't do that *and* shade his eyes at the same time.

The gantry also has to have 15 international commentary positions with two seats each. I mean, 15! I'm almost tempted to buy a couple of South Korean players just to attract their media, because otherwise I reckon that's 30 seats going to waste for most home games. And we have to have a further 15 radio commentary positions (one seat each unless more are requested), along with seven pitch-side presentation positions, which also have to be hardwired. We're going to be spending a bloody fortune on gaffer tape just to stop people tripping over the miles of wire we're putting down.

Then there have to be two separate studios, hardwired obviously. The studios must have windows at least 3 metres wide unless they were built after 2014, in which case they have to be at least 4.5 metres wide. That's not fair. Of course, our studio was built after 2014, so we're already spending an extra metre and a half more on glass than other clubs.

We have to provide a 'visiting club analyst position', a mixed zone for at least 20 people and a safe space for the 'super flash interviews' (that's post-match interviews to you and me), but the players chosen for the interview 'must have featured prominently' in the match. Or, in the case of Conor Gallagher, must have been super flash.

Then there's the media conference room, hard-bloody-wired for at least 70 people; the press working area with at least 25 individual work stations comprising a desk, a chair, an electricity supply and an internet connection; and, not forgetting my particular favourite, the photographers' room, because the snappers get their own space, too. The club must also supply 20 bibs with the word 'photographer' clearly visible and a further 20 bibs with the word 'messenger' clearly visible. Question: if every centimetre of the bastard ground is either hardwired or internet-connected, why do we need 20 messengers in the first place?!

And all of these people, from international broadcasters down to messengers, must be suitably catered for during the course of the matchday. I've been to the press room at many Premier League clubs so I know we are not just talking sandwiches here. Except for the photographers. They may not know it, but their suitable catering is basically a choice between white bread or brown for the tuna sandwiches. Everyone else is getting à la carte. I still remember the full Thai buffet laid on in the Aresnal press room at one game, mainly because I was full of Thai buffet for three days afterwards.

Floodlights are the biggest problem, though. I have never been to an evening game at any level of football and found myself thinking, 'I can't see a bloody thing here.' They are always bright enough. In fact, if you're going to an evening game at a new ground you tend to find your way there by simply heading for the floodlights. Not once at any stage of our progression through the pyramid has anyone ever complained about our murky pitch, but, of course, the Premier League aren't going to take my word for that. The least complicated part of the floodlight requirements is the opening statement: 'There must be a maintained vertical illuminance of an average of at least 1650 lux and a minimum of at least 650 lux at any one location of the pitch measured towards the four vertical planes.' Four vertical planes? How many versions of 'up' are there?! And let's face it, the Premier League aren't that fussed whether someone sitting in row Z can see the game; they want to ensure that someone sitting in Kuala Lumpur can see it on telly. Of the £5 million spent by Leeds United on their promotion to the Premier League, probably around half would have gone on installing new floodlights in the West Stand.

Naturally, a league that is a genuine global brand is going to set very high standards for anyone who joins it. And, yes, the monetary rewards for being in the Premier League are huge, but having to do all that work in such a short space of time is very difficult, in both practical and financial terms, and will nearly always disadvantage the team who is promoted via the play-offs, especially if it is their first time in the Premier League. But also, while the Premier League do concede that the 'nature of the construction and configuration of a stadium' may mean that a club is unable to comply with these new regulations before the season kicks off, any reprieve from punishment will be only temporary. Failure to make all the necessary adjustments could lead to part of the broadcasting money being withheld or an order to share another stadium that *is* fully Premier League-ready. In other words, at a time when our fans are joyously celebrating the promotion and waiting for the fixture list to be announced, the club itself is already in a state of high anxiety – and that's without all the other financial considerations on top.

The main one being, what will our strategy be? When we reached League One, we did talk about planning ahead and setting different budgets, one for being promoted and one for not, but it's different when you actually arrive in the promised land. Do we try to do a Sheffield United and hope that adrenalin and a new way of playing will turn us into a surprise package that stays up? Do we adopt the Norwich approach and stay within our financial means regardless of whether that means inevitable relegation? Or do we adopt the Nottingham Forest policy of spending huge amounts on players and wages to give us a decent chance of staying up, but a decent chance of going bust if we go down with all those wages still to pay for players that no one wants to buy?

And, naturally, all those players who got us promoted now want better contracts for doing so and it's heartbreaking to think that some of them haven't yet realised they are surplus to requirements. I've always argued that any promoted club must play their first five games in a new league with the players who got them there, just so they at least get some sort of reward for their effort. But now, even though I'm only the part-owner of a fictional football club, I realise quite how impractical that idea is – and I'm the romantic one!

When Crystal Palace got promoted to the Premier League in 2013, most fans would assume that Wilfried Zaha would still be flourishing there 10 seasons later, but none of us thought Joel Ward would get anything other than a compensation game or two before being sold to a Championship club to try again. Luckily, he proved us wrong, but without substantial investment in new players (and new managers when things were going wrong) Palace would have been relegated long ago and, given their precarious financial state in the first seasons in the Premier League, that would have been disastrous. We all agree that unless Malky Porter has some unlikely tactical changes up his sleeve then the Sheffield United approach is unlikely to work for us. That leaves safe and sensible against spend, spend and spend again.

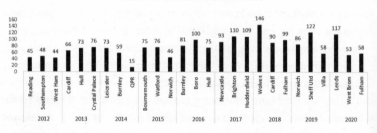

Promoted Teams Income Increase £ m

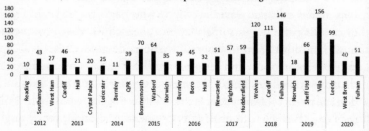

Promoted Teams Wage Increase £ m

Promoted Teams Transfer Spend in Premier League £ m

Source: Kieran Maguire

The good news is that, as a club not in receipt of parachute payments, we can expect to generate about an extra £95 million income in the Premier League, even if we finish bottom. For every additional place up the table it is worth about £2.5 million and, if we are popular with broadcasters, then we'll be in for some extra facility payments, too. The bad news is that the money goes quickly on increased wages and, of course, there will be pressure to compete in the transfer market.

Our winning goal at Wembley was scored by Louis Quatorze, who we signed on loan from a French Ligue Un side in the January transfer window with an obligation to buy for £10 million if we were promoted. It was obviously money well spent, but, amazingly, it turns out that all the other French clubs now seem to have any number of players they reckon we should look at, only they all seem to be that much more expensive now because we are in the Premier League and therefore rolling in cash.

That's a problem Newcastle United will increasingly face in the future. If a selling club knows you are owned by some of the richest people on the planet they are going to automatically add £10 million to the asking price of any player they may be interested in. And it's not just Ligue Un clubs. Most of the phone calls that are driving people mad with a combination of Laurel and Hardy, the Dead Kennedys and Shirley Bassey are from agents offering us a must-see YouTube video of a Brazilian wonder-kid doing keepy-uppies or a deal on that Serbian centre-back West Brom released on a free transfer last year, both of whom are guaranteed to keep us in the Premier League.

15% OF EVERYTHING

I don't think it's an exaggeration to suggest that most football fans actively dislike player agents. While there is often outrage at discovering the wages some players are earning, in my experience most fans don't seem to blame the players themselves. They accept that careers are short and life after football is long. They understand that top comedians and TV presenters get similar sums, and they don't blame a working-class lad or lass for making a few bob while they can. But what football fans do seem to resent is every single penny earned by the agent representing that player who negotiates the deal that makes them both rich.

On the pod, we have interviewed several agents and they have all been intelligent people who genuinely seem to have the welfare of their clients at heart. It makes you wonder, then, why so many fans think of agents as corrupt, venal bastards with no interest in the game other than to take money out of it. Sadly, it's because there are agents like that and they are precisely the ones who refuse to be interviewed by people like us.

The image of the agent wasn't helped in the 1980s by people like Eric Hall and his 'Monster, monster...' catchphrase, which he used to boast of a deal he had done. His background was in music, where he'd done PR work for the likes of Frank Sinatra, Queen and the Sex Pistols (he arranged their notorious appearance on a live early-evening TV show where they delighted teenagers like Kieran and me by swearing at the presenter for five minutes). In 1986, sensing that football was about to emerge from a long period of public disapproval, he became the agent for a number of high-profile players, such as Neil Ruddock and Dennis Wise.

As it happened, the players loved him, because he saw no reason why they shouldn't be paid for everything they did, including personal appearances, ghost-written tabloid columns and image rights. The football establishment, however, and most fans, disliked his brash manner, his open desire to make money from the game and his clear craving to be a celebrity himself. Unfortunately, he set the template for a stereotypical player agent and it's one that still persists.

Until October 2022 when FIFA introduced an actual exam it was very easy to become an agent. As long as you had never been convicted of a serious crime, or a financial crime of any sort, then all you needed was professional liability insurance and you received a certificate from the FA recognising you as a registered intermediary. After you'd paid them £500, naturally. Like many agents, you very rarely get anything for nothing from the FA. In practice, of course, many agents have a legal background or a very good knowledge of contractual law, but there are players who are perfectly happy to be represented by a mate or a family member.

Football fans also tend to be wary of clubs having too close a relationship with one particular agent and conspiracy theories abound of clubs whose transfer policy is not driven by a manager or a director of football, but by a super-agent. And one club more than any other tends to get the wink and the nose tap from conspiracy theorists.

In July 2016 the Chinese conglomerate Fosun bought Wolverhampton Wanderers for £45 million. The previous season the club had finished 14th in the Championship. Fosun had investments in the entertainment sector, such as Cirque du Soleil, but no experience of European football. However, Fosun also had a stake in Gestifute, a Portuguese agency owned by Jorge Mendes.

Mendes was not a board member at Molineux, but was asked by the new owners to advise on player recruitment. He then became, depending upon your level of support for Wolves, a useful sounding board with experience of the football market or a parasite sucking money from the club, using his influence in the game to negotiate deals that benefitted himself first and other parties second. Within two years of the takeover Wolves were promoted to the Premier League, although their transfer spending in those two years was substantially higher than in previous years.

Since arriving in the Premier League, Wolves have spent well over £400 million in four seasons on players. Nineteen players represented by Gestifute have joined Wolves since 2016 and many others have been signed on deals brokered by Mendes or one of his associates. No one knows what he himself has earned on those deals, but it's likely to be at least 15% on each one and 15% of well over £400 million is a hefty amount – and that's just money earned from the player deals. Quite often the club is the client of the agent, not the player, and they are likely to be charged much more than 15%. There are other ways, too, an agent can supplement their income... [The rest of this sentence has been redacted on the advice of the West Park Rovers lawyer.]

Wolves have competed in the Europa League since promotion and some of the players have been *sold* for large fees too, so why should anyone complain? Probably because football and complaining, whether through petty jealousy, xenophobia or making two plus two equal five, is part of the modern game. Mendes has done well from Wolves, Wolves have done well from Mendes, but is there more to things than meet the eye? A run of bad results will see critics claiming that signings are based on agent commission rather than talent. Similarly, some good results will have some saying that having expert knowledge of markets, especially in Portugal, has allowed Wolves to punch above their weight since promotion.

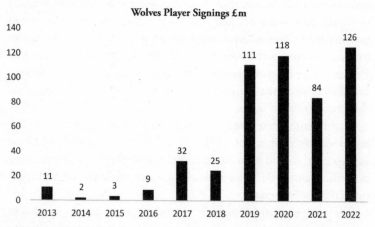

Wolves Player Signings £m

Source: Kieran Maguire

Luckily, all the agents West Park Rovers deal with are very decent people, but now we're looking at some eye-watering transfer fees; fees that we clearly can't pay in one lump, so what do we do? Well, perhaps we could turn instead to some of the encouraging young talent developing in our academy. We've already spent millions on them so surely they must be good? Apparently not. According to Manager Malky they are nowhere near ready for this level, but a few of them have potential, so how about loaning them to Championship clubs for a bit to toughen them up? Meanwhile, here's that list of players he wants, all of them available for a steal at around £30 million a pop.

CAN YOU LEND ME A STRIKER 'TIL TUESDAY?

To be fair to Malky, he has used the loan system very well and has a fine instinct for bringing in players who can help in the short-term or shipping out those players who need a bit of character-building by being kicked all over League Two for a season. Trouble is, it gets complicated keeping up with the contractual stuff and hoping that your promising youngster does well enough at Club X on loan, but not so well that Club X may want to buy him.

It's not just Malky. For previous generations the lending and borrowing of players was an ad hoc and informal affair, usually done only when one of your first team needed to be replaced because of injury or you wanted the same player to go somewhere else to get match fit. Now it's such an integral part of the game that most Premier League clubs have someone like Mark Bright at Crystal Palace, whose full-time job is managing the welfare of those players the club have brought in temporarily and those they have parked elsewhere for a while.

The loan system, a bit like God, works in mysterious ways, although the loan system did not invent the platypus. There are straight (or should that be vanilla) loans, loans with options to buy and loans with obligations to buy, all of which have costs and potential consequences.

The straight loan is where a club has a player who is surplus to requirements, the player wants to get more playing time and another manager thinks the player can 'do a job'. 'Do a job' is football speak for helping the club to succeed and in doing so helping to preserve the manager's actual job.

The loanee players come from a variety of scenarios. They could be young and promising, such as Kasey Palmer and Izzy Brown, who both joined Huddersfield Town in 2016/17 from Chelsea, aged 19, and helped get the club promoted via the play-offs. All parties win from the situation. The players gain experience from a high standard of football, the lending club gets to see how their assets are faring with a view to bringing them into the first team squad or selling them, and the loanee club is able to utilise a talented player who they might not be able to afford to buy. The precarious nature of professional football is highlighted in the case of Izzy Brown who had to retire in 2023 at the age of just 26.

Contrary to the belief of many fans, especially those bending my ear in the pub, loans are not free. Chelsea would have charged a loan fee for those players. This may have been a nominal amount given the loanee was a relatively small club, but with bonuses should certain goals be achieved, such as promotion. Chelsea are a bit coy as to how much they generate from the loan system, but

Manchester United in their accounts usually disclose £2–3 million of loan income, Arsenal have generated as much as £4.5 million and as Chelsea seem to have several tons of talent at other clubs every season you can guess that figure may be higher. Or it was. From 1 July 2022 FIFA limited the number of players who can be loaned internationally out to eight per season to 'prevent the hoarding of players'. That number will reduce to seven in 2024 and six in 2025. Although the loophole which Chelsea will no doubt exploit is that players aged 21 and younger will be exempt, as will those players who have come through a club's academy system, i.e. 90% of them.

The players' wages are usually split between the two parties, but the host club may negotiate a graded contribution from the loanee club. For example, if the player averages less than 30 minutes per match the loanee club pays 60% of the wages, 30–60 minutes 40% of the wages, and more than 60 minutes 10% of the wages. This is to encourage the loanee club to make use of the player. If he is not playing football then he might as well spend his time at his own club or loaned out elsewhere.

Sometimes the player is more senior, but a new manager decides that his face does not fit and so he goes out on loan. Chelsea bought Romelu Lukaku in the summer of 2021 from Internazionale for £98 million, but he only scored eight Premier League goals in an injury- and Covid-impacted season. He was then loaned back to Internazionale for 2022/23 as manager Thomas Tuchel decided Lukaku's style of play was not right for him. The loan fee for Lukaku is quoted by 'sources' as being €8 million, a substantial sum, but only a small proportion of the amount Chelsea paid for the five-year deal that brought the player to Stamford Bridge.

The highest loan fee in football was the €45 million paid by PSG that brought then 18-year-old Kylian Mbappé from Monaco in 2017. The deal included an option to purchase Mbappé 12 months later, taking the total fee to €180 million. PSG did not want to register Mbappé as a signing in the same year that they paid €222 million for Neymar, so this was a way of keeping Mbappé off the balance sheet for a year.

This type of deal offers protection for the buying club, for if the player exceeds expectations then they are able to recruit at a discount. The player would have to agree terms, too, but this is where the agent can protect their client's interests by ensuring that a competitive deal is offered. Otherwise they can refuse to go along with the loan.

An obligation to buy forces the loanee club to purchase the player at the end of the loan period. It is often linked to achievements, such as the number of matches played. Fulham, then in the Championship, signed Anthony Knockaert on a season-long loan deal from Brighton and Hove Albion in 2019. Fulham were promoted to the Premier League at the end of 2019/20 and signed Knockaert on a three-year permanent deal on 8 July 2020. The rumour is that the terms of the loan included an obligation-to-buy clause if he appeared in more than 30 matches in the Championship. He did play those games and he was duly bought, but he never played a game in the Premier League for Fulham. They loaned him to Nottingham Forest just weeks into the season.

Another source of confusion for fans is why a struggling side doesn't just borrow a whole new team to save themselves. It's simply because the loan rules are quite clear. In the Premier League you can have no more than two loan players in any match squad, and in the EFL it's five. Actually, the loan rules are way too complicated to explain here, but I will tell you that, for some reason, a Premier League club can only loan out one goalkeeper a season.

So Manager Malky is going to have to buy in the talent we need, and he is very excited about all the money and new players he thinks are heading his way. He wants an entirely new back four, because he reckons the one we've got is going to struggle to cope with the scrutiny that VAR will bring to their hair-trigger offside trap ('fucked' is the actual word he used) and, of course, along with every other manager in the Premier League, he wants a creative midfielder and a 20-goal-a-season striker.

THE MAGIC WORD

Like I say, despite having that lovely Premier League money safely banked we can't afford to buy those players outright, even if we can lure them here in the first place. If only there was some way of spreading the cost in an instalment type plan... And here we are, it's the moment you've all been waiting for: it's amortisation time! Before I started doing the podcast I don't recall ever using the word 'amortisation' in any context. Now, I reckon after the words 'pint' and 'Guinness' it's the one I use most on a daily basis.

Accountancytools.com describes amortisation as 'a process of incrementally changing the cost of an asset to expense over its expected period of use', while Investopedia calls it 'an accounting technique used to periodically lower the book value of an intangible asset over a set period of time.' Frankly, I'm still none the wiser, but I know just the man to answer my simple questions. One day I will ask Kieran about something normal like cheese, but until then, I wanted to know how a football player can be regarded as an 'intangible asset'. He explained that an intangible asset is one with no physical substance, so you can't touch it. Intangibles include things such as goodwill, trademarks, brands, licences and so on. On the face of it, these things have nothing to do with signing a footballer.

There is, however, a common misconception. When a player is signed, it is their registration certificate that is transferred from one club to another for a fee. The registration certificate gives the club that owns it the exclusive right to have that individual play for the club, to the exclusion of all other clubs. It is those rights given by the certificate that have value, but the rights themselves are intangible as they, unlike the player, cannot be touched or indeed kicked.

I then asked Kieran why so many transfer fees are amortised. Transfer fees are amortised, because the registration fee is effectively a rental agreement. If you rent a house for three years, but pay the landlord £12,000 at the start of the agreement and nothing else, you are effectively paying £4,000 a year in rent.

It's the same with a transfer fee. When Manchester City paid Aston Villa £100 million for Jack Grealish's registration certificate to be transferred to them in the summer of 2021, the player signed a six-year contract. He can't play for anyone else unless City gives their permission and so the cost of the transfer (£100 million) is spread over the contract period (six years) giving an annual amortisation fee of £16.7 million. The longer the contract signed, the lower the annual amortisation fee. This also protects the buying club as the player can leave on a Bosman deal, with no transfer fee, at the end of the contract. Don't worry, you'll learn all about Bosman deals in due course. The downside of this is that if the player turns out to be a bit bobbins* the club is locked into paying the players wages for a long period of time, which can prove to be costly.

Danny Drinkwater was a key player for Leicester City when they won the Premier League in 2015/16. He was signed by Chelsea on a five-year deal for £35 million a year later. This meant that Chelsea amortised his contract by £7 million (£35 million over five years) a season. However, things did not work out professionally or personally for Drinkwater. He only made 23 appearances for Chelsea over that period, although his contract at Stamford Bridge was lucrative, worth an estimated £5 to £6 million per year, which is why he was perhaps not prepared to sign permanently for another club.

As with loans, the actual transfer process is a lot more complicated than the average fan thinks, especially at this level. Back in the old days of the National League South – and I nearly said 'good old days' then, because I'm beginning to miss the simple pleasures of just turning up and playing football – we knew every player at every club within a 50-mile radius and we knew whether they fancied a change of scenery and ten quid a week more by coming to us. And if we didn't know, we asked them.

Well, 'we' didn't, because, of course, that would be 'tapping-up', which is strictly not allowed. But you'd be amazed how many players' dads drank in the same pub as Ena from our canteen, who just happened to mention we needed a left-back and may accidentally have revealed that we paid a very decent petrol allowance.

Things are different now, especially as the Premier League take a very dim view of the whole tapping-up business. The rule is quite clear: 'A contract player, either by himself or by any person on his behalf, shall not either directly or indirectly make any such approach without having obtained the prior written consent of his club.' Simple. A player from another team can't express an interest in moving to you and you can't express the same interest to them without written permission from his club.

All right and proper, except that as Stoke City owner Peter Coates told the *Guardian*, 'Everyone is at it. You could almost say it's part of the fabric of the game' and as one agent, on condition

---

*Bobbins is a Mancunian word. It means shite, but can be said on the radio.

of anonymity, told the *Mirror*. 'No transfer happens without an element of tapping-up.'

Normally it's the agent that does it for you – either by telling you one of your own players wants to go and would you like him to quietly arrange it, because he happens to know that another club is interested, or by telling you that a player at another club wants to leave and his lifelong ambition has always been to play for West Park Rovers, so would you like him to quietly arrange that as well? – but there are other ways. When Malky Porter told Sky Sports in a live post-match interview last season that West Brom's star striker was just the sort of player he'd love at Rovers, that's tapping-up.

When Miranda Nurse murmurs to our Portuguese playmaker that next time he's on international duty could he tell his teammates how happy he is here and drop a hint to Cristiano Ronaldo that we may be just the club for a world-class player to spend the last season of his career – and by the way the canteen does a blinding *bacalhau com natas* – that's tapping-up.

When a tabloid newspaper reveals that a well-placed source, i.e. our press officer, suggests that Rovers are keen to strengthen their squad with a player like Reuben Loftus-Cheek, that's tapping-up. It happens and, just as a controversial penalty delights one set of fans and infuriates another, your view of it will depend on who's doing it to whom. If it's your star striker that's being tempted then you are furious, but if it's you doing the tempting then it's all part and parcel of the modern game, innit?

There's another issue with transfers that most fans are not aware of. I certainly wasn't until I spoke to Steve Parish, co-owner and chairman of Crystal Palace. He told me that, basically, if you want to sign a right-sided midfield player then you need to be speaking to five of them at the same time, because the chances of getting your first choice are slim. That's why so many deals are done at the last possible moment on transfer-deadline day. Your first four choices have turned you down and gone to other clubs for various personal or financial reasons, and now you have just hours to convince choice number five that he was always your prime target and would he like an extra ten grand a week to prove it?

Wages, of course, are the main discussion point in any transfer deal, as well as in any pub where two or more football fans are gathered together. A club like ours has very little choice but to offer any potential recruit a decent wedge if we want to sign them. They know it, we know it, fans know it. Mind you, it still makes me laugh when I hear an irate fan berate an under-performing player with, 'I pay your bloody wages.' One day I will turn to them and say, 'Actually my man, I know a little about football finance and it turns out your matchday contribution is having little to no impact on that player's wages.' Depending, of course, on how big the irate fan is.

No matter how much a player will tweet about joining a club he's always admired and that he looks forward to playing in front of such a passionate bunch of fans, the truth is that he would be saying the same thing about Watford if they'd offered him more money than we did. If only there was a way to amortise a player's wages as well as his fee. I'll put Kieran on to it.

It's strange that with such big sums of money involved we still talk about a player's weekly wage and not his salary – yet another lingering reminder that football is a working-class sport. And it's not that long since footballers were paid about as much as their mates in other working-class jobs and still lived on the same road as them.

THE WAGES OF SIN

Most football historians agree that it was probably in 1878 that a Glaswegian lad called Fergie Suter became the first player to be paid, when he arrived in Lancashire to join Darwen FC. Which means, annoyingly, that those snooty Old Etonian hackers in the FA Cup were right to be suspicious. Suter was, at least, the first to be publicly accused of the heinous and immoral practice of accepting money to play what was considered to be a pastime rather than a job. Well, it was considered to be a pastime in the south, where it was mainly played by toffs who didn't need to dirty their hands with something as grubby as money. In the north, where the game was growing among the working classes, it was a different matter.

No one ever proved that Suter was paid, but the fact that he seemed to be living a comfortable life despite never actually appearing at the stonemason's yard where he was supposed to be employed was enough for the rumours to continue. Suter claimed that he stopped working there because the local Lancashire stone was too hard to work with, but as Manager Malky is living proof that no Scotsman ever would admit that anything in England was tougher than it was north of the border I find that hard to believe.

Nevertheless, the genie was out of the bottle and all the clubs who joined the newly formed Football League in 1888 paid their players a weekly wage. It wasn't much though. Even with the odd bonus thrown in (although sadly no image rights, even if your face did appear on a cigarette card) you weren't getting a fortune, so many players took on other jobs during the summer when they only received around half their normal wage, because they weren't actually playing football. They certainly weren't earning enough for agents to get involved and players were at the mercy of the club secretary when their wage for the new season was set.

Nevertheless, in 1901, alarmed by stories of club owners offering huge financial inducements to lure in the best players, the Football League imposed a maximum wage cap of £4 a week, which according to my calculator (AKA Kieran) is worth around £544.60 a week now – and only Kieran would use the word 'around' about a figure that goes to two decimal points.

The wage cap was still in place in 1961, although by then it had been raised to the princely sum of £20, which ironically works out slightly less than 1901 at around £500 a week in our money. For comparison, the average weekly wage of a teacher in the same year was £22 and an army sergeant £17. Players could supplement their earnings with a nice little signing-on fee if they were transferred, but here again they were entirely at the mercy of the club secretary.

It was a system that was officially known as 'retain and transfer', but was more commonly called 'soccer slavery', because the club basically owned its players. It started in 1893 as yet another attempt to prevent richer clubs poaching players from the less well-off and, given that was just five years after the formation of the professional English league, it shows that football has been a big-dog-eats-little-dog-world right from the start.

Basically, once a player was registered with a club he could never be registered to another without permission from that club. This meant that even if his contract expired and he wanted a move, he didn't get it if the club refused permission. Not only that, but if the contract expired and the club refused that permission *and* retained his registration, then the club were not obliged to either play him or pay him.

It took a strike threat from a man with a spectacular chin to change all that. Jimmy Hill (see Chapter 2 for more details) was in the last year of a modest playing career when he became the head of the Professional Footballers' Association and decided it was time to end both the minimum wage and soccer slavery.

After some preliminary skirmishing with Football League executives, Jimmy went straight for the jugular and, with unanimous support from the players called a strike for Saturday 21 January 1961. The Trade Union Congress (TUC) asked its members to support the strike action and encouraged the public to boycott any matches that went ahead as clubs tried to gather enough reserves and apprentices to cobble a team together. On 18 January the government summoned the PFA and club chairmen to a meeting in Whitehall and an hour later the maximum wage was abolished.

Legend has it that the first beneficiary was Johnny Haynes, star midfielder for Fulham and England. The Fulham chairman was the famous comedian and actor Tommy Trinder, who, the year before, had jokingly told a journalist that Haynes was worth £100 a week, but sadly his hands were tied because of the wage cap. The day after it was lifted Haynes marched into the chairman's office with the newspaper cutting in his hand. He got his pay rise. Other club chairmen, however, got the hump. West Bromwich Albion's Major Wilson Keys called it 'dangerous and unsettling' and predicted that other Fulham players 'would have to starve' to pay for it.

Meanwhile, in 1960, George Eastham, Newcastle United's tricky winger, didn't play for seven months as the club had refused him permission to join Arsenal when he turned down the offer of a new contract to stay with the Geordies. The club relented in October and he joined the Gunners for £47,500, but the PFA now had their tails up and offered to pay all the costs if Eastham took legal proceedings against Newcastle. Accordingly, early in 1963 a High Court judge declared for Eastham and instructed the Football League that clubs no longer be allowed to retain a player's registration. In a pleasing bit of historical irony, the judge was Richard Wilberforce, great-great-grandson of William Wilberforce, the man who led the movement that ended the *actual* slave trade in England in 1807.

So that was the 'retain' gone from 'retain and transfer', but it was three more decades before a bang-average Belgian player saw off the 'transfer' bit. Jean-Marc Bosman's contract with RFC Liege expired in 1990 and he wanted a move to Dunkerque, across the border in France. The French club refused to meet the Belgian club's transfer fee demand, so Liege refused to release Bosman and reduced his wages by 70% as he was no longer in the first team. The system was the same across most clubs in Europe, including the UK: when a player's contract ended the club could refuse to release him for transfer if there was a dispute over the fee.

Bosman challenged his club through the European Court of Justice, suing them for restraint of trade. After just two years, which is lightning fast by their standards, the ECJ ruled in his favour. I like to think that Jimmy Hill raised a glass of Stella Artois to celebrate. The ruling meant that clubs can no longer demand a fee for an out-of-contract player and, if a player has less than six months left on his contract with club A, he is able to negotiate a free transfer with club B in advance. That's why as much attention is paid to the duration of contracts as to their value and it's one of the reasons why we appointed Miranda Nurse in the first place. As she pointed out, if it had been left down to me we'd end up with 23 out-of-contract players going on a free transfer as soon as the window opened. A bit harsh, but to be fair she was twitchy because my phone had been playing Laurel and Hardy all morning.

ZIP, NADA, RIEN

Pre-Bosman there was a bit of a stigma about free transfers. No one got excited if their club signed someone for nothing and 10 minutes into his debut you could usually work out why his old club were happy to give him away. These days, the free transfer is a handy option for clubs and players. Jesse Lingard's move from Manchester United to Nottingham Forest is a good example. United could still reasonably expect a fee of £30 million for him, but that would have put off a lot of potential buyers, even Forest, and they were spending money like a sailor on shore leave. Nevertheless, allowing Lingard to leave for nothing meant they no longer had to pay substantial wages for a player who wasn't part of the manager's plan and it allowed

Forest to sign a decent player and pay him much more in wages than they could have done if they'd had to find the £30 million to buy him, so everybody was happy – apart from fans of other clubs who were furious that Forest would do something so unsporting as pay Jesse Lingard a hundred large a week to keep themselves in the Premier League.

When a club signs a player, they look at the total cost, both amortisation and wages, over the contract period. If the player arrives on a Bosman deal with no transfer fee paid, then the player's agent will aim to ensure that their client is the beneficiary of the transfer fee 'saved' via either a large signing-on fee or big wages. This is why elite players, in particular, such as Paul Pogba at Manchester United, Kylian Mbappé and Zlatan Ibrahimovic at PSG have been happy to let their contracts expire.

Back in 1961, the sort of money players earn now would have been unthinkable. Despite the fears of club chairmen like Major Wilson Keys, no floodgates were opened. Player wages went up for some, but not by much, although there was a bit of public outrage in 1968 when it was revealed George Best was on £1000 a week at Manchester United.

Gary Lineker has done very well out of football, thank you very much, but his playing days were just before wages for Premier League players hit the eye-watering levels they are at now. I asked him recently if he could ever see an end to the huge disparity between the money at the top and bottom of football and his answer was very interesting. 'Not while we have three governing bodies in the game. The Premier League and the EFL are essentially completely separate organisations so where's the real incentive for the Prem to share their money? Because there's really nothing that the EFL or the FA can promise them in return.'

In Gary's heyday, matchdays were pretty much the only source of income for all 92 clubs, so there wasn't that much money to go round and, in general, for three decades after Jimmy Hill's triumph footballers' wages were still only slightly higher than the average worker. If anyone was responsible for the mega-riches of today's players it wasn't Jimmy Hill, it was Rupert Murdoch. It was Sky's broadcasting deal with the newly formed Premier League in 1992 that led us to the situation West Park Rovers are in now, having to shell out millions of pounds to buy a player and tens of thousands a week to keep him. Still, with any luck, we'll do alright in the Premier League, so hopefully we won't have to go through the complicated process of buying a human being for quite some time.

ME AND MY BIG MOUTH

One of my grandads was incredibly superstitious: no walking under ladders, no stepping on cracks, no passing on the stairs, the lot. It must have been a nightmare for him because he worked on a building site all his life, right up until the time he broke his leg tripping over a black cat on Friday the 13th. He would also never tempt fate by wishing for things out loud. I clearly broke that rule and annoyed the universe by hoping out loud that we could stay up with minimal additions to the squad because we are going to have to buy a *lot* of players. Despite a decent start to the season when we took four points off Liverpool and Manchester United, and they said on *Match of the Day* that we would definitely not go down, we definitely/probably/certainly could. That run of six games without a win in the lead-up to Christmas has left us in trouble and if we don't win the New Year Bank Holiday game tomorrow we could be in the bottom four.

I've done it again! Why did I say that out loud? We're in the bottom four. With half a season left we're just a point above the relegation zone and the fans are very fed up with hearing me say we would have taken 17th at the start of the season. Guy, Kieran, Miranda and I have an emergency meeting this afternoon, because we have two very difficult decisions to make. Firstly, do we spend our way out of this and basically panic-buy enough quality players in the January transfer window to keep us up? Secondly, do we trust that Malky Porter is still the right manager or do we listen to the advice of 15,000 fans who seem to be of the opinion that he don't know what he's doing? And to be fair to them, it did seem a bit odd to take off our only decent striker when we went two-nil down, although Malky can't be blamed for our keeper backheeling the ball into his own net for the second goal.

Right, that's that. We've sacked the manager. Or, as the press release says, 'We've reluctantly parted company with a loyal servant who has guided West Park Rovers to the greatest success in our history.' It was reluctant, too. I imagine anyone who has ever sacked Michael Gove enjoyed it immensely, but no one wants to kick a mate out of a job, especially when they realise how much it's actually going to cost them to sack him.

Flush from our promotion to the Premier League, we offered Malky a new contract back in July and it still has two-and-a-half years to run, so that salary is what he will walk away with. He has not been dismissed for gross misconduct and so will not lose his basic income, excluding bonuses, which costs us about £4 million. Blimey, that's a lot of money and the next manager will definitely be staying for a *long* time! Makes you wonder how much serial sackers Chelsea have spent on severance deals in the past few years.

Under Roman Abramovich's Chelsea reign, which started in 2003, the club spent £127 million on managerial payoffs and compensation fees to other clubs. That's before the new owners sacked Thomas Tuchel and replaced him with Brighton's Graham Potter, which cost an estimated £47 million and still sets Kieran off crying.

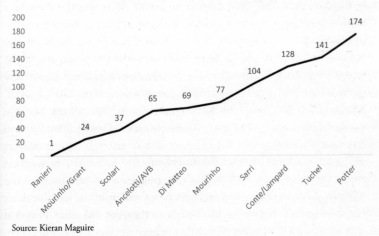

Chelsea Cost of Managerial Changes £m

Source: Kieran Maguire

Those eye-watering figures haven't equated to recent success and are a source of comfort for some. Or even a sauce of comfort. I've known TV chef Ainsley Harriott since he was knee-high to a goal post and he loves Arsenal even more than he loves Percy Pepper.

Just after their valiant but ultimately doomed attempt to fend off Manchester City in the 2022/23 title race I asked him if he thought Arsenal could ever truly compete with the mega-rich clubs. He said, 'You have to believe, Kevin. The really big clubs don't always get it right with their money or their manager'. Then he laughed. A lot.

Right, where was I? Ah, yes. Now all we have to do is find a new gaffer. Although just between you and me, we'd done that already. It's amazing how many fans genuinely believe that a club can sack the manager on Monday then somehow manage to identify a replacement, approach his current club for permission to speak to him and negotiate the deal that enables Sky Sports to film him arriving at the training ground on the Wednesday. The truth is, though, we've been aware of the work of Manuel Borachio for some time now. His combination of flair and grit has worked wonders at several European clubs, especially Anderlecht, where he is now (well, until Wednesday).

The tapping-up of managers is as frowned upon as the tapping-up of players, so I would like to categorically state that everything has been above board. Yes, Miranda may have bumped into Manuel in Eurostar's first-class departure lounge in Brussels and it's true that Kieran may have had dinner with his agent in London a couple of weeks back, but it was Christmas and Kieran's a very sociable chap. Besides, he swears blind that the only thing they talked about was Joy Division and The Smiths, who turn out to be surprisingly popular in Portugal. Anderlecht were surprisingly good about it as well when that journalist from *Le Soir* asked them about the rumours that Manuel had been approached by an unnamed Premier League team who may or may not be hovering just above the relegation zone.

All water under the bridge: Manuel Borachio is the new manager of West Park Rovers, a club he has always admired and relishes the opportunity to manage, yadda-yadda. But he didn't come cheap. As *Le Soir* wrote, 'Il a couté un bras et une jambe.' As did the two coaches he wanted to bring with him and as will those players on his transfer wishlist, which no way did he actually email us on Christmas Eve. And I am perfectly happy to accept the pure coincidence that every single player on that list has the same agent as him.

Which brings us nicely to the other of those two big decisions. Stick or twist? Shit or bust? Do we make a calculated gamble that a huge short-term investment will reap dividends by maintaining our status in the league that offers most in potential and ongoing financial rewards? Or do we ignore Manuel's wishlist and offer him the time and resources to get us back up again if we do get relegated?

Whatever way you describe it, we face a dilemma that could affect not just what happens to us this season, but what happens to us in the next 10. In other words, we have to make a decision now that we are highly unlikely to still be around to see the results of in a decade or so. It's a big responsibility, especially as we have always spoken of being only the stewards of this club, looking after its interests for the sake of the club and its fans rather than ourselves. Sometimes I wish we hadn't been quite so honourable in public. If it works, then another year in the Premier League is worth £95 million minimum in broadcast money, plus we get a third year of parachute payments instead of two. That's worth a gamble, surely?

OK, decision made. If we were 10 points from safety then our hands would stay in our pocket, we'd make the usual statement about fighting to the last whistle of the last match and start planning budgets for life back in the Championship. But we're not even in the bottom three and we have a couple of winnable home games coming up against the teams just above us. Miranda is on the phone to the super-agent as we speak and we're all learning a bit of Portuguese to welcome in our new players.

Luckily, we still have three weeks of the transfer window left. Unluckily, everybody knows we are now in the market and will be bunging a few million on the asking price and, even worse, we are in for three weeks of pointless speculation on Sky Sports as they desperately try to fill 24 hours of live TV by linking us with a move for half the players in Europe and most of the players in Portugal.

WINDOW PAIN

Ah, the transfer window: an attempt to do the decent thing that has been turned into a spectator sport accompanied by a giant clock counting down with the dramatic words that there are only 81 days, 34 minutes and seven, six, five, four, three, two, one seconds to go until transfer deadline day. I'm convinced that productivity rates in offices and factories go down and accident rates on the streets go up as people refresh their laptops and phones every 10 minutes to check umpteen websites for more information gleaned from podcasts or blokes in pubs. I once got very excited when the *Mail Online* reported that a Crystal Palace insider was hopeful they were about to sign a 20-goal-a-season striker until it turned out that the insider was actually me responding to a question in a talkSPORT radio interview about the sort of player we were hoping to sign!

At the start, Premier League clubs could buy or sell players at any stage of the season up to 31 March. It was thought that allowing clubs to do transfer business after that date could lead to the wealthier ones buying players on very short-term contracts to make a late title challenge or try to avoid relegation. According to the Premier League's own history, 'That was not really in the spirit of a season-long league campaign,' which is odd because you'd think that with only five weeks of the season left, clubs would already be in a position to know just what they needed to do to either mount that challenge or stave off that relegation.

In Europe most leagues already had transfer windows at the suggestion of UEFA, who felt that allowing players to move at will at any time would undermine the footballing economy (i.e. Barcelona, Real Madrid and Bayern Munich could buy your star player at any time) and remove the incentive for clubs to develop young talent, because what was the point if Barcelona, Real Madrid and Bayern Munich could also buy *them* at any point as well.

In 2002 the Premier League decided to follow suit and introduced the two domestic transfer windows: summer and winter. As ever, their reasons were purely altruistic. Firstly, to 'enable managers to plan for a set period of time' even though most managers, especially of the big clubs, were furious that their option of a short-term solution had been taken from them. Secondly, 'it gives the opportunity for younger players to play if there are injuries or drops in form from established first-team members whereas before the temptation would always be to go and buy a replacement.' Most big clubs saw a way round that immediately.

They simply spent the windows buying enough players to make sure they wouldn't have to turn to the youngsters. The third reason given by the Premier League is my favourite: 'It is good for fans as well.' Why? Well, 'knowing that your squad is settled for at least two chunks of the season means they can invest in those players, emotionally and with that other modern phenomenon: names on the back of shirts.'

So there you are. One of the reasons we have a transfer window is that you don't have to deal with a shell-shocked nine-year-old when his or her favourite player is transferred the day after they have spent their birthday money getting his name on a shirt. But if the transfer window is good for your child, it still has plenty of critics in the grown-up world. As Graham Potter, then manager of Brighton and Hove Albion, said on 2 September 2022 about his relief at the transfer window closing: 'There are only 13 games until the next one!'

It's the January window that gets most criticism from football heavyweights like FIFA President Gianni Infantino and legendary ex-Arsenal manager Arsène Wenger. Among many things they argue that the January window is mainly a massive opportunity for the biggest clubs in Europe to circulate players among themselves at vastly inflated prices.

The original aim of allowing young players to shine is shown to be nonsense. Chelsea, for example, have a warehouse full of very good young talent, but you can guarantee that every January they will strengthen their ranks with three or four world-class players rather than whistle up one of the kids.

And your nine-year-old may be happy now, but if he supports a club outside the Premier League he or she is likely to spend the entire month of January unable to sleep for fear that their favourite player will be sold from under them, leaving them with only a faded name on a shirt as a childhood memory. Indeed, you could argue that fans of lower league clubs who have bought a season ticket are not getting full value if two of their best players are sold in January and there's no time to spend the money on replacements. The main argument is that, notwithstanding a severe injury crisis (and emergency transfers are already available if so), the summer transfer window should be enough to build your squad to begin with. There are also some players who argue that any transfer window system restricts their freedom of movement, but this chapter is long enough as it is without getting into that argument.

In fact, it's probably a metaphor for something that this chapter on the Premier League is already dominating this book on football finance, but I need to help Miranda get on with signing some players before the window slams shut and then watching them try to keep West Park Rovers in the Premier League. Yes, Miranda, I have turned my bloody phone off.

11

EUROPE

Away days

Wilkommen! Bienvenu! Yassas! Dzień Dobry! Dia dhuit agus failte! Alright my son, we are going on a European tour! Bloody hell, sticking a pin in that list of managers then panic-buying half a new team in three days in January turned out to be a genius bit of strategic forward-thinking on our part, although Miranda, our CEO, has begged me not to say that again the next time a journalist asks me about that amazing post-new year run.

Far from going down, Senhor Borachio led us on a charge that culminated in a late equaliser at Stamford Bridge on the last day of the season, which took us up to seventh on goal difference and earned us a place in the UEFA Europa Conference League. Yes, I know, some people are calling it the Runners Up Runners Up Cup and, yes, there is every chance that Mickey Mouse wears a Europa Conference League watch, but it's a proper tournament and we are in it.

And before you sneer, how many of you have a job where you are actually paid to go to Liechtenstein for a couple of days to watch football? Producer Guy can't believe his luck and is hoping to visit a couple of his favourite bank accounts while we're there. Admittedly it's a bit of a schlep for our fans and they are going to find the beer expensive, but Vaduz, the capital, is a lovely place and the stadium will remind them of the old days back in tier eight of the English pyramid.

I went with a friend to see Liechtenstein play Latvia in a Euros group game (long story) and one clearance saw the ball land in a pond behind the open end of the stadium. And when Ireland played there a season or two later, visiting fans thought they were being taunted when the band played 'God Save the Queen', only to discover it's also the tune for the national anthem of Liechtenstein, only they call it 'Oben am jungen Rhein'. You see, that's two things you've learned already because of the Europa Conference. If you ever win a quiz because you knew which ground had a pond behind it and which country shares our national anthem, then you know who to thank.

It's not just the fans who have cost concerns. Those upcoming trips to Spain and Serbia are going to be expensive for all of us. And the fans don't get anything in return, apart from bragging rights down the pub – 'You buy the drinks, Terry. Me and Sonia spent all our money in Belgrade.'

The club will get €2,940,000 just for being in the group stage. Each victory in the group will net us €500,000 more and you get €166,000 for a draw. Which means, unpatriotic as it may be, Guy will now be watching the exchange rates charts like a hawk as a falling pound is good news for West Park Rovers. Win the group stage and that's another €650,000, thank you very much, or €325,000 if we are runners-up. Getting to the final and lifting the trophy will add another €8,900,000, so altogether we could be looking at about €14 million.

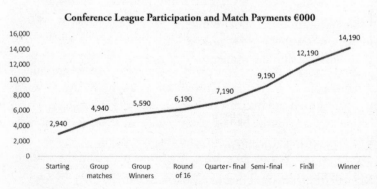

Conference League Participation and Match Payments €000

Source: Kieran Maguire

UEFA also have a series of pots of money that can add to our financial rewards. One is linked to how much domestic broadcasters pay for the rights to their competition (by the way, did I ever tell you how much I love you, BT?). We will earn more from this if we progress further than other English clubs in the Conference. So, Aston Villa, don't take this personally, but I wish you nothing but the worst on a Thursday night in Tirana.

There is also a 10-year coefficient payment, which ranks all 32 teams in the tournament in terms of their results in UEFA competitions over the last decade. Prize money is then allocated as shares, with the worst ranked club getting one share and the highest getting 32. Given that less than 10 years ago we were deciding whether or not we could afford a rope around the perimeter of the pitch, we will be bottom of this outrageously undemocratic distribution model and it only brings us €44,000. Hopefully though we will soon have enough years in Europe for me to upgrade 'outrageously undemocratic' to 'completely fair'.

And how much will it cost us to take part? For every yang there is a yin and chartering flights to Europe (we don't travel with riff-raff) is about £100,000 per match. Hotel rooms for the squad, backroom staff and suites for me, Kieran and Guy will be another £40,000, and coach travel from airport to hotel to stadium and back another £15,000. So seven matches in getting to the final is going to cost us a million, and then there are the player and management bonuses.

Annoyingly, UEFA don't seem to have realised that it costs just as much for women's teams to travel to away games in Europe, so perhaps the prize money should be the same. Sadly not. Or perhaps I should say, of course not. Winning the men's Champions League in 2022 was worth €119.8 million to Real Madrid. Lyon, who beat Barcelona to claim the women's trophy, only earned €1.4 million by comparison.

CONTINENTAL DIVIDES

Most English football fans when asked to name the country's most influential club in European football will probably suggest Manchester United for that first European Cup win in 1968 (while, of course, acknowledging that the wonderful Lisbon Lions of Celtic were the first British team to win it the year before) or Liverpool for their six European Cup/Champions League wins. Nottingham Forest fans will obviously point to their back-to-back European Cup wins in 1979 and 1980, and the occasional Cockney might suggest Spurs for being the first English team to win a major European trophy when they lifted the Cup Winners' Cup in 1963, although the historically minded will add that in 1909 West Auckland travelled from the north east of England all the way to Turin to beat Juventus and win the Sir Thomas Lipton Trophy, arguably the first ever international competition.

Fans of obscure quiz questions will point out that Birmingham City and a London XI took part in the first ever Inter-Cities Fairs Cup in 1955. That was an odd concept for a tournament, because teams could only compete if their city had hosted a trade fair, and the winning team received the splendidly named Noel Beard Trophy. It's wrongly thought to be the predecessor of the UEFA Cup, but, as it was actually organised by a FIFA-led committee, UEFA still refuse to acknowledge it as one of their competitions. Mind you, I wouldn't tell that to Newcastle fans as their victory in 1969 is still their only European win.

For me, though, the answer is Wolverhampton Wanderers. In 1953 the first floodlights were installed at Molineux* and, in order to recoup some of the costs, Wolves, then champions of England, arranged some high-profile friendlies against glamorous opposition like Racing Club of Buenos Aries, Celtic and Spartak Moscow. The biggest, however, was against Honved of Budapest in December 1954. They were not only one of the greatest club sides on the continent, they also supplied half the players in the Hungary team that had humiliated England the year before, beating them 6–3 at Wembley and 7–1 in Budapest. Billy Wright, captain of Wolves, had played for England in both games. After the first game, the *Guardian* said England had been given 'a severe lesson in the arts of Association Football' and the *Times* said that Wright played like 'a fire engine going to the wrong fire.'

---

* I wonder what the minimum requirements were back then? A 'pylon' and 'some searchlights left over from the war' would be my guess.

So on that night in Wolverhampton revenge was in the air and the press had called for Wolves to prove that English football still ruled the world. The game, a friendly, remember, attracted a crowd of around 54,000 and was considered so significant that the BBC showed the second half live on TV, which was an honour previously only reserved for FA Cup finals. Wolves won the game 3–2 and the English press responded with its usual modest understatement. The *Daily Express* went with 'English football is the genuine, unbeatable article... the best in the world.' The simple headline in the *Mirror* was 'Wolves the Great', but it was the *Daily Mail* that inadvertently set in motion the events that eventually led to West Park Rovers qualifying for the group stages of the Europa Conference League. They said that in beating Honved, Wolves were now 'champions of the world'.

In Paris, Gabriel Hanot, ex-French international footballer and now editor of sporting newspaper *L'Équipe*, disagreed: 'Before we declare that Wolverhampton are invincible, let them go to Moscow and Budapest, Milan and Real Madrid.' UEFA liked the idea and, with suggestions from Hanot, a list of 16 teams was drawn up to be invited to take part in the first ever European Cup competition in 1955. Chelsea, the new league champions, were to be the team from England, but the FA and the Football League banned them from taking part, arguing that it would disrupt the domestic season and that Wolves had just proved we were the best anyway, so what was the point? Plus, I am sure, they also said that the food was terrible and no one over there spoke English, so it's not for us, thank you. They soon changed their minds, however, allowing Manchester United to take part in the European Cup the following year, a tournament that became dominated by Real Madrid for the first decade, but which since then has been rich pickings for English teams.

As a kid, I loved the European Cup. There was something pure about the fact it was a simple knockout competition contested only by the teams who had won their country's league title. And the champions of England could just as easily meet the champions of Germany in the first round as the champions of Malta. And the names – oh the names! Not just the great teams of legend like Benfica, Bayern Munich, Ajax, and Real Madrid, but Carl Zeiss Jena of East Germany, Wacker Innsbruck of Austria, Viking of Norway and Jeunesse of Luxembourg, all wearing different and exotic kits to drool over when we finally got a colour TV.

Never ones to miss out on potential ways to make money, UEFA soon added the UEFA Cup for teams who had finished second, third or fourth in their league, and the Cup Winners' Cup for, well you can work that one out for yourself. So why did those exciting and unpredictable cup tournaments become league tournaments and why did UEFA decide to add a third one in the shape of the Conference? Spoiler alert: the answer is money, broadcasting and keeping the big clubs happy.

UEFA has to answer to a variety of stakeholders. The elite clubs, who thought (and privately still think) that the European Super League Franchise Competition was a good idea, want guaranteed revenues. They know that while it is possible to lose a match over two legs to a lesser talented team, over six matches, or eight from 2024, there is a much greater chance of making it through to the next stage of the competition. Also, by having a seeding system the big clubs are kept apart in the early stages of the competition and, therefore, once again they are more likely to make it through to the later, more lucrative, rounds, which generate higher viewing figures and more money for the elite.

The European Cup final in 1991, for example, was between Red Star Belgrade and Marseille. Both qualified for the competition by virtue of winning their domestic leagues. Neither of them are likely to be on Florentino Perez's wish list for Super League Version II, coming to you at some point over the next few years if he and his cronies get their way. The 10-year coefficient is similar to parachute payments in the sense that it gives clubs extra money for prior achievements. Therefore, in the 2022/23 Champions League, Real Madrid, with 32 shares, 'earned' €36.4 million and Maccabi Haifa, with just one share as the lowest ranked club, €1.1 million.

The Champions League is where we hope to be one day, because that's where the real glamour lies. And the real money. And you don't have to play on a Thursday. I don't know why, but for some reason Thursday just doesn't feel like a football day, even in the bright lights of downtown Vaduz. And the Thursday, Europa Conference/ Sunday, Premier League routine is really going to stretch our squad, which means, guess what, Manuel Borachio our Portuguese manager has already presented us with a list of Portuguese players that he reckons his Portuguese agent could attract to the club if only the British owners are willing to cough up a considerable amount of money. We don't want to throw away all that hard work it took to stay up for the lack of a player or two, he says. What if the Vaduz players get really physical and injure a couple of the fringe players who finally get a game when we play them, he says.

All valid points, but Guy and Miranda have pointed out to him that there may be players available in, I don't know, the Championship here, or, you never know, there may be a couple of gems in that academy of ours that I know for a fact Manuel has never actually visited. I will never get bored with being in the Premier League or Europe, but I never realised quite how relentless the constant search for the money to keep us there would be. Kieran and Guy insist that's because I never listened when they told me – and they have a point.

FUNDING GAP

We need to look for new ways to raise money before the season starts. As it happens, our contract with shirt sponsors Montague Insurance is coming to an end. They are very keen to renew it and Miranda is just as keen to allow them to renew it, but is less enthusiastic about the offer they've made to do so. Obviously we will be releasing a new kit for the new season, plus a rather natty fourth kit that we will only be wearing in Europe, so that's a handy bonus. Some of those new players Manuel is after also have some very long names, so that will bring the club shop a few bob when they print them on the shirts. However, Miranda reckons there is a lot more flexibility in the sponsorship deal, i.e. we can get much more money out of it than Montague are offering.

As usual, Miranda is right. While kit deals are commercially sensitive, some clubs do disclose more details than others. Manchester United are presently in the midst of a 10-year deal with Adidas that brings in a guaranteed £75 million and a commission on each sale, up to a maximum of £79 million. If the club fails to qualify for the Champions League two seasons in a row, or is relegated to the Championship, then Adidas can reduce the amount payable by up to 30%. Liverpool's deal with Nike is more incentivised. They are estimated to have an annual retainer of £30 million, but earn 20%

commission on each shirt sold (the average for other clubs is 7%). We can't ask for that sort of money, although, as it happens, we already know that there is someone willing to pay significantly more than Montague are offering, but it's given us a dilemma.

HKOK are an online gambling company based in the Far East. Where in the Far East they seem strangely reluctant to say, but Kieran reckons it's Macao. They are definitely a legitimate company, they seem to have members all over the world, their advertising campaign, fronted by a well-known hard man actor, is all over the telly and they have offered us nearly half as much again as Montague, so we have to take their approach seriously.

But, it just seems ever so slightly, I don't know, grubby. None of us co-owners are against gambling as such. I'll put a tenner on something in the 2.30 at Sandown, preferably a horse, but I don't bet on anything else and I don't have an account. Guy has the occasional flutter on football and Kieran is one of those terrible people who will bet on the other team to beat Brighton, just so he has at least some consolation.

It's the type of gambling that surrounds football which bothers us. The constant urge for (mainly) young men to bet again and again on the next goal, the next card, the next corner or on an accumulator consisting of an unlikely combination of all of them. It's the free credit offered to new customers; it's the money back as a free bet if you lose and the offering of 'best odds, guaranteed!' For all the accompanying warnings to 'gamble responsibly' and 'when the fun stops, stop' we are fully aware of the terrible social and mental health problems associated with gambling. So, for a club that publicly talks of its responsibility to the community, taking huge amounts of money from a company that, unknowingly or not, damages that very community, seems hypocritical to say the very least.

And it's not just the community. The PFA have some very stark warnings on the danger of gambling for players. The Players Foundation, their charitable organisation, reported that problem gambling was a 'root issue' in members seeking help with mental health. In fact, 15% of members contact the organisation for gambling addiction issues directly and 44% who have low mood or anxiety issues say gambling is usually the trigger.

What is really baffling is just how little football actually makes from the gambling industry, while that industry makes vast amounts of money from football. Mind you, getting clear figures from the gambling industry is challenging. Many publish their 'revenue' as being the difference between the amount wagered in total, less the amount paid out. If you toss a coin 100 times and call heads or tails, betting £1 on each bet, with a £2 pay-out if you're successful, that means you've wagered £100. You will probably have won or lost a very small amount of money though, so using wagers is an imperfect metric.

Gambling companies are, however, loathe to disclose the amount of wagers they generate from punters, with one exception: Bet365. As I've said previously, Bet365 are a very successful company and their owners, the Coates family, have done many positive things for the local community and elsewhere. In 2000, when Bet365 started trading, they generated £90 million in wagers. By 2019 this had increased to over £64 billion, about half of the NHS budget that year. Kieran presented these figures to an All Party Parliamentary Group on gambling in sport in 2020. By an amazing coincidence, Bet365 stopped publishing its wager totals from 2020 onwards, but if the profit margin, which for Bet365 was about 5%, was applied to the other members of the 'Big Four' gambling companies – Flutter, Entain and William Hill – their collective wagers earned would exceed £200 billion, of which football is a significant element.

There's nothing inherently wrong with gambling (if it's controlled, which is a big if) and it's perfectly legal, but the betting companies involved are the ones to gain most from the formation of the Premier League and the Champions League. I am totally opposed to prohibition. It doesn't work and encourages criminality, but the industry could do more to help both gamblers and the football industry itself.

Horse racing is another sport that attracts gambling and there is a gambling levy of 10% on operators' profits from horseracing bets. This has raised as much as £90 million in a single year and football betting exceeds horseracing, so if there is political will then football could benefit from at least £100 million a year. I think most of us would be slightly less uneasy about the issue if we knew that much money was coming into the game, particularly if it was directed towards grassroots football or used to help those struggling with gambling addictions. Sadly, there is no political will. The gambling industry and politicians on all sides have a very amicable relationship.

Just look at the Register of Members' Financial Interests to see how often MPs are entertained by the industry.

Seven out of the current 20 Premier League clubs have shirts sponsored by gambling companies. The Championship and Leagues One and Two are sponsored by a gambling company, and many top clubs here and in Europe have official betting partners. Of course, in the current economic climate, gambling is one of the few industries that has the money available to sponsor top-flight football, but there are also practical reasons for our misgivings.

Firstly, having a gambling company as the main shirt sponsor means that we need to find a separate sponsor for the youth team shirts and the ones that we sell to our younger fans because, by law, they can't have a gambling brand on them. We sell too many of them to consider plain shirt fronts for the little darlings and we've got thousands of young fans, so it would be a waste to not use them as tiny advertising hoardings. Secondly, the climate is definitely turning against sponsorship from gambling companies, just as it did in recent years when sponsorship by tobacco companies and alcohol brands were eventually banned. In 2022, the government announced plans to phase out gambling sponsorship, but then backed down and suggested that football looks at a voluntary ban. The Premier League announced a voluntary ban on front-of-shirt gambling sponsorship in early 2023, but the ban only comes into effect in the 2026/27 season. Shirt sleeve gambling sponsorship is still allowed, as is perimeter advertising. There is no similar ban proposed in either the EFL or Scottish football.

Finally, we are very keen that our men and women's team carry the same sponsor, but HKOK are already adamant that the numbers who watch our women's team don't justify that, so we would need to find a separate sponsor there, although we could do a deal that covers the shirts for the women and the club shop kiddies. Figures for those women's teams who have separate sponsor deals are very sketchy, but Newcastle United's men's team was sponsored by Fun88, for an estimated £8 million a year, whereas the women's team announced a deal with local construction company Straightline NE Ltd, likely to be in the thousands of pounds.

What to do, what to do? Turn down HKOK is what to do. In the end it was an easy decision. We are one of the clubs who declined the opportunity to offer our fans another way to lose money by 'investing' in fan tokens or Socios, so it would have been odd to embrace actual gambling just a season after.

Just a reminder: what Socios offer is also perfectly legal. Fan tokens can be bought, using their own cryptocurrency, the Chiliz (or $CHZ for you kids in the know). You can buy $CHZ by depositing 'real' money into your Socios account and these are used to buy tokens. The tokens can be used to predict results, influence polls, earn rewards and so on. The more you deposit, the more influence you can potentially have. According to Socios' own marketing, this helps you to be 'more than a fan' and there is a lot of talk of 'engagement', 'utility' and so on. Individual clubs have their individual tokens, too, which you can buy with $CHZ. Arsenal launched their token in November 2021. By September 2022 it had fallen in value by two-thirds and it is by no means the worst performing on the market.

If fans want West Park Rovers to play a song by S Club 7 at the half-time break or name the club mascot Dobermann Dave, then I'm more than happy for them to email me their preferences or shout them out to me after a match instead of just yelling about how rubbish the team had been. I do not feel comfortable asking them to do the same thing for money via a convoluted process.

Besides, Montague Insurance upped their offer slightly and are only too glad to carry on sponsoring the women and the kiddies; not only that but I reckon our shirts are too classy to have a gambling brand on, even though some of our fans think the introduction of a new shirt for European games is slightly less classy. They'll thank me when they run out of Christmas present ideas in a couple of months' time.*

Speaking of which, the club shop has taken on a life of its own. Long gone are the days when Jean sold a few bits of green and black tat from that hole in the wall with the corrugated shutter. These days, it's not even a shop, it's a 'store', a 'retail outlet that should be an essential part of your matchday experience' containing

---

*Cat lovers will be pleased to know we still have Feliway as our secondary sponsors. Turns out that since lockdown ended there's a lot of money in the feline anxiety business.

'everything you need to show your support for the club you love and wear your colours with pride.' I would argue that you don't actually 'need' a West Park Rovers autograph book or official West Park Rovers shinpads, all sizes available. And I reckon even the most fashion-conscious 10-year-old could do without a temporary tattoo sheet, even if it does include a green and black union flag and a fierce-looking Rover the Dog. Nevertheless, you can't argue with success. There's always a queue on matchday, so I'm happy, and with figures like these so are Kieran and Guy. On a matchday we hope for a footfall (get me with the management lingo) of about 3000 to 4000 fans through the store. If they spend an average of £25 each, then that's £100,000 gross and about £2 million a year. A lot of that goes in wages and the cost of buying the merchandise, but overall we should be clearing half a million pounds from the shop.

I'm less happy with those blokes selling half and half scarves outside the ground on a matchday. To be honest I'm baffled by the whole concept of half and half scarves anyway, but who are these blokes and where are they getting the scarves from, because they don't look like knitters. And why aren't we stopping them? Not just them, but I had a quick walk down our local high street the other day and counted at least three stalls selling hooky West Park Rovers merchandise. The black stripes were alright but the green stripes were a colour I could only describe as Kermit with a hangover. I should have challenged the stallholders I know, but I was on my way to lunch and, to be honest, they looked like quite hard blokes, so I've passed their location to our retail manager. She'll sort them out.

We're not the most glamorous club in the league, so it's not a huge problem for us, but unofficial or, if you prefer, fake merchandise can cost the bigger clubs a lot of money. It is difficult to generate accurate numbers, as counterfeiters are not known for completing accurate tax returns, but the global fake goods market is estimated to be worth £400 billion – which does make me wonder whether we're in the wrong business… Perhaps I should ask Uncle Terry.

THE RIGHT IMAGE

It can also cost players a lot of money as well. Image rights have always been part of football, it's just that for the first century or so they weren't called that. In the 1930s, superstar striker Dixie Dean's image was used to advertise Carreras cigarettes – 'the cigarette with a kick in them'. In the 1950s Denis Compton's face was all over a Brylcreem hair oil campaign and in the 1960s, while hardman full-back George Cohen was earning a few bob for telling us that Elliman's Athletic Rub was 'vital and stimulating' for his tired legs, George Best was putting *his* name to products ranging from aftershave to sausages, pausing only to do a commercial for eggs in the meantime. He was just a rasher away from the breakfast hat-trick.

Not long after they won the World Cup for England in 1966, Martin Peters and Bobby Moore were the stars of a cinema advert for pubs. Not a specific pub, pubs in general, which according to Bobby, were a 'great place to meet the wife.' So it went on through Kevin Keegan splashing Brut all over to Gary Lineker earning millions flogging us crisps and Gareth Southgate advertising pizza just days after his penalty miss saw England lose the semi-final of Euro 96.

Some big clubs now can have upwards of 70 commercial partners across the globe and all of them will want to tap into the selling power that a star name like Cristiano Ronaldo or Harry Kane will bring. Finally, even West Park Rovers have reached the stage where we are buying the level of player whose agent wants a separate contract for commercial activities and image rights – which is where it gets complicated.

If our star striker, let's call him Christophe Magnier, because that's his name, or his agent realises that Rovers want to feature him more heavily than other players in commercial deals (which we do, because he's a handsome bugger and very charming) then it makes perfect sense for us to make a special arrangement with the image rights company his agent has set up; especially as our standard employment contract states that he, or his image, must be available for various sponsor promotions, but only to the same extent as other players are.

So we do a deal whereby 80% of the money we pay him each year is considered as salary, but the other 20% is considered as payment to his image rights company. The problem – or benefit if you're the player – is that the 80% salary is taxed at a rate of 45% through HMRC's pay as you earn (PAYE) scheme, but the payment to the image rights company is subject to corporation tax of just 19%. Not only that, but the club doesn't have to pay National Insurance of 13.8% on the image rights money, so if a club has a lot of players on separate image rights contracts then everyone can save a lot of money each season.

It also means that HMRC began to wonder whether all these players with image rights deals actually had much of an image to make a deal with in the first place, or whether this was just a tax-avoidance scheme. According to Daniel Geey, a partner in the Sports Group at law firm Sheridans, in 2010 HMRC investigated a large number of clubs and almost all Premier League clubs entered into settlement arrangements. He says, 'Many paid large sums to resolve the matter.'

According to Kieran Maguire, who needs no introduction, HMRC are a bit more relaxed these days. They understand that the Premier League is a huge global brand and that the top players are offered fortunes for off-field activities, so as long as a club can justify paying a certain amount per year through image rights companies – and a maximum of 20% is deemed to be a fair figure – then they are happy to nod it through. Or, as Kieran more succinctly puts it, 'If we don't take the piss they'll leave us alone.'

But it's not just HMRC who are keeping their beady eye on image rights payments. The Premier League and UEFA seem to be very aware that such payments could be used as a way round FFP regulations. They certainly form part of UEFA's long running legal battle with Manchester City. The club sold their players' image rights to a third party for £24.5 million, a lump sum that helped their 2012/13 financial results comply with UEFA's financial regulations, except UEFA disagreed. They claimed the sale artificially inflated City's income and in 2017 declared their belief that City were still making millions from image rights they claim to have sold and were therefore in breach of all sorts of rules. UEFA and City's battle was long and expensive in terms of legal fees for both parties. The Premier League have now also charged Manchester City with breaches of financial rules and that will also result in lawyers cheerfully thumbing through Range Rover brochures and booking an extra Caribbean holiday.

So our more marketable players are being paid properly for those lovely pictures of them proudly wearing our club shirt, but as those shirts are not now embossed with the brand name of HKOK we are still looking for new ways of improving our short-term income. Barely a month goes by without Lincoln City issuing shares in order to release funds, so, as the Imps are a team that Kieran thinks is exceedingly well run, maybe that's an option we also need to explore?

On 23 August 2018, Manchester United plc became the first football club in the world to be worth $4 billion dollars as their share price finished that day at a record high of $24.60 on the New York Stock Exchange. Unfortunately, as the small print always says, investments can go down as well as up and, my word, they certainly have gone down. By the summer of 2022 the Manchester United share price had fallen to an all-time low of $10.41, not only valuing the club's shares at 'just' $1.7 billion, but also being worth substantially less than when the Glazer family first listed United on the New York Stock Exchange a decade earlier. Within a year Manchester United's shares were trading at as high as $27 each after the Glazer family announced they were open to 'strategic alternatives' in terms of finding potential new owners.

In the 1980s and 90s it became quite fashionable for clubs to raise money by becoming a public company listed on the Stock Exchange and selling shares. Spurs, Millwall,* Sheffield United, Southampton and Hearts were just a few of many whose eyes turned into cartoon-like dollar signs at the thought of the riches to come. Within 20 years most of them had gone private again, 'chastened', as Kieran once wrote, 'by their experience of the additional scrutiny and costs of being members of the stock exchange.'

STOCKS AND SHARES

So what are the pros and cons of floating on the Stock Exchange and raising money through a share issue? Public companies can issue shares to anyone, through what is called an initial public offering (IPO), whereby the company publishes a prospectus, where it sets out its intentions in terms of a business strategy and budget. The benefit to the club is that it can raise money from anyone and

---

*At one stage Millwall had 78 billion shares in issue, each one worth two-hundredths of a penny each.

everyone, thereby broadening the number of people who are willing to invest and raising more money to be spent on the playing squad, improved facilities for fans and so on. The benefit to shareholders of buying shares in a public company is that they can easily sell their shares on the open market and know the price of those shares from day to day.

From a fan's point of view they could own anything from a single share in the club upwards. The shareholders are not, however, involved in the day-to-day running of the club and are not consulted on strategic or operational decisions, which are delegated to the board of directors and the manager/coach. Therefore, if a fan thinks that buying 100 shares in their favourite club will allow them to have a say in transfer, ticket price and away shirt colour policy they are wrong. They need to buy Socios for that sort of thing.

There are significant downsides to being a publicly quoted football club. The club is subject to greater compliance costs, as it is necessary to abide by the rules set down by the relevant stock exchange, as well as more complex and detailed company law requirements. Millwall estimated these costs to be about £100,000 a year when they made the decision to return to being a private company in 2011. The club may have to answer to analysts and commentators in the media to a greater degree on its financial dealings. Analysts give advice to their clients as to which companies they should invest in and so tend to want to know the intricacies of the club's finances. The club directors may feel this is time wasted and prefer to focus on running the club rather than being grilled and observed with keen interest by a bunch of bankers. The majority of shares in publicly quoted companies are owned by institutions, such as pension funds and insurance companies. These shareholders have little interest in the club as a sporting institution; their aim is to maximise a short-term financial return rather than the longer-term success of the club.

For an owner, going public means potentially losing control of the club. The Glazers at Manchester United have prevented this by having two types of shares in the club. Class A shares carry one vote each and are the ones traded on the New York Stock Exchange. Class B shares carry 10 votes each and are owned by the Glazers. This allowed the Glazers to generate £140 million in 2012 by taking United public. Half of this was used to pay down debt and the other half went to the Glazers. The A shares represent about 25% of the total number of shares in Manchester United, but carry just 3% of the votes. This allows the Glazers, provided they do not fall out with each other, to make whatever decisions they see fit without worrying too much about unhappy third-party investors.

As a club owner I really like the sound of dividends. Manchester United's owners, the Glazer family, have paid shareholders, mainly themselves, £165 million in dividends and in 2011 the Oyston family, owners of Blackpool, newly promoted to the Premier League, paid themselves £11 million. The fans of both clubs were, and still are, furious, with huge protests from both. So, as responsible owners who would, of course, immediately reinvest any dividends back into the club, I reckon the share option is more trouble than it's worth. Yes, I would think differently if the dividends were quietly sneaked into my own bank account.

EUROPE – THE FINAL COUNTDOWN

Now, there comes a time when even the most hard-working club owners and CEOs need to step back from the everyday money worries and just try to enjoy the football – and the sangria. West Park Rovers are just weeks away from our first ever European game, a home tie against Villareal AKA El Submari Groguet – the Yellow Submarine, a club not much bigger than us but one with an illustrious recent history in Europe. It may be polite to do a little bit of research about the game in Spain and the other major countries on the continent before they arrive. And perhaps we should get some tapas in to make them feel welcome.

It's a cliché that Spanish football is dominated by the two teams of Barcelona and Real Madrid, but in fact only nine teams have ever won La Liga since its inception in 1927, and, taking out Atlético, only six teams from outside Barcelona and Madrid have been champions. In the same period, 20 different teams have won the title in England.

Spain has its own football pyramid, but with two main differences. Firstly, their third tier (equivalent to our League One) is Segunda Division B and it has 80 teams, split into four divisions of 20 teams, and the fourth tier (our League Two) has 360 teams split into 18 regional groups. The promotion and relegation play-off system is really complicated, but I reckon even the most patriotic director of Villareal won't be too upset if I haven't mastered the intricacies by the time we're sharing a sherry at half-time. The other big difference is that the reserve teams of the major sides also compete in the league system, but are not allowed in the same league as the first team, meaning that a reserve side has never competed in the top division.

Spanish football is not just dominated by the two giants, it's dominated by an obsessive interest in the finances of the two giants, and currently at one of them those finances can only be described as '*un completo y absoluto desastre*'. Barcelona lost €133 million before tax in 2020, a poor performance, but less than both Everton and Manchester City in the Premier League. Unlike either of those two clubs, Barcelona did not have billionaire owners who could underwrite those losses. Barcelona were hit very hard by Covid and the following year announced a €555 million loss, resulting in a lot of shit hitting a very big fan. Some of those losses were there for political reasons. The Barcelona ownership model, which is that of a fan-owned club, also involves voting for a president. Joan LaPorta was elected on a manifesto of spending money, but there was not much to spend. He therefore did what many presidents do and blamed the problems on his predecessor.

La Liga cost control rules are complex, especially for Google Translate, but basically, at the start of each season each club is told what their transfer and wage spend can be, based on recent financial performance. That's why Barcelona had to reduce their player spending on wages and transfers to just €97 million in 2021/22. This resulted in an exodus from the club, including losing Lionel Messi, among a series of big names.

Initially La Liga's financial boffins calculated that Barcelona's player budget for 2022/23 was going to be MINUS €144 million. The club therefore had to either cut costs (and even I know you can't have a negative wage bill) or increase the money coming into the club. Barcelona therefore announced a series of 'economic levers'. Few in the world of finance had heard of this phrase before, whereas many had heard of 'payday loans' with which the economic levers appeared to have a lot in common.

Barcelona sold part of their broadcasting and licensing rights to financial and media institutions. The good news is that this immediately brought in cash, which was used to increase the player budget, which suddenly shot up to €656 million. The bad news is that Barcelona will only receive a fraction of their rights for up to 25 years – so very much a case of paella today and pain tomorrow.

Employing the financial restraint of a lottery winner in a champagne hot-tub, Barcelona started signing players such as Raphinha from Leeds and Lewandowski from Bayern Munich. This prompted Bayern Munich coach Julian Nagelsmann to ruefully say, 'It's the only club in the world that can buy players without money. It's kind of weird and crazy.'

Barcelona have pulled off financial gymnastic routines of the highest degree of difficulty in order to continue signing players, presumably secure in the knowledge that no bank in Spain is ever going to call in their debts, but you do wonder how they are getting round the FFP rules in Spain, which normally seem to be rigorously applied.

French football seems to have as many leagues and divisions as they have cheeses and is one of the few where the title has been regularly won by a foreign team, in the shape of Monaco, albeit a foreign team from a mega-rich micro-state where everyone speaks French for the simple reason that it is actually surrounded by France. It may be some time before Monaco win Ligue Un again though, because if Spanish football is dominated by two teams, French football has recently come to be dominated by just the one in the shape of Paris St Germain. (Fans of other French teams may suggest that they are also a foreign team as well, being wholly owned by the Qatar government.)

PSG were only founded in 1970[*] and for the first three years were wholly owned by supporters, before being taken over first by a business consortium, then in 1991 by satellite TV company Canal +. Despite being slap-bang in the middle of the capital city of France, they were far from an overnight hit. In fact, for decades

---

[*] It's odd to think that despite the illustrious history of French football, Paris did not have an elite football team until 1970.

'Les Parisiennes' had the double-whammy of being hated *and* unsuccessful.

All that changed in 2011 when they were bought by Qatar Sports Investments (QSI), the sovereign wealth fund of the Emir of Qatar. Some people will argue that as they are owned by QSI, they are 'state-backed' rather than 'state-run', but QSI are wholly owned by the Qatar government, so it's a fine distinction and to all intents and purposes, like Manchester City and Abu Dhabi, and Newcastle United and Saudi Arabia, PSG are owned by Qatar.

And Qatar is one of the wealthiest countries on the planet, so it's not surprising that PSG's fortunes have changed since 2011, on and off the pitch. It may or may not be a coincidence that QSI began negotiations to buy the club at the same time as Qatar were one of the countries bidding to host the 2022 World Cup. And it may or may not be a coincidence that shortly before the vote took place in 2010, UEFA president Michel Platini met with the Emir and the Prime Minister of Qatar, then publicly declared he would be giving his backing to their campaign and not that of the USA. The World Cup duly went to Qatar and six months later so did PSG.

It's clear that Qatar acquired the club in order to establish some sort of footballing credentials in the decade before the World Cup was to take place in a country that has absolutely no footballing credentials, but right from the start they also declared their ambition to dominate French football and win the Champions League.

And, bugger me, they've spent a lot of money succeeding. Well, with the first part of the plan at least. A spend of roughly €1.3 billion has bought multiple Ligue Un wins, but, to date, no Champions League trophy. What it has also bought them, though, is almost constant UEFA scrutiny into their finances and their effect on FFP rules.

In 2013, PSG signed a huge sponsorship deal with the Qatar Tourism Authority (QTA) worth more than a €1 billion over five years, but backdated to cover the 2011/12 and 12/13 seasons, which conveniently wiped out their losses for that period. UEFA don't like payments that look like they come from a third-party and not the actual club owners, and they particularly don't like deals that look artificially inflated. Consequently, in 2014, UEFA's Club Financial Control Body halved the value of the deal, which meant

PSG's deficit was now more than double the amount allowed for FFP, and imposed transfer sanctions and a €60 million fine. God knows where they got the money to pay that!

In August 2017 PSG activated a €222 million release clause to bring in Neymar from Barcelona then took Kylian Mbappé on loan with the option to buy for €180 million over three instalments – good to know that even the wealthiest need to manage their cash flow sometimes. A fresh FFP investigation followed. In June 2018 UEFA cleared PSG of breaching the rules, but once again devalued the deal with the Qatar Tourism Authority and one with the Qatar National Bank. PSG appealed to the Court of Arbitration for Sport and won, but since then have realised their deal with the QTA may be more trouble than it's worth and, in a radical change of direction, have ditched it in favour of a massive deal with Qatar Airways as front-of-shirt sponsor, after a brief hiatus with hotel chain Accor. By an amazing coincidence the airline is part-owned by the Qatar Investment Authority.

For my generation, it was Italian football that really caught the imagination. A combination of cool kits and a kind of fascinating yet sinister glamour added to a win-at-all-costs mentality made their teams the ones our newspapers really wanted to see beaten by good old-fashioned English teams who were above the hair-pulling, little kicks and the moaning to the referee of the Italians.

Personally, I quite liked the dark arts. They made a pleasant change from the good old-fashioned and apparently more honest leg-breaking tackles we saw every week in the English game. Consequently, I was delighted when Channel 4 began to show live Italian games in 1992. They were accompanied by the Saturday morning highlights programme *Gazetta Football Italia*, an incredibly stylish espresso of a show that added to the country's reputation as the home of cool football.

At the time, Serie A was arguably the biggest league in the world and Italian clubs were probably the wealthiest in Europe, so they were able to pay the transfer fees and wages to attract international superstar players. Their own players were pretty good, too, which is why their teams won 17 European trophies between 1990 and 2010. But since Inter lifted the Champions League trophy in 2010, only two Italian teams have even reached the semi-final, and the year before that AC Milan and Inter sold two of the game's biggest names, Kaka and Zlatan Ibrahimovic to Real Madrid and Barcelona in a clear indication that Italian football was losing its cool appeal.

It's easy to identify where that process started. In 2006, the country was rocked by the match-fixing scandal known as *Calciopoli*, which involved Juventus, Fiorentina, AC Milan, Lazio and Reggina. An investigation into the finances of a football agency called GEA World uncovered evidence that they were leaning on officials in an attempt to influence the appointment of referees for big games, and offering financial inducements to both the officials and the refs.

In an historical irony of which I heartily approve, transcripts of recorded telephone conversations about referees were passed to newspapers by an unknown whistle-blower. Public outrage was followed by severe punishments, including fines, points deductions and expulsion from European tournaments. Juventus were hardest hit: they were stripped of two league titles and relegated to Serie B. Many individuals involved were banned from football for life or imprisoned. Interestingly, no blame was attached to any of the referees whose names were mentioned in the scandal.

It led to an orgy of 'I told you so' across Europe as club after club came forward to voice their suspicions about unlikely results against Italian teams in European tournaments going right back to the 1960s. Italian football still hasn't quite thrown off the taint of match-fixing, but there are other factors in the decline of Italian football in the past decade. The lack of success in Europe has seen crowds fall, leading to a loss of matchday income and that process is exacerbated by the fact that most Italian clubs don't own their own stadium, leaving them reluctant to invest in infrastructure and making them far less attractive to potential overseas investors. That's why Juventus recently took the decision to build their own new stadium, a choice less available to AC and Inter who share a ground.

Italian football has also way less appeal to broadcasters these days, which is not helped by the fact that Roma were the last team outside that big three to win the Scudetto and that was back in 2001, with Juventus winning it nine times in a row between 2011 and 2020. All of which means that Italy now rank last of the traditional big five, certainly in terms of spending power. And, yes, I do know that Napoli won the Scudetto in 2023 and Inter reached the Champions League final, but I'm not changing the whole chapter because of them!

In one of those countries, however, it seems that money is less important to fans than culture. Any British fan who goes to a game in Germany is invariably hugely impressed by the experience. Personally I prefer my flag displays and singing to be a little more spontaneous, but there is no doubt that the *tifos* and *choreos* of German games present a thrilling sight and sound.

The Bundesliga, of course, is dominated by the wealth and buying power of Bayern Munich – they've won the last 11 – but many Bayern fans consider them to be a Bavarian club not a German one, an attitude that makes them just as unpopular to other fans as their constant success does. In fact, German clubs tend to have very strong rivalries based on regional identity or historical connection. The centres of Dusseldorf and Cologne may be 26 miles apart, but one is on the left bank of the Rhine and one is on the right, which is more than enough reason for their football fans to continue an animosity that dates back to a battle in 1288 (and you thought the Scots had long memories!).

Borussia Dortmund, and Schalke 04 from the town of Gelsenkirchen, are almost adjacent to each other in the Ruhr region, for centuries the heart of German coal and steel production. Even the Bundesliga's own website describes games between them as 'the mother of all derbies' and notes how in 1969 two Schalke players were bitten by a police dog called Rex as they celebrated scoring a goal in the game at Dortmund. Rex is still a hero in the city. Not to be outdone, in the next game at Schalke, the home team were accompanied on to the pitch by two lions – actual lions, not Millwall players.

From a distance of 76 miles, even further apart than Palace and Brighton, Hamburg and Werder Bremen dislike each other so much that the *Nordderby* or Derby of the North is one of the few where alcohol is banned inside the ground; and in Berlin, Union fans consider themselves to represent the tough working-class values of the city with Hertha fans cast as the bourgeoise elite, so much so that when their stadium needed to be re-built in 2008/09 it was fans who did the building, with more than 2300 volunteers providing 140,000 hours of labour.

I know that because I've been to a game at Union Berlin's Stadion An der Alten Forest or, in English, the Old Forest Stadium. Not only was the atmosphere electric, but following a friendly against Crystal Palace a few seasons before, they even adopted a couple of our songs, so we felt right at home.

You get the picture: Germany is a very passionate football country where fans get very involved in the culture and politics of the game. Ticket prices are low and usually include free travel on public transport to the grounds, and, despite the fierce rivalries, crowd trouble is rare.

And as we have seen, pride in the culture of German football and its 51/49 ownership model is why, as we saw in Chapter 6, Bayern fans probably secretly admire RB Leipzig, because they are the only club hated more than they are.

One thing clear from even a cursory glance at the current finances of clubs in Spain, Italy, Germany and France is that even the traditional powerhouses of the European game are being left behind by the growing economic muscle and global popularity of the English Premier League (as a glance at spending in the summer transfer window of 2022 will show) with broadcasting deals telling a similar story.

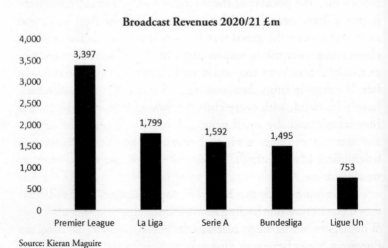

Broadcast Revenues 2020/21 £m

Source: Kieran Maguire

As a result of Juventus nearly always winning, Italian football now generates less than half of the amount made by the Premier League from broadcasting. The more unpredictable the outcome, the more sets of eyeballs are going to be watching matches on screens. PSG generate three times as much revenue as the second largest club in France, Lyon, and five times as much as the next biggest, Marseille. With such a financial advantage it is no wonder that PSG win nearly every tournament in France and this predictability does not attract viewers.

Those figures go part of the way to explaining why AC Milan, Atlético Madrid, Barcelona, Inter, Juventus and Real Madrid made up some of the clubs to announce the formation of a new mid-week competition, the Super League, in 2021. What it doesn't explain is why the other clubs were Arsenal, Chelsea, Liverpool, Manchester City, Manchester United and Spurs.

The Super League press release announcing the competition said the aim was 'to deliver the best outcomes for the new League and for football as a whole.' Not only that but 'the global pandemic has accelerated the instability in the existing European football economic model' and now 'a strategic vision and a sustainable commercial approach are required to enhance value and support for the benefit of the entire European football pyramid.'

All absolute bollocks, of course. The aim was to deliver more money into the pockets of the biggest clubs. It was so transparent it would have been banned on Brighton beach. And what was even worse than the greed was the arrogance which led to those clubs being completely unprepared for the apoplectic backlash, not only throughout the world of football but from their own fans – *especially* from their own fans. Some furious backtracking hastily followed, with every club involved anxious to explain that they hadn't read the small print and genuinely intended to give any extra money they made to Battersea Dogs Home. Besides, it was all Real Madrid's fault, honest. They kept flicking our ears 'til we signed.

Most people think the European Super League is dead in the water, but I know one leading football finance expert who disagrees. While there was a huge reaction from fans against the original European Super League in England, in other countries the response was more muted, possibly because some of the newspapers in some European countries are little more than in-house publications for big clubs. As such, these publications were happy enough to toe the party line on the benefits of having an invitation-only, relegation-free 'European' league with clubs from just three countries and seven cities across the continent. PSG did not join as perhaps their owners took the view that being seen to oppose the project shortly before Qatar hosted the FIFA World Cup would be good publicity. German clubs, mindful of that famous fan culture and less interested in making money than some owners elsewhere, decided to have nothing to do with it.

However, there is still a resentment towards the Premier League and its success, especially from Spain and Italy, so a Super League where clubs have to share less money with the plebs of Europe and can sell streaming rights direct to viewers, with more marquee fixtures, perhaps taking place in America, Asia and other lucrative markets, is certainly alluring to the elite. The Super League may be dead for now, but it lies in a shallow grave and until someone has driven a stake through its heart do not rule out an attempt to revive it in a season or two.

Hmmm. If there is a Super League, West Park Rovers are unlikely to be asked to join, but for now we're just going to enjoy the novelty of our first season in Europe. Viel Glück! Bonne chance! Kalí týchi! Powodzenia! Ádh mór! The Best of British, my son!

12

A GLOBAL TEAM

The world is our oyster

You should have wished us more luck. I knew that was a difficult group, but I genuinely thought we could get out of it. Trouble is, if you finish third in the Europa Conference there is no consolation prize. The Conference *is* the consolation prize for teams that are shit in the proper tournaments. Never mind, we beat Vaduz home and away and had a sherry nice time in Villareal. Sorry, 'very' nice, but the sherry did take the edge off the 4–0 hammering and luckily we'd arranged to land at a different airport to our less than impressed fans.

I know it cost a lot to get out there, but it also costs a lot to get to Altrincham and Scunthorpe, which is where they could still be going were it not for the imaginary millions that Kieran, Guy and myself have invested in this club, or, at the very least, persuaded other, richer people to invest. And our media team have been only too happy to show me the tweets/blogs/graffiti blaming me for our early exit from European competition. Like it was me who announced at a press conference the day before our first group game that this tournament was not his priority and if anything it was a nuisance.

Sorry, they don't like to be called a media team. They refer to themselves as the 'comms team', which all sounds a bit *Star Trek* to me, not that they would get the reference, because they are all so bloody young. We have just over 300 full-time staff now and half of them seem to be employed merely to share the skipper's favourite pasta recipes on Instagram. Actually we only have seven people in the comms team and two of them are interns, so they may be inefficient but, more importantly, they are cheap. They are all adamant, though, that the fans reckon our failure to qualify from the group was my fault for two reasons.

Firstly, that new European kit I was so keen on apparently offended the gods of football and my greed bought bad karma. It also didn't bring in much money, because hardly anyone bought it, but it certainly wasn't the reason we got knocked out and I'll stick pins in the doll of any superstitious idiot who thinks so. However, I may have to hold my hands up to the second reason, although not in public obviously. In public it was very much an honour to be asked and an opportunity too good to be missed, but in private I will admit it was me who was most keen to embark on that money-spinning tour of Australia, stopping off to take part in that meaningless tournament in Singapore.

Who knew that professional footballers could still be exhausted from three weeks of travel and seven games played in searing heat just before the European group stages were due to begin? But come on, how could we turn down the chance for our players to test themselves against a Liverpool XI, Albirex Niigata and some of Real Madrid's reserve team? Or more to the point, how could we turn down the money offered by that billionaire supermarket owner who was so keen to invite us to take part in the first ever Fusion Tea Bag Series Trophy? And I don't care what our fans say, Albirex are one of Singapore's top teams, so taking a point off them was actually a very impressive result. Luckily, they got absolutely battered by the Liverpool XI and Real Madrid's reserves, so we finished above them on goal difference. Third in a group seems to be our default setting. As it happens, we fielded a weakened team, as we did for our tour of Australia, which drew some pretty healthy crowds considering how few of our line-up anybody would have recognised from watching the Premier League on Aussie TV.

West Park Rovers weren't the only Premier League club to clock up the airmiles in the summer of 2022. Liverpool travelled a total of 14,133 miles in their tour of the Far East and Austria. Yes, Austria. Not Australia as I originally assumed, because that would have been a far more sensible choice travel-wise, although I suppose it is possible that they flew Ryanair and Vienna turned out to be their airport for Bangkok.

Chelsea criss-crossed America taking part in the Florida Cup Series: Clash of Nations,* before flying to Italy to meet Udinese and extend their total trip to 13,363 miles, and Manchester United managed a whopping 22,238 miles flying to Thailand then on to Australia and back to Old Trafford via Oslo, where they played Atlético Madrid for some reason. Spurs went to South Korea then Scotland then Israel for a modest total of 15,532 miles, but it was the first leg of the journey that illustrates why these tours have become so popular with Premier League clubs.

Heung-Min Son, captain of the South Korean men's national team, and Cho So-Hyun, captain of the women, both play for Tottenham, so a trip there was a no-brainer for Spurs and especially for their commercial department, looking to capitalise on the huge passion for Premier League football there and, in particular, the huge number of South Korean fans who support Tottenham because of those two national heroes.

Spurs played two games. The first was in Seoul against a side made up of top players from the K League; the second was against Sevilla, just a short coach ride away in Suwon. Both games sold out in minutes, which is not bad considering the stadia hold 110,000 between them, and, according to *Forbes*, tickets were being offered online for upwards of $3000, which is pretty impressive considering the actual retail price started at a reasonable $30. The cheapest tickets for Liverpool v Man United in Bangkok were $135, although that too sold out within minutes.

Meanwhile, Paris St Germain commemorated their tour of Japan by offering three lucky fans the chance to buy non-fungible token tickets for a bargain price of 30 million yen, roughly $218,000. The tickets guaranteed full VIP hospitality and a photo opportunity with the players. I should think it did. For that money I'd want more than a bloody photo with Lionel Messi, I'd want dinner and tickets to *Hamilton* at the very least.

*Which with true American understatement featured three whole nations.

Apart from the actual games, Spurs players had a full schedule of open training sessions, media appearances and a barbeque with local dignitaries. Poor players, they must have been exhausted, but it was all worth it. The club received a few million quid to help pay those poor exhausted players; their brand image in the region was enhanced even more, which will lead to more money from selling shirts and giant sponge fingers; and the sponsors were delighted.

The tour itself was sponsored by Coupang, Korea's answer to Amazon (the delivery service, not the river) and the only way to buy tickets was through their app. The only way to watch the game on TV was via Coupang Play (think Amazon Prime) and to access it fans had to sign up for a four-week trial, which bagged the service their highest ever number of new subscribers in a month. Tottenham's shirt-front sponsors, AIA, a leading Asian insurance company, also used the tour to make headway in the Korean market, running prizes to win tickets as a way of accessing customer data.

It's no wonder, then, that we are not the only team keen to accept invitations to tour abroad, even if the manager would secretly prefer to have his players doing laps round the training ground rather than the planet. Indeed, *Forbes* claims that a pre-season game in Shanghai in 2012 helped Manchester United land a then world-record sponsorship deal, because, 'Chevrolet were reportedly blown away by United's popularity in China.' Equally impressively we sold out of West Park Rovers giant sponge fingers in Singapore.

For the big clubs, pre-season tours are serious money. Manchester United make up to £15 million a year from travelling to play exhibition matches. This perhaps explains why their owners are so keen on a smaller Premier League, so that they can squeeze in a few more tour games. Manchester United are a global brand and according to one public relations agency have over 1.1 billion followers on social media. Even allowing for the fact that PR companies are prone to exaggerate and/or talk bollocks, that's a big target audience.

West Park Rovers on the other hand, like Palace and Brighton, are local teams and therefore less able to extract large amounts of cash from promoters as we do not have a legion of fans who will fill a stadium in Indonesia, Australia or elsewhere. Nevertheless, any Premier League team will attract some interest around the world, so we still made a fair bit of money and we got around 200 new followers on Twitter. I hope they enjoyed the photos of our players titting about during training that our comms team post roughly every three minutes.

Football is a huge global business now, so it's no surprise that top players should be flying here, there and everywhere to represent their clubs, but, annoyingly, they also have to fly here, there and everywhere to represent their countries. It's a great honour for them, of course, but a bit of a nuisance for us, because we still have to pay them even while they're pulling on their country's shirt and, in the process, risking an injury that could stop them playing for us for several months, during which time it's us that still has to bloody pay them!

I reckon if there is one thing that winds up fans more than a pre-season tournament in South-East Asia that they can't afford to fly to, it's those pointless international friendlies that seem to interrupt the season just as it's getting started. The FA, on the other hand, would happily have an international break every week, because England games are a huge money-spinner for them.

England is probably the only international team in the world that will nearly always sell out a 90,000-seat stadium for a friendly game, no matter who the opposition is. And following the success of the Lionesses in 2022 it may not be long until England Women are getting similar numbers for every game.

Many of the 90,000 are, of course, children and children do a wonderful job of pestering grown-ups into buying them shirts, scarves and must-have Three Lions covers for their iPhones. Then you have the fans who can't get to Wembley, but will watch the game on telly, either at home or in a pub, where, apparently, it's fun to end up with more beer on you than in you should England score a goal.

There were many eyebrows raised when the rights to broadcast England games between 2022 and 2024 were bought by Channel 4, with the deal to include UEFA Nations League games, Euro 24 qualifiers and friendlies, although the Qatar World Cup was still shown exclusively on BBC and ITV as part of legislation ensuring certain sporting events, the so-called crown jewels, are always free-to-air. No one thought that the publicly owned Channel 4 could afford to spend the sort of money that would end the previous FA deal with ITV and Sky, but the *Guardian* claimed the deal was 'part of a rearguard action to avoid privatisation' after the then Culture Secretary Nadine Dorries had announced her intention to sell off the channel, so that it could more easily compete with the likes of Netflix and Amazon. And it must have cost Channel 4 a considerable amount of cash to acquire them because they outbid Sky Sports in UEFA's central auction of rights to show Nations League matches, as well as wresting the other games from ITV and Sky.

The Nations League is the relatively new and largely unloved tournament established by UEFA to replace a lot (although by no means all) of those meaningless friendlies I've already moaned about and also to help some of the smaller countries financially. The logic is that England are unlikely to ever agree to play a friendly against San Marino, even if San Marino could afford to pay for the privilege, so that's one potential income stream denied to the smaller nation,* but as I said, the TV contract for Nations League games is centralised, which means that UEFA auction the broadcasting rights for the whole competition and split the money equally between all the countries, rather than each country making individual deals as before, which left the likes of San Marino, Andorra, dear old Liechtenstein etc at a serious disadvantage.

International team managers don't like it, however. Because the Nations League is competitive (nominally at least) they feel the need to pick a strong team rather than having the opportunity to try fringe players that friendlies give them. Many were also surprised that the FA deal went to a channel with no real sporting pedigree, but that overlooked the millions who have watched Channel 4's ground-breaking coverage of successive Paralympic Games since 2012.

However, despite ooh, upwards of 20 minutes of deep research on the internet I couldn't find any details of exactly how much Channel 4 actually paid for the rights to those England games, so I asked Kieran, the human equivalent of Google, instead. According to his sources, which are mainly WhatsApp groups for swapping Panini stickers, Channel 4 paid about £50 million for the 20 live matches in the package. Whether they felt this was still good value after England were beaten 4–0 at home to Hungary and relegated to the next tier of the Nations League has not been clarified. Neither

---

*They may know they will get hammered, but my goodness do teams like San Marino pray to be drawn in the same Euro qualifying group as England.

do we know whether they realise that some fans blame Channel 4 for the relegation.

Those of you who think I may have exaggerated the superstitious nature of some football followers should be aware that I have at least three friends who think England were relegated solely because the games were no longer on ITV. The fact that two of those friends work for ITV Sport is immaterial.

Regardless of whether international games are friendlies or qualifying games, there are still a lot of them and that means, with more than half of our Premier League squad representing their countries, we are spending quite a few weeks in each season paying players for not playing for West Park Rovers. And the lucky buggers are paid by their countries as well. Admittedly they are not paid much and traditionally money is not a factor for players desperate to represent their country.

In 1974, England players were less than impressed when the new manager Don Revie (a man known for his ability to sniff out any opportunity to fill his pockets) gathered the team together and said, 'Listen, lads. I've managed to get your appearance money raised from £100 to £300.' Team captain Emlyn Hughes is supposed to have replied that every single one of them would be happy to pay *for* the privilege of pulling on the white shirt.

To a previous generation, £300 a game to represent England would have been a fantasy. Long after he retired from boxing I met Jim McDonnell, who had been the British and European featherweight champion in the 1980s. I said how much I liked his nickname, the Camden Caretaker, because of the way his punches took care of opponents. 'Actually,' he said, 'they called me that because I used to be a caretaker for Camden Council.'

So it was with legendary English footballer of the 1940s and 1950s, Tom Finney, who was known as the Preston Plumber, not because many of his goals were 'tap-ins' or he 'overflowed' with talent, but because he was a plumber and was from Preston. North End were the only club he ever played for, partly because he played in the bad old days of soccer slavery, so when he was offered a move to Italian club Palermo in 1952, which included a £10,000 signing-on fee, a villa and a sports car, his chairman Nat Buck said, 'If tha' doesn't play for Preston then tha' doesn't play for anybody.'

That stubborn attitude could be costly, though. Preston lost the 1954 FA Cup final 2–1 to West Brom with Tom Finney admitting that 'he had a stinker'. Later he revealed that was maybe because he had exhausted himself before the game, spending hours trying to persuade club directors to increase the £25 win-bonus they had offered. Tom was equally unimpressed by England's treatment of its players at the time. After his retirement he claimed that the FA made around £50,000 a game on gate money from Wembley internationals: 'The 11 players would share £550 and the rest, all £49,450, went somewhere else.'

To this generation of England players, £300 a game would be loose change down the back of the sofa, but still, representing their country seems to be more important than being paid for it – although getting a hundred grand a week from your club must soften the blow a bit.

The FA doesn't release any information about appearance fees for England's men, but it doesn't really matter because, since 2007, the men decided that all their appearance money should go instead to the England Footballers Foundation, which has distributed more than £5 million to charities. Note to cynics: yes, they can afford it, but most players are actually decent human beings and that's £5 million that charities wouldn't have got elsewhere.

Extrapolating from that figure, though, you can calculate (or at least Kieran can) that England players are on around £2000 a game plus bonuses believed to be in the region of £1500 for a win, £1000 for a draw and £500 for a defeat, although why they're getting a bonus for losing is beyond me – even the cheekiest of agents wouldn't ask our CEO to bung a defeat bonus into a player's contract.

There are also bonuses for winning tournaments, or so we are led to believe. The FA would not confirm reports that England players would share £5 million if they won the 2018 World Cup or whether that bonus would also go to the players' charity pot. The FA would be able to afford that bonus, though. The winners of the 2022 World Cup trousered around $40 million.

England winning the World Cup would be marvellous, but it wouldn't be my favourite source of FA income. That honour goes to England international Ashley Cole, who was fined £90,000 for tweeting that the FA were 'a bunch of twats'. Which led to one of those pointless arguments that football fans love so much about whether 'a bunch' was the best collective noun for twats.

For some reason, most national FAs are strangely reluctant to reveal how much their players are paid to represent their countries. Apparently Scottish players only receive expenses, the German FA did confirm that the team would get a bonus of €350,000 each for winning the 2018 World Cup, but won't disclose the normal match fee and, likewise, the Spanish FA confirmed a bonus of €125,000 for winning the World Cup, but also won't confirm how much they pay per game.

Brazil offered their team a whopping $1 million each if they lifted the Jules Rimet trophy, but, guess what, no details on match fees. If they do pay generous match fees then the Brazilian players are laughing – recurring financial problems mean that the national team is almost constantly touring the world to play money-spinning friendlies, although if they do have such financial problems you wonder how they can afford to offer a $24 million bonus for winning the World Cup.

The only country for which we can make an accurate guess at appearance fees is France, but that is only because Kylian Mbappé revealed that he was donating his £17,000 fee for each World Cup group game to charity.

And how about the women? Well, in the course of my research I browsed several reputable news sources only to find that the figures and opinions quoted in most of them came from a mysterious football finance expert known only as Kieran Maguire. I could have saved weeks writing this by just asking him in the first place. According to ITV.com, Kieran Maguire reckoned that the Lionesses' potential earnings from winning Euro 22 'can be compared to those of the men's World Cup champions of 1966'.

Of course, it is those 'potential' earnings that can make winning tournaments so lucrative for footballers, even for those who claim they only play for the pride. The money to be made from sponsorship deals, endorsements, TV adverts etc is enormous for victorious teams, particularly for those players who are already household names.

Those earnings for the Lionesses, however, still don't make up for the fact that they received a total of £1.74 million from UEFA for winning their tournament and Italy's men received £28.5 million for winning theirs the year before. Add to that the fact that, as you may remember, the average salary in the Women's Super League is just £27,000 a year and it's clear that we are still a long way from equality. No information is available as to whether the England Women players donate any match-fees to charity. My guess is that they do, but given the huge discrepancy between their weekly earnings and the men's, no one would blame them if they didn't.

It's not just European players who are proud to represent their countries. I'm sure players of every nation are thrilled when they pull on the national shirt, but that just adds to the problems for their club side.

The past 20 years have seen an enormous growth in the number of African players in English football. To some extent that was down to an extension in our clubs' global scouting networks, but, sadly, in part, it was also initially down to clubs on the continent of Europe reckoning that players from the continent of Africa may be happy to accept lower wages than others, because they would still be higher than anything they had been paid before.

Now, West Park Rovers, like just about every other Premier League team has players from Cameroon, the Ivory Coast and Ghana. And every other year we lose them to the African Cup of Nations, meaning, again, that for four weeks of the season, usually in January, we are paying them to play for another team and praying they don't get injured in the process.

The upside is that Premier League interest has raised the profile of what was already a great tournament and, like every other Crystal Palace fan, I was immensely proud when our player Cheikhou Kouyaté won AFCON with Senegal.

Every tournament in football is played under the remit of the Federation Internationale de Football Association, otherwise known as FIFA, otherwise known by themselves as 'the most prestigious sports organization in the world' and otherwise known by Kieran Maguire as 'a bunch of bloody pirates'. FIFA was established in 1904 by seven national associations – Belgium, Denmark, France, the Netherlands, Spain,* Sweden and Switzerland – to 'promote the game of Association Football to foster friendly relations among National Associations by promoting the organisation of games at all levels, and

---

*Although it was actually just Madrid. The Spanish equivalent of the FA wasn't formed until 1913.

to control every type of association football by taking steps as shall be deemed necessary or advisable.'

Basically, FIFA is football's ultimate administrative authority and governs all facets of the game, including the rules of play, overseeing transfers, organising international tournaments, establishing standards for refereeing and encouraging the global growth of the game. They have certainly achieved that part of the deal. According to FIFA's last count, in 2006, there were more than 150 million registered players (men and women), which is roughly 2% of the planet with most of the rest of the planet watching at grounds or on TV – the 2022 World Cup Finals in Qatar were broadcast in more than 180 countries. You might have thought that FIFA would have updated their figures for the number of people playing the game since 2006, but to be fair they have been a bit distracted since then, what with the scandals and the court cases.

FIFA have found time to introduce new types of football, though. Beach soccer and futsal both have their own world cups and, as I write, that original membership of seven countries has now grown to 211, with Russia currently suspended. England, joined in with Johnny Foreigner surprisingly soon after FIFA's formation, possibly because they correctly guessed that FIFA would want to organise the football games at the 1908 London Olympics.* South Africa, in 1909, was the first non-European team to join, followed by Argentina, Canada, Chile and the USA.

Scotland and Wales would also catch up with England by joining in 1910. Not for long, though, because when FIFA re-grouped after World War I, the Home Nations refused to re-join as they were unwilling to face recent enemies in tournaments. Even when FIFA offered England and Scotland a place (without having to qualify) in the 1934 Italy World Cup they declined, with one FA member saying they and the Welsh had enough to do with their own Championship 'which seems to me to be far better than the one to be staged in Rome.'

In fact it was 1950 before England took their place in a World Cup Finals. Scotland should have joined them in host-nation Brazil, but said they would only travel if they won the Home International

---

*The first ever tournament between national teams.

Championship that acted as the qualifying group. They finished second and withdrew in a huff. Actually all the early World Cups were rather amateur and ramshackle affairs characterised by withdrawals, boycotts and questions about the process of choosing the host nation. FIFA may no longer be amateur and ramshackle, the World Cups are no longer subject to withdrawals and boycotts, but, oh boy, the questions about the process of choosing the host nation still persist.

These days FIFA are a huge and professional organisation employing over 800 staff, the vast majority of whom do a superb job in relation to the governance of world football, with a turnover of up to $5 billion in a World Cup year and a salary for President Gianni Infantino, including bonuses, of $3 million (plus expenses, of course). However, it only took until the second World Cup in 1934 for the boycotts to start, with the holders Uruguay refusing to travel to Italy, because only four European teams had travelled to them for the first tournament in 1930, most of the others claiming they couldn't afford the fare.

In 1938 the entire South American continent was outraged when the finals were awarded to a European country (France) for the second time running and several of their countries refused to take part, including Uruguay and Argentina. In 1950, most of the countries of Eastern Europe refused to even take part in the qualifying tournaments, presumably because they now thought that football was a decadent bourgeois pastime. Austria withdrew because their team was too young and Belgium withdrew because they couldn't afford to travel to Brazil. They were joined by Argentina who could afford to travel, but didn't because of an argument with the organisers. Argentina also boycotted the 1954 World Cup in Switzerland. No one seems to know why. Habit, I suppose. In 1958, Turkey, Indonesia and Iran boycotted the tournament because they refused to play Israel in a qualifying group.

Nowadays the odd geo-political dispute may cause a boycott problem or two, but everyone can afford to take part in the tournament and would be reluctant to miss out on the commercial income that it can bring. The questions over choosing the host nation still persist, though. The bid for the 1934 tournament was a straight choice between Italy and Sweden, and many people at the time thought Benito Mussolini had bullied or bribed FIFA into choosing Italy, so he could show the world the fascist architecture of Rome.

The South American anger over the 1938 World Cup were fuelled by accusations that FIFA was controlled by the European countries and, for the 1950 World Cup, many European countries were outraged that FIFA had asked if any of them wanted to bid to hold the tournament, not because they knew it was South America's turn, but because their city centres were still smouldering ruins. Maybe it was because FIFA were based in Switzerland and hadn't noticed.

The whole world was baffled when the USA was chosen as the host nation for the 1994 World Cup Finals. Despite FIFA's claim that they awarded the USA the tournament because it was potentially a huge new market in which to grow the game, many suspected that palms may have been greased. As it happens, financially it was the most successful in World Cup history and the game has indeed become big business there.

However, it was the choosing of the host nations for the most recent World Cups in Russia and Qatar that really raised eyebrows. Actually, that's a bit mild. Let me re-phrase it. It was the choosing of Russia and Qatar as hosts that really made people think that FIFA was a stinking hotbed of corruption. On their official website, FIFA proudly boasts that it was 'the first sports body to adopt a human rights policy.' It also says, 'Our aim is to create and continuously develop an environment that celebrates diversity and inclusion.' Strange, then, that the 2018 World Cup went to a country which very much does *not* celebrate diversity and inclusion, and the 2022 tournament went to a country where diversity and inclusion can land you in prison, and where, as Human Rights Watch reports, 'Women must obtain permission from male guardians to marry, study abroad and receive some forms of reproductive health care.'

The standard FIFA response to both choices is that hosting a World Cup shines a light on human rights issues and may help to drag governments kicking and screaming into the 21st century, although in Qatar's case dragging them into the 19th century would be a start. To be fair, with Qatar, FIFA also said that they were motivated by their desire to see the World Cup hosted in a Muslim country for the first time, even if it was one with absolutely no tradition of football at all.

Even before the World Cup Finals take place, FIFA already do very well financially out of the standard bidding process. Prior to making a final decision, there are a series of inspections by FIFA staff as to the infrastructure, travel, accommodation, security and other considerations. These are all carried out diligently and meticulously. The inspector reports are part of the consideration when the votes take place as to who should host the tournament.

FIFA also insists that it has charitable status in the host country of the competition. FIFA is registered as an association in its base in Switzerland, so paid just $28 million tax in 2018 on a profit of $1.75 billion – a tax rate of 1.9%. FIFA also requests that players are not required to pay taxes on their fees and fringe benefits in the country hosting the World Cup.

Once the venue is chosen the FIFA money-making machine really kicks in. Twenty-First Century Fox paid $400 million for the TV rights to the 2022 World Cup. Marketing rights between 2018 and 2022 totalled $1.66 billion and for the period 2015–18 (the last figures FIFA revealed) they made $600 million from licensing rights and $712 million in hospitality and ticket sales. And all that is profit, because it's the host nation that has to shell out a fortune on infrastructure costs.

Suspicions had already been raised when it was decided that the bidding war for 2018 and 2022 would take place at the same time, with the results announced simultaneously on 2 December 2010. Not unexpectedly, there was particular cynicism in those countries, like the USA and England, whose bids were unsuccessful and it didn't help that some FIFA officials were already under heavy suspicion of financial mismanagement.

In 2006, Andrew Jennings, a British investigative journalist, released a book called *Foul! The Secret World of FIFA: Bribes, Vote-Rigging and Ticket Scandals*. It did exactly what it said on the tin, detailing an international cash-for-contracts scam and alleging that Sepp Blatter had used bribes to rig votes to maintain his position as President of FIFA. Sepp Blatter, by the way, is one of only nine men (no women, obvs) to head FIFA in its 118-year history, which is probably not good governance and also suggests that it is a job worth clinging onto. A year later, building on Jennings' work, a BBC *Panorama* documentary claimed that Blatter was being investigated by the Swiss police over a secret deal to repay more than £1 million in bribes taken by FIFA bosses.

In 2010, again following investigations by Andrew Jennings, a further *Panorama* documentary claimed that a company called International Sport and Leisure had made over 175 bribes to FIFA in order to secure marketing contracts for successive World Cups. They also alleged that Jack Warner, President of CONCACAF (the FIFA confederation that oversees football in North America, Central America, and the Caribbean), had not only taken bribes, but had resold World Cup tickets on an industrial scale.

Lord Triesman, part of the England bid, who had just stepped down as head of the English FA, described FIFA as 'a Mafia family' with 'a decades-long tradition of bribes, bungs and corruption' and using parliamentary privilege he made specific claims of bribery against four FIFA executive committee members, including Jack Warner. All four members denied the allegations and FIFA launched no investigation. By an amazing coincidence, however, all four were subsequently found guilty of a whole host of other offences.

In April 2020, after years of investigation, the United States Department of Justice formally charged three media executives and a sports marketing company called Full Play with a number of crimes, including money laundering in connection with bribes to secure TV rights for major tournaments. The indictment also said the Department of Justice had proof that a number of FIFA bosses had taken bribes, among them the former head of the football federation in Brazil, who took money from Qatar, and our old friend Jack Warner, who was paid $5 million dollars through various US shell companies to vote for Russia.

Did FIFA do anything in response to all those allegations of bribery and corruption over the years? They certainly did. In 2018 they revised their code of ethics to make it an offence to make public statements of a defamatory nature against FIFA.

What seems peculiar about the money that some countries will spend to acquire a World Cup tournament is how little money they can actually make back by hosting it. In fact, in some cases, those four weeks of football have been an ongoing economic disaster.

The bigger the party, the bigger the hangover, and the bigger the clear-up afterwards when everyone has left. South Africa 2010 was by all accounts a superb World Cup for anyone who attended and also for the millions who watched on TV. The South African people were wonderful hosts, their team did reasonably well, beating France and only missing out on the knock-out phase on goal difference. As part of the commitment to the World Cup the South African government spent about $5 billion on constructing and renovating 10 stadiums for the tournament. This was great for the fans who attended the matches, at grounds such as the 64,000-capacity Green Point Stadium in Cape Town, which was the venue for eight games. The problem is, once the tournament finished there was little demand for a stadium of that size and it was left to slowly deteriorate. By 2016 there were calls for it to be demolished as the maintenance costs exceeded the income generated from the few events that it hosted.

The 2014 World Cup in Brazil was a similar affair, which may seem strange for a country considered to be a hotbed of football. The decision to build some stadia in provincial areas with no significant local teams meant that, once again, local authorities were left to clear up the financial mess after a few weeks of attention.

And both governments had to spend money the country didn't have on building or improving roads and hotels in those same provincial areas, again, facilities that were barely used when the tournament was over. No doubt each would argue that there were financial benefits, especially a long-term boost to tourism, but that is difficult to quantify and it's hard to imagine people are still booking holidays to the safari parks and beaches of South Africa because of their happy memories of watching the World Cup on telly in 2010. Arguably, hosting a successful tournament will boost the morale and civic pride of a nation, but it's a lot of money to pay to put a spring in your step for a few weeks.

I'm happy to repeat what I said earlier about FIFA, on a daily basis they are doing a good job of organising the game around the world. It's just that at management level it seems that nothing they do can't be interpreted in more than one way. Chief Executive Gianni Infantino (who now lives in Qatar) earns around $3 million dollars a year, having rejected his first pay offer of $2 million, but was he unanimously re-elected in 2023 because he is doing such a good job or because he lobbied national associations not to nominate an opposing candidate?

From 2026 the number of teams in the World Cup Finals has been expanded from 32 to 48. Is that because he genuinely wants more teams to be able to share the experience or because FIFA will get hugely increased broadcasting income from 16 more countries? And the move to that many teams means it is unlikely ever again that only one country can host the finals, meaning smaller countries can now bid to jointly host, meaning, of course, more opportunity to stay in nice hotels.

Infantino recently announced that from 2027 prize money at the Women's World Cup will match that of the men's, and rightly so: at Qatar 2022 the men shared $440 million, while for Australia 2023 the women's prize pot was $110 million. However, shortly before the women's tournament began, Infantino invited Visit Saudi, the Saudi government's tourism agency, to be one of the main sponsors, an invitation that was only dropped after howls of outrage from hosts Australia and New Zealand, because of huge issues with women's rights in the Saudi Kingdom. Even then, Infantino had the last word, questioning why the Australian FA took that stance when the Australian government had many trade deals with Saudi Arabia: 'There is a double-standard here which I don't really understand.'

The World Cup may be getting bigger, but Planet Football seems to get smaller every year. West Park Rovers are an outward-looking club, keen to welcome people from all over the world to play for us or to visit our stadium. Sadly, we are not currently in a situation that allows us to engage with the world in a meaningful way financially, by which I mean that we can't afford the increasingly popular multi-club ownership (MCO) model.

Having just one club in your wallet is becoming decidedly uncool for a new generation of owners. Barnsley FC are part-owned by New City Capital. New City also have significant holdings with French club Nancy and Belgian club KV Oostende. And Swiss club Thun, Danish club Esbjerg and Dutch club Den Bosch. Oh, and German club Kaiserslauten.

David Blitzer, one co-owner of Crystal Palace FC, also owns part of German club Augsburg and has shares in Den Haag of Holland and Sportkring Beveren in Belgium. Another co-owner of Palace, John Textor, recently bought a 90% stake in Brazilian club Botafogo, then acquired a controlling share in Olympic Lyonnais in France, and PIF, the new owners of Newcastle United, are reportedly in talks to also buy Polish club Śląsk Wrocław.

This MCO is allowed to happen because UEFA regulations are very clear, but only up to a point. Two clubs in which one person has 'decisive influence' cannot enter the same tournament. The Premier League defines the level of 'decisive influence' as 10%. In other words, if you own 100% of Crystal Palace you can own no more than 10% of Brighton and Hove Albion, albeit that would be one of the weirdest and potentially most dangerous things that any billionaire could do. However, in other countries, the definition is different, so UEFA stepped in and allowed one person to own one club and have a 'non-decisive influence' in any other. Most countries take that to mean anything under 50%, so even in Germany where the 50+1 rule is near sacred, 49% of a club can be acquired by the owner of another. Of course, it is the City Group that has taken most advantage of the UEFA rule, with Manchester City being the eldest sibling of a family of 11 clubs, including New York City, Melbourne City, Montevideo City, Mumbai City and several other sides round the world who don't have the word 'City' in their name.

What then are the advantages of being under a multi-club umbrella, particularly as many of the clubs I have mentioned between Barnsley and Mumbai are not in the top division of their countries' leagues. KPMG is a global audit and tax advisory service with a reputation that even impresses Kieran. On their Football Benchmark website they explain that diversifying a football portfolio is done for the same reasons as any other company would diversify a business portfolio: 'growing the brand, gaining global exposure and optimising operations.'

In practical terms the main benefit is what they call 'vertical integration', which seems to be a fancy term for servicing the needs of a dominant club, if there is one, which in the case of City Group, there certainly is. Vertical integration in this case is a way for your young players to get valuable playing time at your satellite clubs, which they wouldn't get at home. Once a player reaches their full potential they either return to the first team of the alpha-male club, get a permanent deal at the smaller club or get sold for a handsome profit. Since Brexit, playing for the satellite clubs may also be a way of earning enough experience points to get around the UK government's new eligibility rules for signing European players.

If a group consists of two more or less equal clubs (can there be a group of two?) like Watford and Udinese, both controlled by the

Pozzo family, then there is also the benefit of being able to fill holes in either squad from each club – those two clubs completed more than 50 transfers between themselves in just over 10 years. The smaller clubs in the group can benefit as well. Manchester City can negotiate global, centralised deals with kit manufacturers, sponsors, branding partners and so on. Even the percentage of that which, say, Mumbai and Montevideo get will be much bigger than any deal they negotiate on their own.

There are those, though, who claim there are ulterior motives for a big club to acquire a string of mini-clubs to trail in their wake, whether it's for tax purposes, to avoid FFP (by shifting losses between the clubs) or to avoid the normal rules of the transfer market. Plus, with UEFA themselves claiming there are now well over 100 clubs in Europe which are part of a multi-club organisation, there is always the potential that ever-larger conglomerates could actually end up threatening the power of the governing body on the continent.

While there are checks and balances in relation to what happens on the pitch to try to preserve some integrity, off the pitch things are a bit more creative. There is nothing to stop teams under the control of an MCO from transferring players at favourable rates. This would allow clubs under pressure from FFP constraints to either book profits from player sales at favourable prices in the accounts of the club that needs them or undervalue prices to reduce the amortisation cost in the books of the buyer. An MCO model also allows the organisation to 'park' central costs and revenues wherever it is needed from an FFP (or tax) perspective. Finances aside, I guess that the opinion of most fans on multi-club groups depends on where in the pecking order their club sits.

PUTTING THE GREEN INTO GREEN AND BLACK

So we know about the impact the increasing growth of football round the world is having on fans' pockets and club finances, but there is another impact it may be having on us all. One recent report claimed that it takes 20,000 litres of water a day to maintain a football pitch in a Premier League stadium. Each match in the same league will generate around 40 tonnes of waste food and drink and, according to footballforfuture.org: 'The global football industry emits about thirty million tonnes of carbon dioxide every year. About the same as a small nation such as Denmark or Tunisia.'

Sadly, smaller clubs and fan groups seemed quicker to acknowledge the problem than some of the giants of the game, those very clubs that spend much of their time criss-crossing the planet by air and by road to take part in tournaments and those lucrative pre-season tours we love so much. Sorry, they love so much.

Forest Green Rovers FC are owned by Dale Vince, owner of Ecotricity, a green energy provider. It is one of the smallest of the 92 clubs, based in the Gloucestershire town of Nailsworth, which looks as though you might see Miss Marple cycling up the High Street at any moment. In 2018, Forest Green became the first football club in the world to be certified carbon neutral by the United Nations. It is also totally vegan and fully powered by green energy, some of it generated by solar panels on the stadium roof. The pitch is organic and nourished by recycled rainwater, the lawnmower is also solar-powered and they have electric car charging points all around the stadium.

None of those things are particularly expensive and if Forest Green can afford them then surely so can every club in the Premier League. With hindsight, it's clear that West Park Rovers' climb up the table was remarkable, but the further we rose, the less sustainable we became.

The Huddersfield Town Supporters' Association recently launched the Sustainable Stadium Campaign to help raise awareness of pollution and climate issues, and tackle both by making the John Smith's Stadium more environmentally friendly. They are backed by local faith and community groups as well as fans of the Giants, the rugby league team that shares the ground. As they say themselves, their aims are 'modest' and include the phasing out of single-use plastics, access to free water and working with the caterers to redistribute unsold food and other waste. Nothing drastic, but eminently do-able and easy to repeat across the UK and beyond.

Individual players such as Hector Bellerin have become high-profile environmental campaigners and Sky Sports, often maligned in these pages, have removed 90,000 water bottles per year plus disposable beverage cups and plastic cutlery as part of their attempt to become carbon neutral by 2030.

There are signs, too, that Premier League clubs are stepping up to the re-usable plate. In 2021 the United Nations highlighted four, in particular, that had signed up to the UN Sports for Climate Action Framework, which aims to support and guide sport to achieve realistic climate change goals. Arsenal were the first PL team to sign up to the framework and also the first to switch to 100% green electricity back in 2016, as well as planting 29,000 trees to create the brand new Colney Wood. Spurs have committed to cut carbon emissions by 10% in one year and their new stadium is impressively green with, for example, re-usable beer cups and a total ban on plastic straws and cutlery. All Liverpool FC's energy now comes from renewable sources and as part of their Halo Effect sustainability campaign, Southampton FC plant 250 trees every time an academy player features in the first team. At the other end of the scale, clubs like Shoreham FC of the Southern Combination and Hanwell Town of the Southern Premier League have also signed up, proving that environmental responsibility is possible throughout the pyramid.

The Premier League itself is now a UN signatory and aims to reduce 50% of its own emissions by 2030 and all of them (known as net zero) by 2040. Their website shares their laudable aim to 'reduce environmental impact' and 'inspire long-lasting behavioural change'.

The FA's Sustainability Team (FAST) governs their wide-ranging environmental strategy and the Scottish FA is doing the same with the Power of Scottish Football. In 2015 Wales became the first country in the world to enshrine a duty to those who will inherit our earth into law, and the FA of Wales is building on that Well-being of Future Generations Act. The FA of Ireland doesn't have a fancy name for its sustainability programme, but there is one and it includes a commitment to 'a national stadium powered by renewable energy'. UEFA has signed up to the European Climate Pact, the EU's attempt to transition to a net zero economy, and it's clear from examining all these strategies in detail that clubs and leagues are genuinely attempting to at least try to reduce their environmental impact.

Ah, but what about those of you who are worried about the planet as a whole? Don't worry, FIFA are all over it, sort of. FIFA were the first international sports organisation to sign up to that UN framework and their website is certainly not shy about their green credentials. But there is always a but when it comes to FIFA. According to environmental group Climate Trade the 2018 World Cup Finals in Russia generated 2.16 million tonnes of greenhouse gas, the equivalent of 465,000 cars worth. The figure was based on the construction of facilities, player and supporter travel, energy for light, heat, broadcasting etc, as well as the manufacture of merchandise. Before the finals in 2022, FIFA itself predicted that around 3.6 million tonnes of greenhouse gas were on the way into the atmosphere – or they would be if they and the Qatari organisers hadn't given a 100% cast-iron guarantee that the tournament would in fact be entirely carbon-neutral. I'm not sure how much energy a flying pig actually generates, but there must have been a lot of them soaring above that particular press conference.

That's right, FIFA actually promised that a tournament which involved building seven new stadiums, a brand-new city, an entire metro system and umpteen hotels in the middle of one of the globe's hottest deserts would be carbon-neutral. This was to be achieved by a process called 'offsetting' whereby you reduce your CO_2 in one area to compensate for increasing it in another, the most basic example being planting trees. I'm not a scientist, but I reckon you'd need a forest the size of Wales to offset 3.6 million tonnes' worth.*

Figures are not yet available to confirm whether FIFA's promise was a valid one, but expectations from experts weren't high. Bloomberg called it 'a fantasy', *Le Monde* said 'it lacks credibility,' the *Economist* went for 'fanciful' and *Scientific American* simply said the Qatar World Cup would be 'a climate catastrophe'. Besides, as campaign group Earthly recently explained, carbon offsetting is an increasingly outdated idea and the real aim should be carbon removal.

The trouble is you and I are also part of the problem. Most of us are not travelling to games, home or away, by electric car and chomping a vegan burger while we are waving our organic locally made bamboo scarves. We may be aware that the replica shirt we are wearing came from the other side of the planet, but are we demanding that our club changes that? Are we demanding, rather than suggesting, the end of single-use plastic cups or that our pitch is only irrigated by rainwater. I'm not. I try to do my bit at home,

*Don't ask me why it's always Wales we measure the size of things by. It just is. Wales and double-decker buses.

but I go to football for release, for excitement, for outrage. I want to be annoyed by referees not climate change. I think, probably like many of you, that by now I expect that all clubs should be working towards sustainability as a matter of course. And, actually, as a (fictional) club owner I agree with me. Yes, some of the measures may cost a bit to adopt but, eventually, the cost of *not* adopting them will be even higher.[*]

FOND FAREWELLS

Well now. Here we are. I'd be lying if I said I never expected West Park Rovers to end up playing in Europe. That was always the plan and it's difficult to surprise yourself in a story when you're the one actually writing it. But I've enjoyed our meteoric rise so much I almost wish there was a Kleanwell Stadium where I could go to watch this rather lovely club of ours. I like the sound of Miranda Nurse and if Malky Porter has forgiven us yet I would love to share a few more drams with him. Lisbon is one of my favourite cities, so a real-life West Park Rovers would give me the ideal chance to visit more often and, let's face it, I'm unlikely to meet Ryan Reynolds in real life am I? Being on the inside of a successful football club has been a real privilege and I depart regretting only that I haven't learned even more about the price of football. Like 99.9% of football fans, the green and black army have been a joy and it's been enormous fun to join them in pubs and bars across the country and Europe. They are passionate, funny, knowledgeable and bolshie, just as fans should be.

Except, a bigger part of me is incredibly relieved that West Park Rovers are fictional. Running even a fictional club is bloody hard work it transpires and I've found myself genuinely fretting about what's right for it and how we pay for it. If it was a real club I would have had a breakdown by the middle of Chapter 4. I imagine, too, that the pressure of running an actual club and being the steward of the hopes and dreams of actual fans would have caused Kieran, Guy

[*] Although at the moment it is actually very difficult to assess an average cost for adopting sustainable practices.

and I to have fallen out long ago, which would be a shame, because I am ever so fond of both of them.

Also, drinking with West Park Rovers fans would mean missing drinking with Palace fans in the Pawsons Arms and beyond (although sadly not in those European bars so far) and that is a prospect I cannot imagine. And of course the biggest reason I am glad to leave West Park Rovers behind is that I am absolutely terrible with money. In real life, I would be a disastrous club owner. I shall miss it, though, but as there doesn't appear to be much football currently being played anywhere else in the universe that we can discuss, I guess we must be coming to the end of the book.

13

POST-MATCH ANALYSIS

In an ideal world we'd be having this discussion live in the studio with Roy Keane and Graeme Souness scowling at each other in that strange homo-erotic way and Micah Richards laughing for no apparent reason. Of course, in a book it's impossible to bring you slow-motion highlights of the meteoric rise of West Park Rovers,* but we can at least tell you what happened to the club after Kieran and I sold our shares, leaving us older, wiser and, more importantly, considerably richer. Well, in the short term anyway, because we are both still older and wiser, but only Kieran is still richer.

Naturally he invested his profit wisely (he bought a quinoa farm and a substantial chunk of the company who make Wonky Chomps who, of course, have made a fortune off the back of all that free advertising on the pod). While I embarked on what my accountant, Bobby Numbers, said was 'one of the most remarkable and irresponsible bouts of frittering' he had ever seen, although how he can describe buying three racehorses, two life-size models of Kate Bush and one pub as 'frittering' is beyond me. And I notice he didn't turn down my invitation to an executive box at Sandown for West Park Boy's first race or the after-party at the Pawsons Arms, which he ruined by constantly telling me that offering free drinks all night wasn't going to help my new pub make money, especially as West Park Boy fell at the first hurdle.

*Although you could always go back and re-read some bits more slowly.

But never mind what happened to me and Kieran, what happened to the football club we created, nurtured and grew? Let's look into the crystal ball. It's 15 July 2027. As soon as the new owners took over they made good on their pledge to invest heavily in building the squad. Mauricio Pochettino led West Park Rovers to fifth place in his first season and then, in 2025, into the Champions League, where they were edged out by Bayern Munich in the quarter-final. Revenge came just a year later: with Cristiano Ronaldo having a golden last season as player/coach, West Park Rovers won the Premier League title and beat Bayern Munich in the final of the Champions League.

Today, the fans get their first look at the club's brand new 55,000-seat stadium, the Dubai Arena. There is a gold statue of the chairman, Guy Kilty, outside the main entrance with a plaque that simply says, 'Legend'. The new owners toyed with the idea of naming one of the bars the Kevin Day Lounge, but instead they called it Finlay's, after Kieran's dog. I found that a little insulting, especially as they paid the dog five hundred quid to come and open it. However, there is a Maguire Refreshment Kiosk, which offers organic coffee and cheese and marmite pies at eight quid a pop.

Well, that's brilliant. I couldn't be more pleased, but let's just check another crystal ball just to make sure. Hang on, the mists are clearing… It's 23 January 2025. The TV cameras capture the booing from hundreds of football fans as the chairman of West Park Rovers, Guy Kilty, known as Muppet the Puppet, is hurried into the High Court under a blanket. Under new owners he has helped to establish West Park Rovers as a mid-table Premier League club, but that isn't important, because it turns out the new owners were part of an organised attempt to turn English football upside down. In February 2024, WPR were 'acquired' by a Michigan-based manufacturer of driverless cars, which brought the number of clubs in the Premier League under American control to 14, enough to give them a straight majority in any vote.

The 14 pushed through their plans to entirely separate the Premier League from the rest of the game. There would be no promotion and no relegation, and clubs were now considered as franchises, which can be moved to any town or city if the price is right. If you think Chairman Guy is unpopular, Kieran and Kevin have been moved to safe houses, because the sale of their share of West Park Rovers was the catalyst for the whole thing and the two men who spent their entire lives arguing for the soul, the romance and the poetry of football are now seen as traitors. Gary Neville, live on TV, threatened to 'hunt them and hurt them' as soon as he was back from his after-dinner speaking tour of Qatar.

The new Labour government are now fulfilling their election campaign pledge to challenge the American move and the first legal hearing is today. This has led FIFA to threaten to expel England, because of political interference in FA matters. Kieran and Kevin are being blamed for that as well. All of which would be a fantastic story for *The Price of Football* podcast had the police not warned them that it may be possible to track their location via the download link, so it would be safer not to record any more.

Whoa, I'm not sure I like that future. Maybe I should reconsider selling my shares to the Americans? Let's give the crystal ball a polish and see whether we can come up with a more optimistic future… It's 7 February 2024. Probably owing to my lack of experience in high-level financial negotiations, I 'forgot' to mention to the new Turkish owners that outstanding bank loan of £10 million I negotiated for the club from an associate of Uncle Terry, which was technically only a bank loan because the money did originally come from a bank.

The interest on the repayment is 2%, which would have been very reasonable had that been an annual rate as I had thought, rather than the weekly one that the associate of Uncle Terry insists is the case. He has a photocopy of the back of the envelope on which the deal was drawn up to prove it. The new owners' silver-tongued lawyers have no problem using this as a reason to declare the sale invalid, and Kieran and I are once again co-owners of West Park Rovers, much to their chagrin, especially Kieran's who has had to sell the house in the Bahamas and move to a flat just outside Brighton. Well, about 48 miles outside Brighton, just south of Croydon.

Without the Turkish investment, but with massive legal fees to pay, not to mention the ten million quid that Uncle Terry's mate wants back 'like, yesterday', players had to be sold, staff had to be laid off, wages had to be cut. What's more, West Park Rovers seem very unlikely to avoid relegation from the Premier League given that they are currently 18 points from safety and the prospects for next season look bleak.

Jesus, that's even worse than the last glimpse into the future. I can almost feel the ghost of Jacob Marley rattling his chains at me. Let's give the crystal ball one more try... It's 29 November 2025. Two weeks after they bought the club the new American owners, during a 'welcome to soccer' dinner with Ryan Reynolds, are informed of the concept of relegation. They finish their cocktails and after a brief discussion they put the club back on the market.

It is purchased at a considerably lower price by a betting and soft-porn company based somewhere in the Far East, who announce in their first press conference that they intend to change the club nickname and colours to something luckier. In their second press conference they announce that the money they used to buy the club technically doesn't exist and they have therefore sold it at a considerably lower price to the sovereign wealth fund of Umm Al Quwain, the second smallest state in the United Arab Emirates.

Just one month later... Alright, alright, we get it. Sliding door moments, millions of alternative universes in which any outcome is possible. How about we split the difference and assume that whenever you are reading this, just at this moment Producer Guy is having the time of his life negotiating a cheaper deal for toilet paper, Kieran is in the boardroom creating a new spreadsheet and I am sampling a new range of white wine for the executive lounges, we're all content. West Park Rovers are currently 12th in the Premier League and are financially comfortable, because, as we have learned on *The Price of Football* podcast, for most football clubs in England that would be the happiest of endings. And if you are about to start a new team, then we wish you the happiest of beginnings.

References

CHAPTER 2

Burnley FC conducted a six-month investigation into the comments after the Board of Deputies of British Jews suggested that the Bob Lord Stand at Turf Moor be renamed because of the comments: https://www.thejc.com/news/news/burnley-fc-decides-not-to-rename-stand-dedicated-to-antisemite-former-owner-4ciSoPEKjQmTvGZ5LusCOX

Salford City announced they had received an extra £2.5 million in investment from existing shareholders in the previous six months, which was an interest-free loan on top of a further £2.5 million generated by issuing new shares in the 12 months before that: https://d3d4football.com/salford-city-receive-2-5m-in-extra-investment-from-shareholders/

Accrington Stanley's entire wage bill for 2022 was £1.8 million: https://salarysport.com/football/sky-bet-league-one/accrington-stanley/

'The owners' and directors' test (also known as the "fit and proper person test") is a test that is applied to directors and prospective directors of English football clubs…': https://www.lawinsport.com/topics/item/a-guide-to-the-owners-and-directors-test-in-english-football

CHAPTER 3

Maidstone United, in the National League, charge a minimum of £350 for a two-hour slot: https://maidstoneunited.co.uk/stones-pitch-hire/

For Sutton it also meant they had to find (and pay for) somewhere else for their academy, their women's and girls' teams, and their disability sides to play and train: https://www.bbc.co.uk/sport/football/57336301

In November 2021 City had signed a deal with 3Key, announcing 3Key as an 'official retail partner in decentralised trading analysis': https://www.sportspromedia.com/sponsorship-marketing/sponsorship/manchester-city-3key-technologies-partnership-suspended-cryptocurrency/

CHAPTER 6

'These leagues are formed of real, honest clubs with real, honest fans and that resonates with us': https://www.vanarama.com/blog/national-league/national-league-sponsorship

Humphrey Ker did give them a word of warning: *Four-Four-Two*, September 2021

A quick browse of the websites of the surprisingly numerous companies who make these costumes shows that even the most basic one starts at around £1600: https://www.frenzycreative.co.uk/

CHAPTER 7

Those so-called 'Scotch professors' who signed for English clubs changed the way football was played for ever, and Scottish immigrants also did much to establish the game in northern Europe and South America: https://www.thenational.scot/

When Hibs won the 1887 Scottish Cup Final in Glasgow, the Irish population of the city were so overjoyed they started a team of their own, called, of course, Celtic: https://www.nutmegmagazine.co.uk/

As Alan Burrows, CEO of Motherwell, told the *New York Times* they are being 'squeezed at both ends': https://www.nytimes.com/2021/08/19/sports/soccer/scotland-football-brexit.html

Colwyn Bay FC/CPD Bae Colwyn… have an average home attendance of 626 in Cymru North: https://cbfc.wales/bay-in-line-to-top-cymru-attendances/

Until 2011, those Welsh teams in the English League were still under the jurisdiction of the FAW: https://footballhandbook.com/how-can-welsh-teams-play-in-the-premier-league/

Colwyn Bay are a bit of a problem child for the FAW, having a tendency to flit across the border and back on a regular basis: http://twohundredpercent.net/colwyn-bay-existential-dilemma/

AFC Newport declined the offer to join the new Welsh league: *Who Are Ya?* by Kevin Day, Bloomsbury, 2020

These figures came from information provided to Sport NI, who demanded a full audit of all their clubs before they allocated money to help them through Covid, the biggest crisis football faced outside two World Wars: https://www.newsletter.co.uk

Scotland has the highest per capita match attendance in Europe: Sky News, 23 February 2023

CHAPTER 8

The EFL… promised to review any future Saturday screenings and also promised that clubs would be consulted: https://www.theguardian .com/football/2018/sep/07/accrington-stanley-attack-efl-over-live -streams-of-saturday-3pm-games

'We put a lot of money in and aren't embarrassed': https://www.lancs.live /sport/accrington-stanley-owner-andy-holt-14931672

'It is most essential that the members of one team should be distinguished from those of the other and to have a distinct uniform…': http://www.historicalkits.co.uk/Articles/History.htm

…uproar over prices for Lioness replica shirts during Euro 22: https:// www.dailymail.co.uk/sport/football/article-10852995/England -Women-Fans-slam-price-new-home-away-shirts-costing-114-95.html

Having to wear men's boots is causing foot injuries, deformations and stress fractures for women players: https://www.standard.co.uk/news/ uk/football-kits-women-injuries-lionesses-b1040458.html

CHAPTER 9

Teams were still 'playing in a patchwork of local friendlies, few venturing beyond the most parochial of boundaries to play games': https://www .thefa.com/news/2016/nov/02/history-of-the-fa-cup

Darwen were drawn to play the Old Etonians at the Kennington Oval in the quarter-final: https://www.theguardian.com/books/2012/mar/21/ underdogs-football-keith-dewhurst-review

Failure to send an English team to FIFA's new tournament would damage England's bid for the 2006 World Cup: https://www.thesportsman .com/articles/remember-when-manchester-united-killed-the-fa-cup

UEFA introduced the concept in 2011 and the basic FFP idea is a sound one: https://www.financialfairplay.co.uk/

When Gary tweeted his support for the idea, he was challenged by Simon Jordan…: https://fanbanter.co.uk/hypocrisy-gary-neville-and-simon -jordan-come-to-blows-over-salford-city-revelation/

As Gary Neville points out, if they do that in advance, is that a bad thing?: https://fanbanter.co.uk/gary-neville-hits-back-at-fans-mocking -salford-city-over-latest-revelations/

CHAPTER 10

That minor miracle was matched by the heroics their stadium operations team achieved off the pitch: https://theathletic.com/2056700/2020

/09/12/explained-premier-league-promotion-cost-fulham-west-brom
-leeds/

Legend has it that the first beneficiary was Johnny Haynes…: *When Footballers Were Skint* by Jon Henderson, Biteback Publishing, 2019

CHAPTER 11

Just look at the Register of Members' Financial Interests to see how often MPs are entertained by the industry: https://www.parliament.uk/mps
-lords-and-offices/standards-and-financial-interests/parliamentary
-commissioner-for-standards/registers-of-interests/register-of-members
-financial-interests/

'Many paid large sums to resolve the matter': https://www.danielgeey
.com/done-deal-blog/image-rights-in-uk-football-explained

On 23 August 2018, Manchester United plc became the first football club in the world to be worth $4 billion dollars as their share price finished that day at a record high of $24.60 on the New York Stock Exchange: *Price of Football* podcast, 16 October 2018

Even the Bundesliga's own website describes games between them as 'the mother of all derbies': https://www.bundesliga.com/en/bundesliga
/news/why-borussia-dortmund-and-schalke-are-such-fierce-rivals
-revierderby-explained-13308

CHAPTER 12

West Park Rovers weren't the only Premier League club to clock up the airmiles in the summer of 2022: All figures from Chris Wright, ESPN, 11 July 2022

Tickets were being offered online for upwards of $3000: https://
www.forbes.com/sites/steveprice/2022/07/16/the-business-behind
-tottenham-hotspurs-pre-season-korean-tour/

A pre-season game in Shanghai in 2012 helped Manchester United land a then world-record sponsorship deal: https://www.forbes.com/sites/
steveprice/2022/07/16/the-business-behind-tottenham-hotspurs-pre
-season-korean-tour/

'Profiting from one's country is a taboo among footballers – and has long been so': https://www.bbc.co.uk/news/uk-44683574

'The 11 players would share £550 and the rest, all £49,450, went somewhere else': *When Footballers Were Skint* by Jon Henderson, Biteback Publishing, 2019

Once the venue is chosen the FIFA money-making machine really kicks in: https://www.investopedia.com/articles/investing/070915/how-does-fifa-make-money.asp

The United States Department of Justice formally charged three media executives and a sports marketing company... The indictment also said the Department of Justice had proof that a number of FIFA bosses had taken bribes: https://www.nytimes.com/2020/04/06/sports/soccer/qatar-and-russia-bribery-world-cup-fifa.html

Was he unanimously re-elected in 2023 because he is doing such a good job or because he lobbied national associations not to nominate an opposing candidate?: https://www.independent.co.uk/sport/football/gianni-infantino-fifa-president-election-salary-b2302804.html

One recent report claimed that it takes 20,000 litres of water a day to maintain a football pitch in a Premier League stadium: chrome-extension://efaidnbmnnnibpcajpcglclefindmkaj/https://www.cardiff.ac.uk/__data/assets/pdf_file/0010/348661/the-environmental-impacts-of-sport-the-case-of-football.pdf

'The global football industry emits about thirty million tonnes of carbon dioxide every year. About the same as a small nation such as Denmark or Tunisia': https://footballforfuture.org/blog/kicking-off-the-conversation

In 2021 the United Nations highlighted four, in particular, that had signed up to the UN Sports for Climate Action Framework: https://unfccc.int/blog/four-premier-league-clubs-taking-climate-action

The 2018 World Cup Finals in Russia generated 2.16 million tonnes of greenhouse gas...: https://climatetrade.com/the-carbon-footprint-of-football/

Earthly recently explained, carbon offsetting is an increasingly outdated idea and the real aim should be carbon removal: https://earthly.org/the-guide-to-carbon-offsetting

Acknowledgements

We'd like to thank Martin Searle and Julian Chenery for their continued dedication. Kevin would especially like to thank his long-suffering accountant Bobby Numbers aka Robert Kent. And we offer the humblest of thanks to all the listeners of *The Price of Football* podcast. None of this would have been possible without them. I'm happy to say there are far too many of them to name in person.

We'd also like to mention all the charlatans, fraudsters, tyre-kickers and wrong'uns in the beautiful game. None of this would have been possible without them either. Sadly, there are also far too many of them to name in person.

Finally, of course, we'd like to say a huge thank you to Matt Lowing and Megan Jones at Bloomsbury for their help, encouragement and coffee.

Index